Sadness Expressions in English and Chinese

Corpus and Discourse

Corpus linguistics provides the methodology to extract meaning from texts. Taking as its starting point the fact that language is not a mirror of reality but lets us share what we know, believe and think about reality, it focuses on language as a social phenomenon, and makes visible the attitudes and beliefs expressed by the members of a discourse community.

Consisting of both spoken and written language, discourse always has historical, social, functional, and regional dimensions. Discourse can be monolingual or multilingual, interconnected by translations. Discourse is where language and social studies meet.

The *Corpus and Discourse* series consists of two strands. The first, *Research in Corpus and Discourse*, features innovative contributions to various aspects of corpus linguistics and a wide range of applications, from language technology via the teaching of a second language to a history of mentalities. The second strand, *Studies in Corpus and Discourse*, is comprised of key texts bridging the gap between social studies and linguistics. Although equally academically rigorous, this strand will be aimed at a wider audience of academics and postgraduate students working in both disciplines.

Research in Corpus and Discourse

Conversation in Context
A Corpus-driven Approach
With a preface by Michael McCarthy
Christoph Rühlemann

Corpus-based Approaches to English Language Teaching
Edited by Mari Carmen Campoy, Begona Bellés-Fortuno and
Mª Lluïsa Gea-Valor

Corpus Linguistics and World Englishes
An Analysis of Xhosa English
Vivian de Klerk

Evaluation and Stance in War News
A Linguistic Analysis of American, British and Italian television news
reporting of the 2003 Iraqi war
Edited by Louann Haarman and Linda Lombardo

Evaluation in Media Discourse
Analysis of a Newspaper Corpus
Monika Bednarek

Historical Corpus Stylistics
Media, Technology and Change
Patrick Studer

Idioms and Collocations
Corpus-based Linguistic and Lexicographic Studies
Edited by Christiane Fellbaum

Investigating Adolescent Health Communication
A Corpus Linguistics Approach
Kevin Harvey

Meaningful Texts
The Extraction of Semantic Information from Monolingual and
Multilingual Corpora
Edited by Geoff Barnbrook, Pernilla Danielsson and Michaela Mahlberg

Multimodality and Active Listenership
A Corpus Approach
Dawn Knight

New Trends in Corpora and Language Learning
Edited by Ana Frankenberg-Garcia, Lynne Flowerdew and Guy Aston

Rethinking Idiomaticity
A Usage-based Approach
Stefanie Wulff

Working with Spanish Corpora
Edited by Giovanni Parodi

Studies in Corpus and Discourse

Corpus Linguistics in Literary Analysis
Jane Austen and Her Contemporaries
Bettina Fischer-Starcke

English Collocation Studies
The OSTI Report
John Sinclair, Susan Jones and Robert Daley
Edited by Ramesh Krishnamurthy
With an introduction by Wolfgang Teubert

Text, Discourse, and Corpora. Theory and Analysis
Michael Hoey, Michaela Mahlberg, Michael Stubbs and Wolfgang Teubert
With an introduction by John Sinclair

Web As Corpus
Theory and Practice
Maristella Gatto

Sadness Expressions in English and Chinese

Corpus Linguistic Contrastive Semantic Analysis

Ruihua Zhang

B L O O M S B U R Y

LONDON · NEW DELHI · NEW YORK · SYDNEY

Bloomsbury Academic

An imprint of Bloomsbury Publishing Plc

50 Bedford Square	1385 Broadway
London	New York
WC1B 3DP	NY 10018
UK	USA

www.bloomsbury.com

Bloomsbury is a registered trade mark of Bloomsbury Publishing Plc

First published 2014

British Library Cataloguing-in-Publication Data
A catalogue record for this book is available from the British Library.

ISBN: HB: 978-1-4725-1066-2
ePDF: 978-1-4725-0767-9
ePub: 978-1-4725-0661-0

Library of Congress Cataloging-in-Publication Data
Zhang, Ruihua (Linguist)
Sadness Expressions in English and Chinese : corpus linguistic contrastive semantic analysis / Ruihua Zhang.
pages cm
ISBN 978-1-4725-1066-2 (hardback) — ISBN 978-1-4725-0661-0 (epub) —
ISBN 978-1-4725-0767-9 (epdf) 1. Emotive (Linguistics) 2. Language and emotions.
3. English language—Grammar, Comparative—Chinese. 4. Chinese language—Grammar,
Comparative—English. 5. Emotions—Cross-cultural studies. 6. Comparative linguistics.
7. Psycholinguistics. I. Title.
P325.5.E56Z53 2014
420.1'43—dc23
2014006174

Typeset by RefineCatch Limited, Bungay, Suffolk
Printed and bound in Great Britain

Contents

List of tables   viii
List of figures   x
Acknowledgements   xi
Abbreviations and typographical conventions   xii

1   Introduction   1
2   Emotions   9
3   Contrastive lexical semantics   21
4   Corpus linguistics, parallel corpora and cross-linguistic research   27
5   The corpus-linguistic framework   33
6   Methodology   49
7   Contrastive analysis of sadness expressions in English and Chinese   69
8   Implications   207
9   Conclusions   211
Appendix   215

Notes   223
References   225
Index   239

Tables

7.1	The common pattern of *sorrow* and *grief* in the BOE: and/or	73
7.2	Chinese equivalents for *sorrow** and *grief** in the BPC	80
7.3	Definitions of *bēishāng*, *bēitòng* and *bēiāi* in XHCBL	80
7.4	Significant collocates of *bēitòng* in the CCL corpus	82
7.5	Significant collocates of *bēiāi* in the CCL corpus	84
7.6	Significant collocates of *bēishāng* in the CCL corpus	88
7.7	Contrastive analysis: *sorrow* & *grief* vs *bēitòng*, *bēishāng* & *bēiāi*	90
7.8	The most frequent Chinese equivalents of *unhappy** in the BPC	94
7.9	Significant collocates of *bù gāoxìng* in the CCL corpus	95
7.10	Significant collocates of *bù yúkuài* in the CCL corpus	98
7.11	Significant collocates of *bú kuàilè* in the CCL corpus	101
7.12	Comparison of some collocates of *bù gāoxìng*, *bù yúkuài* and *bú kuàilè*	103
7.13	Features of *unhappy* expressions	103
7.14	The most frequent Chinese equivalents of *sad** in the BPC	108
7.15	Significant collocates of *shāngxīn* in the CCL corpus	111
7.16	Significant collocates of *nánguò* in the CCL corpus	113
7.17	Comparison of the collocates for *shāngxīn* & *nánguò*	114
7.18	Significant collocates of *yōushāng* in the CCL corpus	115
7.19	Chinese equivalents of *heartbreak** in the BPC	120
7.20	Significant collocates of *xīnsuì* in the CCL corpus	122
7.21	Chinese equivalents of *woe** in the BPC	129
7.22	Chinese equivalents of *mourn** in the BPC	135
7.23	Significant collocates of *āidào* in the CCL corpus	136
7.24	And/or pattern for *depression* in the BOE	140
7.25	Top three Chinese equivalents of *depression** & *melancholy** in the BPC	146
7.26	Significant collocates of *jǔsàng* in the CCL corpus	147
7.27	Significant collocates of *yāyì* in the CCL corpus	148
7.28	Significant collocates of *yìyù* in the CCL corpus	150
7.29	Significant collocates of *yōuyù* in the CCL corpus	151
7.30	Significant collocates of *shānggǎn* in the CCL corpus	154

7.31 Significant collocates of *huīxīn* in the CCL corpus 163

7.32 Comparison of *dejected**, *despondent** and *disheartened** and their Chinese equivalents 164

7.33 Chinese equivalents of *gloom** in the BPC 168

7.34 Significant collocates of *yīnyù* in the CCL corpus 169

7.35 Significant collocates of *mènmènbúlè* in the CCL corpus 170

7.36 Chinese equivalents of *bitter** in the BPC 179

7.37 Chinese equivalents of *agony** in the BPC 185

7.38 Chinese equivalents of *anguish** in the BPC 185

7.39 Significant collocates of *tòngkǔ* in the CCL corpus 187

7.40 Comparison of metaphors in sadness expressions in Chinese and English 192

7.41 Major differences between English and Chinese sadness expressions 200

Figures

6.1	A screenshot of the collocates of 伤心 by WordSmith 5.0	54
6.2	A screenshot of searching result by ParaConc	57
6.3	The interface of the concordancing options of word sketch	59
7.1	Concordance listing of *mínzú de bēiāi*	85
7.2	Concordance listing of *dolefully*	125
7.3	List of instances of *mourning*	133
7.4	Concordance listing of *melancholy*	145
7.5	Concordance listing of *dishearteningly*	158
7.6	Concordance listing of *despondently*	160
7.7	Diagram for contrastive corpus-based analysis	198
7.8	Equivalence network of sadness expressions between English and Chinese	199

Acknowledgements

This book has grown out of my PhD thesis developed at the National University of Singapore (Zhang 2011). I would like to express my deepest appreciation and thanks to my supervisor, Associate Professor Vincent B. Y. Ooi, for his detailed guidance, constructive advice and tremendous support throughout the writing of this book. I also wish to give my sincere thanks to Professor Wolfgang Teubert, who inspired me to work on the present topic and offered me substantial assistance and continuous support during my writing.

I owe special thanks to Professor Bao Zhiming and Dr. Peter K. W. Tan for their critical but highly valuable comments on the earlier versions of this book, to Associate Professor Joseph Sung-Yul Park for his insightful remarks on my research, and to Professor Chang Baobao for his permission to use the Babel English–Chinese Parallel Corpus for my study. In addition, I would like to express my gratitude to my husband and daughter for their understanding, support and encouragement, without which this book would not have been possible.

I am deeply indebted too to the National University of Singapore, which offered me the chance and scholarship to complete my PhD project, the staff members of the Department of English Language and Literature and the Division of Research and Graduate Studies, Faculty of Arts & Social Sciences for their full support, and the Central Library and the Chinese Library at NUS for their massive academic resources.

Abbreviations and typographical conventions

The following abbreviations are used in this book:

BOE = The Bank of English
BPC = The Babel English–Chinese Parallel Corpus of Fiction
CCL = The Chinese corpus compiled by the Centre for Chinese Linguistics, Peking University, China
CDA = Critical Discourse Analysis
COBUILD = *Collins COBUILD Advanced Learner's English Dictionary*
LDCE = *Longman Dictionary of Contemporary English*
OALECD = *Oxford Advanced Learner's English–Chinese Dictionary*
OED = *Oxford English Dictionary*
POS = Part of Speech
XHCBL = *Xiandai Hanyu Cidian: Bilingual Edition* (*A Dictionary of Modern Chinese*)
5th XHC = *Xiandai Hanyu Cidian* (*A Dictionary of Modern Chinese*) 5th Edition

With regard to typographical conventions, I use italics for word forms in English and Chinese (e.g. *sorrow, grief, bēishāng, bēiāi*) and * after an English word form (e.g. *sorrow**) for the word family. The English glosses in single quotation marks are mine. In parallel examples, if the English part is put in single quotation marks, it means that the example is from the CCL corpus and the translation is mine; otherwise, it means that the example is from the BPC. The English segments in square brackets are mine to explain the Chinese definitions from the dictionaries.

1

Introduction

The issues of universality versus cultural specificity of emotions have long been debated among psychologists and biologists. Biologists tend to believe that emotions are innate and universal because they have biological bases. The dominant view among psychologists, mainly based on some psychological experiments, is that human beings have some basic emotions, which are universal. The cultural specificity of emotions cannot be discussed without recourse to the cultural specificity of language, which has often been overlooked by psychologists. To what extent does language shape the way we perceive things and therefore influence our emotions? Whorf (1956) tells us that the way we cut the world into objects and actions is not a true reflection of reality but a division imposed upon us by our language. Although the strong version of the Sapir-Whorf hypothesis—language entirely determines thought and cognition—is probably not tenable, more and more linguists have begun to support its weak version, i.e. language does influence our thoughts to some extent. According to this hypothesis, the emotional lexicon of a language constrains the thoughts of its speakers about feelings. Each language has its own set of emotion words to characterize emotional experience, but apparently there are more distinct human emotions than those words can describe (Wierzbicka 1992a). A language has not lexicalized a particular emotion because its culture has not found it worthy of a specific word; it does not mean that its speakers have never experienced that emotion or cannot perceive it as a recognizable feeling (Wierzbicka 1992a). This is why we reject the Sapir-Whorf hypothesis in its strong form. However, the embracing of its weak version means that the ways in which the speakers of a language characterize, discuss and communicate their emotional experience are largely shaped by the ready-made emotional lexicon in their language.

'Emotion words reflect, and pass on, certain cultural models, and these models, in turn, reflect and pass on values, preoccupations, and frames of reference of the society (speech community) within which they have evolved' (Wierzbicka 1999: 32). The close relation between language and culture can be explained by the newly rising enterprise—cognitive linguistics,[1] represented by the works of Lakoff and Johnson (1980), Lakoff (1987), Langacker (1987) and the like. Its basic assumption is that human language cannot be viewed as an abstract system isolated from socio-psychological settings in which it is used; on the contrary, it reflects the way people experience the world. In other words, a wide variety of factors such as perception, reasoning, the nature of the body, the emotions, memory, social structure, and cognitive development, etc. determine the structural characteristics of language. Langacker (1999: 16) reveals the correlation between language and culture:

> ... the specific conventions of a given language are culturally transmitted through social interaction. Language is an essential instrument and component of culture, whose reflection in linguistic structure is pervasive and quite significant.

At the outset of communication, speakers of a language need to characterize the objects and events in their world. If we reject the innate hypothesis, their characterizations are unavoidably influenced by the way in which they perceive and construe things around them. Such characterizations are then encoded into various layers of their language and culturally transmitted from generation to generation; of course, they have been gradually enriched in the later development of the language. Hence, the organization of a language is shaped by the way in which its speakers perceive the world and conceptualize the phenomena around them. This explains, in large measure, why different languages have different structures and lexicons. The lexicalization of a concept is to 'present it as an established category of human thought' (Fillmore 2003: 258). As the established categories of human thought, the lexicon of a language will no doubt reflect its cultural features, including its emotional lexicon. Semantically similar emotion words in different languages might overlap. The comparison of the emotion lexicon of a language with that of another can therefore suggest similarities and differences in conceptualizations of emotion.

In lexical contrastive semantics, one of the thorniest problems is how to establish equivalence of lexical items across languages. One common belief would be that equivalent lexical items in different languages can be decomposed into identical sets of features. This sort of decomposition presupposes the existence of primitive or universal concepts, which can serve as *tertium comparationis* to establish lexical equivalence across languages. However, this will bring numerous problems. Krzeszowski (1990) presents a detailed analysis of this difficulty (see Section 3.2). It seems that the establishment of equivalence of lexical items across languages, by decomposing words into primitive concepts, is more than difficult to achieve. This is because the idea of primitive concept itself is problematic: we have to express it in a natural language, where the great majority of words are polysemous and ambiguous. Traditionally, their meanings in the dictionary have to rely on other words there, which in turn will unavoidably lead to circularity. Meaning is far more subtle than a componential analysis based on discrete features can account for, and far more complex than any print dictionary can describe. To carry out a cross-linguistic lexical study, the better choice is to start with 'a perceived or assumed similarity' between contrasted items (James 1980: 168) rather than to seek primitive or atomic units. What we can do is to refine the 'initial assumptions of similarity' (Altenberg and Granger 2002: 16). The analysis is only to 'add explicitness, precision, perhaps formalization' (Chesterman 1998: 58); it may also provide 'added information, added insights, added perception' (Chesterman 1998).

Most of the traditional contrastive lexical studies are incomplete and inadequate, for they are not supported by empirical quantitative data and fail to present linguistic information on frequency of use, collocations, colligations, semantic preferences/associations of the examined items. Their lexical descriptions have been largely based on individual researchers' introspection, dictionaries or scanty empirical evidence. Due to the inadequacy of previous contrastive lexical studies, there has been a growing tendency to base such studies on corpora.

The methodology of corpus linguistics is based on scientific principles. It relies on authentic texts and computational tools to detect and classify linguistic phenomena; the datasets and computer programs are open to scrutiny by the peer community; the results they produce are reproducible. This approach to lexical studies aims to arrive at the meaning of a word by observing its external linguistic behaviour in various contexts rather than looking for its primitive units intuitively. Such a practice can be justified by Firth's (1957) dictum that a word shall be known by the company it keeps. In keeping with Firth's observation, Levin's (1993: 1) central claim that the behaviour of a verb is to a large extent determined by its meaning can also be extended to other classes. Thus, the semantic information encoded in the word can be revealed by examining its linguistic behaviour. By using corpus tools, we can read its concordance and examine its collocates. As long as we have sufficient instances, anything significant about the node word will be disclosed. Hence, to know the meaning of a word does not necessarily follow that we have to decompose it. Computer corpus linguistics will tell us in exactly what way collocation is related to meaning.

Corpus-assisted contrastive lexical studies will show that distinctions of semantically similar words in the same language or in different languages can be drawn without decomposing them.

1.1 Aims and objectives

Emotions are not innate but constructed in various cultural contexts through the process of socialization (e.g. Santangelo 2003). Different cultural groups conceptualize their emotional experience in different ways, as they categorize other human actions and thoughts (e.g. D'Andrade 1995; Palmer 1996; Strauss and Quinn 1996). The conceptualizations emerging at the cultural level of cognition are referred to as 'cultural conceptualizations' (Sharifian 2003, 2008), which are negotiated and renegotiated by its members through time and across generations (Sharifian 2003, 2008). The cultural conceptualizations of emotions are encoded in the emotional lexicon of a language, which reflect the ideas, beliefs and cultural models of emotions of its speech community. Analysis of the emotional lexicon of a language helps reveal the concepts available to its speakers through which they categorize and describe their emotional experience. Where lexicalized in a single word, the presence of a word implies the existence of the concept it expresses. Language-specific emotion words might overlap semantically across languages. By comparing and contrasting the semantic features of the emotion words in a language and their equivalents in another, we can know what they share and how they differ.

Sadness has been proposed as one of the basic emotions by many psychologists. However, what are considered basic emotions in the Chinese culture are markedly different from those proposed for the English language. The disparity between sadness concepts across these two cultures seems to be more significant, as compared with happiness, anger, etc. The primary goal of this book is to investigate the general concept of 'sadness' within the English and Chinese contexts by examining lexical sets of sadness expressions. The exploration will be conducted by applying corpus-linguistic theories (Teubert 2005, 2010; Teubert and Cermakova, 2004) on meaning (as a social construct, usage and paraphrase), i.e. meaning is language use and it is constructed and negotiable through paraphrases in discourse, and by employing Hoey's (2005) or adapting Sinclair's (1996, 2004) corpus-linguistic lexical model, i.e. to look at lexical items in terms of colligations, collocations and semantic preferences/associations.

In this book, I will describe the colligational properties of sadness expressions and formulate their semantic preferences/associations on the basis of their collocates, compare and contrast the semantically similar items within and across languages to capture their semantic similarities and differences, uncover the respective cultural distinctiveness, and explain why they exhibit such differences from a cultural perspective. Their semantic information will become vivid when we look at the empirical language data in corpora. As long as our corpora are large enough, our quantitative tools will yield sufficient data, on the basis of which the exact meanings of these sadness expressions and the finer distinctions between them can be accurately captured. By comparing the semantic features of sadness expressions between Chinese and English, their emotive content will be revealed and the cultural difference of emotion between English and Chinese can be highlighted.

The sadness expressions to be examined include (cf. Section 7.1): *sorrow, grief, unhappy, sad, heartbreak, mourn, doleful, woeful, woebegone, depression, melancholy, gloomy, upset, dejected, disheartened, despondent, bitter, anguish, agony* in English, and *bēitòng, bēishāng, bēiāi, shāngxīn, nánguò, yōushāng, bù gāoxìng, bú kuàilè, bù yúkuài, xīnsuì, āidào, chóuméikǔliǎn, jǔsàng, yāyì, qíngxùdīluò, yìyù, yōuyù, shānggǎn, yīnyù, mènmènbúlè, huīxīn, sàngqì, chuítóusàngqì, huīxīnsàngqì, xīnhuīyìlěng, tòngkǔ* in Chinese. The above English items will be looked at together with their cognate items. For instance, *sad* will be examined along with *sadness, sadden, sadly*. Finally, an equivalence network between English and Chinese sadness expressions and a summary of their semantic similarities and differences across languages will be presented.

1.2 Methodology

There has been an increasing awareness that cross-linguistic studies cannot rely on introspection or dictionaries, but must be firmly based on naturally occurring language used in a variety of situations. With the aid of computer technology, we can observe semantic similarities and differences across languages objectively; we can identify clearly what elements they share with similar expressions from the other language and what elements are specific to their own language. Basing my research on corpora ensures that my investigation leads to tenable results and a more accurate description of English and Chinese sadness expressions.

Discussions of emotions can be cleared from the charge of being impressionistic by means of an examination of empirical data. To retrieve reliable information on lexical use, large corpora are needed, particularly for less frequent words. Sufficient instances of the examined item from various texts are required to give a reliable picture about its use. The data resources of my investigation will be the Chinese corpus developed at the Centre for Chinese Linguistics, Peking University, the Bank of English and the Babel English–Chinese Parallel Corpus of Fiction compiled at Peking University. This corpus-based approach is embedded in a corpus-linguistic theoretical framework. The purpose of incorporating a parallel corpus into this methodology is to base cross-linguistic lexical links on quantitative data.

This analysis will involve, by means of examining their collocates, describing the colligations and semantic preferences/associations of the English and Chinese sadness expressions respectively. Colligations 'provide an objective view from the outside. They describe the observable behaviour of a social group' (Stubbs 2009: 125). According to Stubbs, semantic preferences/associations 'provide a subjective view from the inside' and they can only be identified intuitively (p. 125). Sometimes it is not an easy task to label them adequately. Once this is achieved, I will then look for real paraphrases (explicit paraphrases) and typical examples (implicit paraphrases, see Section 5.2.2) that contain information contributing significantly to revealing meaning. The final step of the analysis is to compare and contrast cross-linguistically and qualitatively the meanings of the semantically similar expressions within the same group on the basis of the previous corpus findings and provide a cultural explanation for the differences.

1.3 Significance

Psychological approaches to emotions have led to a number of important insights. Nevertheless, such studies have the disadvantage of seeming less objective because they are either based on introspection or the subjects studied are unlikely to behave in a natural way under observation. On the other hand, the corpus-based approach to the study of emotions offers a number of advantages. First, there is no 'observer's paradox'; in other words, since the study is based on texts written independently, the results will be less distorted by the subjects. Secondly, it is easier to achieve accuracy and reliability in such an analysis because the number of texts to be examined is much larger than can be looked at in psychological studies.

This study extends the corpus-linguistic framework to analyse and compare lexical meaning in depth. It proposes a unique theoretical approach that integrates corpus-linguistic theories on meaning (as a social construct, usage and paraphrase) at the macro level with lexical items at the micro level. It also develops a new complex methodology, which combines computational tools with manual examination to tease meaning out of corpus evidence, to compare and contrast lexical meaning within and across languages. Hopefully, this will provide fresh insights into how developments in corpus-linguistic theories as well as in the application of computer corpus technology can advance the field of lexical contrastive linguistics. By so doing, we can have a nuanced description of similarities and differences that epitomizes the descriptive potential of the corpus-linguistic approach to contrastive lexical semantics. This book will be the first large-scale corpus-based examination of the 'sadness' expressions. By analysing a large quantity of contrastive corpus data, I will uncover differences in the use of emotion words, and a large part of this book will be devoted to explaining them. I will show to what extent the differences can be explained through cultural differences. This is a relatively recent field of enquiry and investigations are still few and far between. My own contribution will hopefully offer new insights not yet described in the literature. In addition, the corpus-linguistic approach can throw new light on psychology, contrastive lexical studies, bilingual lexicography and language pedagogy.

1.4 Summary

This book explores, with reference to large corpora, the semantic disparities between sadness expressions in English and Chinese by applying the corpus-linguistic approach. It aims to probe into the cultural reasons that caused these differences, based on the corpus findings. Chapter 1 gives the rationale, objectives, methodology and significance of this research. It is grounded in three research areas: emotions, contrastive lexical semantics and corpus linguistics, so Chapter 2 addresses topics of emotions in psychology and emotion research in linguistics, Chapter 3 deals with contrastive lexical semantics, focusing on the frequently discussed issues of lexicalization and decomposition, and Chapter 4 is concerned with corpus linguistics, parallel corpora and cross-linguistic research. Chapter 5 explicates the theoretical framework on which the research is based and Chapter 6 deals with its methodology. Chapter 7 mainly reports, with great detail, on the corpus findings from the semantic-contrastive analysis of English and Chinese sadness expressions. The corpus-based analysis is also complemented by a contrastive-qualitative analysis of metaphorical sadness expressions in

English and Chinese. Chapter 8 discusses possible implications of this research for psychology, contrastive lexical semantics, bilingual lexicography and language pedagogy. The final chapter summarizes the research findings, discusses the limitations of this research and envisages the further development of cross-linguistic lexical studies with the aid of the corpus-linguistic approach in the near future.

Emotions

2.1 Emotions in psychology

There has been a heated debate about whether emotions are culture-specific or universal among anthropologists, biologists and psychologists. In 1872, Darwin addressed the behavioural manifestations of emotions in his *The Expression of the Emotions in Man and Animals* (1872/1965). Much of the research on emotion in the field of psychology maintains his tradition by documenting universal aspects of human emotions. The basic emotion theory has drawn the most attention, which argues that there are 5–7 basic emotions common to all human beings. Proponents of this theory have used facial-expressions recognition studies as their central source of evidence. Their assumption is that facial expressions are the translations of psychological states or processes. For example, Izard (1971) shows that facial expressions of Americans in photographs expressing 'basic' emotions can be recognized above chance level in both pre-literate and literate cultures and she concludes that these facial expressions of emotions are universally recognized. Ekman (2007) has carried out similar experiments over many decades and draws a similar conclusion, namely that basic emotions are inborn and everyone understands them. In these experiments, people in different countries—Papua New Guinea, the United States, Japan, Brazil, Argentina, Indonesia and the former Soviet Union—listen to stories and later are asked to match these stories with one of the photographs of facial features expressing seven basic emotions (sadness, anger, surprise, fear, enjoyment, disgust and contempt). These studies, which aim to demonstrate universality, have been criticized on the grounds that their methodology biases their outcome. In particular, it seems unreliable to tell participants to view expressions and enter multiple choice responses from a predetermined list. As Russell (1991) argues, what such experiments can show is that people from different cultures give similar (but not necessarily identical) interpretations to facial expressions. He says, suppose you are asked to match one of the terms to a face wearing a bright smile:

> Most likely, you'd select happy. But now suppose that happy had been replaced on the list with elated. Given the alternatives, you'd have no choice but to select elated. If happy were successively replaced with serene, satisfied, excited, grateful, and triumphant, you'd again select any of these words in turn.... Indeed, substitute for happy any clearly positive word ... and the conclusion remains the same.
>
> (Russell 1991: 435)

Moreover, it remains unclear how translation equivalence is assured. For instance, in the experiment of happiness in Papua New Guinea, Ekman (2007) uses 'His/her friends have come and s/he feels very happy' for the examinees to match with photographs of emotions. However, after being translated from English to Pidgin and then to Fore, the stories are told to the examinees finally in Fore, a local language in Papua New Guinea. Due to the great semantic variations between languages, it is problematic to assume, on the basis of such experiments, that the people in those isolated areas understand emotions in the same way as western people do and claim further that all these emotions are universal and have a genetic foundation.

Furthermore, often the same studies demonstrating universality also imply cultural specificity of emotions (Elfenbein and Ambady 2002). In Ekman *et al.*'s (1969) study, the recognition accuracy of the pre-literate participants from New Guinea, albeit above the chance level, is apparently lower than that achieved by the literate participants, revealing that there is still cultural difference in the recognition accuracy. The cultural variations are also marked in Izard's (1971) study, in which American & European, Japanese and African groups identify 75–83 per cent, 65 per cent and 50 per cent of the facial photographs respectively. It has been argued that collectivistic cultural groups are less accurate in expressing and perceiving negative emotions due to the risk of disrupting social disorder (Matsumoto 1989). Emotional communication may be more accurate when the expresser and the perceiver are both from the same cultural group rather than from different cultural groups (Elfenbein and Ambady 2002).

On the other hand, cultural constructionists claim that emotions are culturally organized or moulded, and thus are culture-specific. Some early ethnographic work on emotion has shown convincingly that cultures vary in which emotions are aroused in a given situation and how particular emotions are conceptualized and labelled (Briggs 1970; Lutz 1988). Durkheim (1911/1961) terms 'collective conscience' the ideas, norms and social expectations held important in the minds of all members of a society, and points out that feelings are closely linked to social situations. Kleinman (1980) suggests that affect comes into consciousness when a state of psychological arousal is given shape by a cultural judgement, the process of assigning an emotion label, made by an individual who suffers the arousal. Some recent work in the anthropology of emotion has also critiqued the notion that human emotional expressions are universal and have their basis in biology (Shweder 1994) by investigating affect as a cultural category and symbolic system. Secondary or cognized affects in different cultures, once labelled, differ in quality or intensity. Culture provides the cognitive and social environment to which the individual must learn to accommodate.

Goddard (1997) argues that psychology has yet to fully come to grips with the problem of translation between languages; researchers in cultural psychology and ethnopsychology (e.g. Harre and Finlay-Jones 1986; Lutz 1988; Shweder 1991, 1993; White and Kirkpatrick 1985) are well aware of the semantic variation between languages, while it is not the case in the field of psychology at large. Goddard takes as an example a recent edited volume entitled *The Nature of Emotion* (Ekman and Davidson 1994), where the terms 'translation' and 'language' are not included in the index, and only one of over twenty contributors acknowledges that languages issues would pose 'any great conceptual or methodological dilemma' (p. 155). Statements like this are more often seen in books of psychology: 'Equivalents for most of the emotion terms commonly considered part of the "basic" category seem to exist in almost all major languages of the world' (Scherer 1994). In some translation-sensitive studies of emotion, the researchers first decide on the emotion terms in English, then translate them into the respective other languages, and finally back-translate them into English. However, it is questionable that the procedure of 'back-translation' can really ensure semantic equivalence across languages. In a series of studies by Jerry Boucher and associates (Boucher and Carlson 1980; McAndrew 1986), a pair of Malay expressions (*marah* and *naik darah*) is used as an equivalent of English 'anger'. But Goddard's study (1996) shows that *marah* is closer to English 'offended' than to 'angry', and *naik darah* is more like 'to lose (one's) temper'. If cultures and languages differ in conceptualizing and expressing emotions, how can the exact equivalents across languages be found? What they can get are only close or near equivalents available in those languages.

Goddard's contrastive study (1997) of 'surprise-like' words from Malay (*terkejut, terperanjat, hairan*) and English (*surprised, amazed, shocked, startled*) shows that the English word *surprise* does not have an equivalent counterpart in Malay. He finds no semantic core shared by the various 'surprise' expressions either, only 'a loose set of cross-cutting and overlapping semantic correspondences' (p. 153). His findings are at odds with the traditional 'basic emotions' theory, which would regard *surprise* as one of the universal human emotions. Actually, it has also been argued that traditional psychological categories, such as 'emotion', 'sensation' and 'cognition', are also cultural artefacts of western society (Harre 1986; Lutz 1988). In the same article, Goddard (1997) points out that English should not be used uncritically as the metalanguage of cross-cultural research; English folk taxonomy should not be assumed as objective psychological reality and indigenous emotions concepts should not be tagged with English glosses. He claims that cross-cultural psychology can ill-afford to ignore the extent of semantic variation between languages; recent developments in linguistic semantics can benefit psychological research by overcoming 'some of the conceptual confusions and methodological difficulties impeding the development of a soundly based cross-cultural psychology' (p. 154).

2.2 Emotions in linguistics

To understand emotion is to ask for its origin in development. Psychological research shows that the emotional development of the child is deeply embedded in the emotional culture. From this developmental perspective, the child is 'constantly experiencing complex, constantly changing, internal and external emotional "stimuli", including the continuously changing expression of other people, filtered by cultural rules and norms, and the ongoing flow of language; [i]n these highly complex situations emotional meaning is co-constructed' (Josephs 1995). This is exactly what cultural constructionists claim: emotions are culturally organized or moulded, and thus are culture-specific. The cultural specificity of emotions cannot be discussed without recourse to the cultural specificity of language, the discussion of which originates from Sapir (1933: 166):

> Languages differ widely in the nature of their vocabularies. Distinctions which seem inevitable to us may be ignored in languages which reflect an entirely different type of culture, while these in turn insist on distinctions which are all but unintelligible to us. Such differences of vocabulary go far beyond the names of cultural objects such as arrow point, coat of armour, or gunboat. They apply just as well to the mental world.

Vocabulary is the best evidence of the reality of 'culture' because it reveals the specific concepts and classifications of categories and has been historically transmitted. Emotion words in different languages favour different distinctions as well, reflecting their respective cultures. The emotional lexicons of various languages differ significantly, and this reflects considerable differences in ideas and beliefs about emotions and cultural conceptualizations of emotions. These culture-bound emotion words might overlap. And, 'presumably, the closer two cultures are, the greater the overlap between their respective sets of emotions words' (Wierzbicka 1992a: 124). Interpretative categories that have been applied to emotions, such as *surprise* in English, or *jingya* in Chinese, are language- and culture-specific. In turn, the categorization of feelings depends mainly on 'the introspective vocabulary of the seeker' (James 1890: 485). In other words, the emotional lexicon in one's native language, to a great extent, constrains what kind of feelings people think they might have.

In cross-cultural lexical semantics, the theory that has drawn the most attention is the Natural Semantic Metalanguage (NSM) framework mainly developed by Wierzbicka (1972, 1992a, 1995, 1996, 1999). Within this framework, the meaning of a word is phrased in terms of small, standardized and translatable metalanguage, i.e. 'universal concepts' or 'semantic primitives' (also called 'conceptual primitives' or 'lexical universals') such as GOOD, FEEL, LIKE, HERE, THINK, WANT, DO and HAPPEN. These concepts are said to exist in all or most of the world's natural languages. Wierzbicka argues that the great majority of the words in natural languages are culture-bound, including emotion terms. She believes that each language with its own lexicon imposes its own classification and interpretative categories upon the world, which vary a great deal across languages and cultures. However, she also believes that there are some semantic components, be it a separate word, an affix or a fixed phrase, which are present in almost all languages, such as PEOPLE, GOOD, DO or HAPPEN. These universal concepts (about 60 have been identified) can be employed to define or explain other more complicated culture-specific concepts without the danger of 'terminological ethnocentrism'. The central claim of this theory is that the interpretation of any word (other than the universal concepts) in any language can be reduced to a combination of these semantic primitives. In other words, what Wierzbicka and her followers have been endeavouring to do is to deconstruct the words in natural languages, compare them and find what semantic components in them are common and what different. She states, '[T]he use of conceptual primitives allows us to explore human emotions . . . from a universal, language-independent perspective' (1995: 236).

Wierzbicka's search for conceptual universals has led to a substantial body of findings on cross-linguistic lexical semantics. Examples examined are from English, Russian, Polish, Ifaluk (Wierzbicka 1986, 1992a, 1992b, 1995, 1999),

Yankunytjatjara and Malay (Goddard 1990, 1991, 1995, 1996, 1997), Aboriginal English and Maori (Harkins 1994, 1996) and Chinese (Ye 2001), among other languages. To give a clear illustration of this approach, three 'anger-like' words from English, Malay and Ifaluk (cf. Goddard 1996; Lutz 1987, 1988; Wierzbicka 1992a) are used to show how their meanings are described by using so-called 'semantic primitives' (adapted from Goddard 1997: 160–1):

> It will be seen that the meanings are depicted by reference to a prototypical cognitive scenario in which a person thinks certain thoughts (often in association with certain desires) which give rise to a pleasant or unpleasant feeling. The cognitive scenarios for these three words all begin with the thought 'this person did something bad' and give rise to an unpleasant feeling.

    (a) *anger* (English)
        when X thinks of Y, X thinks something like this:
          this person did something bad
          I don't want this
          I want to do something to this person because of this
        because of all this, X feels something bad

    (b) *marah* (Malay) =
        when X thinks of Y, X thinks something like this:
          this person did something bad
          this person knows I do not want him/her to do something like this
          I feel something bad because of this
          I want this person to know this, not because I say anything about it
        because of all this, X feels something very bad

    (c) *song* (Ifaluk)
        when X thinks of Y, X thinks something like this:
          this person did something bad
          I don't want this
          it is bad if people do things like this
          I want this person to know this
          I want to do something because of this
         because of all this, X feels something bad

We can see that the definitions are 'stated in the form of an explanatory paraphrase' (Goddard 1997: 159), which are made up of 'semantic primitives' all languages have in common. According to Wierzbicka and Goddard, the NSM approach can show what the cross-cultural concepts have in common and how they differ. In this example, the three words all denote a bad feeling evoked by the thought that someone has done something bad. But *anger* is 'active and focused on retaliation', and *marah* is 'muted and restrained', while *song* is 'righteous and not necessarily directed toward the offering party' (Goddard 1997: 161).

Though the NSM theory's aim to reveal the cultural-specificity by using cultural-free and language-independent concepts is laudable, Bamberg (1997) argues that 'the methodological tool in the form of a universal inventory of lexical items' is unable to perform this job (p. 183). He gives the following reasons (p. 183):

> First, . . . the natural semantic metalanguage falls short of delivering more or better insights than traditional interpretative approaches to human actions and texts. Second, the discursive orientations and perspectives within which emotion terms are put to use in actual talk are washed out. Consequently, in order to achieve some richer understanding of emotion terms, particularly those of a foreign language, fuller contours of emotion talk need to be taken into account.

As the quote shows, he thinks the NSM theory is no better than the traditional interpretative approach. Goddard (1997), a keen follower of Wierzbicka, claims that the NSM methodology will lead to a better understanding of word meanings. However, Bamberg casts doubts on it by saying that 'most interpretative ethnographers, including Geertz or Garfinkel (1967), as well as semanticists of the Fillmore/Lakoff tradition, have always stressed that the explication of lexical meanings is never complete, but at best an approximation' (1997: 187). Bamberg's second reason concerns perspectives. The descriptions of the emotion scenarios under the NSM are presented through the shifting of roles from the first-person to a third-person perspective, assuming that it does not make any difference whether the person is the undergoer, instigator or onlooker. Nevertheless, Bamberg's work repeatedly shows that 'perspective matters tremendously in how emotion scenarios are construed and understood' (1997: 187). For example, a presentation of an anger event from the first-person perspective (when I once was angry) is different from one from a third-person perspective (when John once was angry) both in structure and content.

Josephs (1995) also makes some critical comments on Wierzbicka's approach. He points out that the NSM has brought novel analytic schemata to the semantics of emotions, but it still overlooks a number of relevant issues. First, 'her static and exclusively structural approach to emotion excludes functional aspects of emotions' (p. 279). Emotions are not static but ongoing processes.

Also, emotions are 'deeply-rooted in human action and functional in intrapersonal and interpersonal communication' (p. 286). So we cannot cut them off from their context of usage. The meaning of the emotion, i.e. its functional significance, should be found within the socio-cultural system (Averill 1980). Besides, Wierzbicka's understanding of semantics is problematic in the sense that she analyses the meanings of feelings, isolated from its usage, from the process of encoding and decoding. She assumes that words can be decomposed into cognitive components, 'the sum of which makes the whole—an assumption over which advocates of gestalt psychology especially would stumble' (Josephs 1995: 282). Furthermore, Wierzbicka's position on universality is questionable. If we believe that lexical universals do exist, then where are they? Are they in dictionaries or people's brains or somewhere else? The descriptions of the cognitive scenarios under her framework are actually highly individual choices, thus having little to do with universality (Josephs 1995).

To sum up, first, it remains problematic whether the notion of 'semantic primitives' itself can hold water since they are English words themselves. It is also unclear whether we can treat them truly neutrally or language independently. Wierzbicka and Goddard would take 'I' as a semantic primitive, but Harre's (1993) investigation shows that 'I' does not mean the same across all languages. Similarly, what is taken as 'good' or 'bad' is not the same across all cultures. For instance, *missing* is a beautiful feeling in the Chinese culture, while it is a negative one in the English-speaking society. So it is unnecessary to approach culture-specific concepts by inventing or discovering lexical universals. The understanding of foreign practices is possible by looking at them from your own perspective and 'not by giving up one's own, adopting a neutral universal one, and from there approaching the foreign' (Bamberg 1997: 190). Concerning this, Bamberg makes the following comments (1997: 190):

> The idea of a full, complete and objective understanding lurking behind the metaphor of semantic universals may even obstruct a better understanding of other cultures and their communications, because it posits the possibility of perfection and truth, while traditional interpretative and hermeneutic approaches are satisfied with the approximations that are desirable and in constant need of being reflected in light of historical changes and cultural affordances. In sum, then, I do not see any reason to give up well-established interpretative practices that have been tested in the interpretation of foreign texts and cultures in exchange for the promises of the natural semantic metalanguage approach.

Besides, Rosch's (1973) position that concepts are not defined by giving a list of features but by describing 'typical' examples is certainly not right in every way, but it is reasonable in some sense.

Secondly, it is highly simplistic to think the description of the world can be broken down to 60 basic universal concepts. It is hard to imagine words with complicated meanings can be defined or explained by these so-called semantic primitives. Thirdly, Wierzbicka has been trying to capture and depict the isolated meanings of single words without looking at their contexts, frequencies, colligations, collocations or semantic preferences/associations. As corpus linguists have observed, words are usually embedded in contexts, and rarely occur in isolation. To find out what a word means, we have to examine its contexts. It is the contexts that determine its meaning (for the interpretation of meaning, see Chapter 5). As corpora contain directly observable language data, they enable us to have a proper discussion of contextual meanings of words. There is no point in discussing the meaning of a word in isolation solely on the basis of researchers' intuitions, or 'highly individual choice and description', in Josephs' words (1995: 284).

Analysis of the affective lexicon of a language can reveal the classifications and interpretative categories imposed upon its speakers. Most of the discussions of cultural specificity of emotions, however, are impressionistic and therefore not very reliable. To give a solid and sound documentation of cultural specificity of emotion expressions, we have to look at directly observable language data. Goddard also agrees that it is time to embrace open data-gathering methods, including 'recourse to corpora of naturally occurring texts' (1997: 156). As far as I know, Teubert (2000) is the first linguistic study on emotion using corpus-linguistic methodology. In this study, by focusing on the semantic field of *trauer* in German and *sorrow* in English, he addresses the deficiencies of the dictionary approach and the conceptual ontological approach to bi- and multilingual lexical semantics, and proposes corpus linguistics and parallel corpora as a new potential and promising approach to this issue.

In another study on emotion, 'When did we start feeling guilty' (Teubert 2004b), he claims that *guilt* as a feeling has not entered into the Western discourse before roughly the second half of the nineteenth century, on the basis of historical evidence from dictionaries, psychological and cultural anthropological researches, early modern literature and a corpus. *Guilt* is, as we know, fuzzy and ambiguous. It means both 'the state of having committed a wrong' and 'a feeling, a state of emotion'. In this study, 4114 occurrences (excluding the occurrences referring to the first sense) of *guilt* as a feeling are found in the Bank of English.

Its collocation profile contains words like *inferiority, remorse, inadequacy, shame, intense, terrible, anger, failure, stress, self, deep, parents, strong, burden, release, painful*, etc. Here are some citations for *guilt* as a feeling extracted from the corpus (pp. 154–7):

- *Despairing, filled with remorse, guilt and self-pity, Kevin could not forgive himself*
- *the profound disruption in basic trust, the common feelings of shame, guilt and inferiority*
- *profound feelings of failure, guilt, self-loathing, and shame for having given in*
- *most females who are unable to control their eating behaviour feel intense guilt*
- *shame and guilt are stuff that makes us hide ourselves*
- *passions can be aroused by liberation from these guilts*

We can see that, in the first four citations above, *guilt* is caused by being unable to forgive oneself or to control one's eating behaviour, by 'a disruption of basic trust' (p. 155), for giving in when one should not have. The last two citations talk about the consequences of *guilt*. We can also see that, if *guilt* is conjoined with *shame, remorse, self-loathing* and the like, the purpose seems to be 'less a differentiation of these feelings than an intensification of the overall effect' (p. 155). These relevant context words of *guilt*, along with the concordance lines (or contexts) in which it occurs, would help capture the meaning of *guilt* as a feeling.

Following Teubert, Kondo (2004) makes a comparative study of *unhappy* on the basis of a small Japanese-English newspaper corpus. Although her study focuses on syntactic patterns rather than meaning and the data from that small corpus is not sufficient to allow a real statistical analysis, it is still a meaningful pilot empirical study to show, in some respects, the similarities and differences of *unhappiness* in English and Japanese.

Apart from what has been mentioned, some other corpus-based studies on emotions can be found. For example, Stefanowitsch (2004) analyses the metaphors of *happiness* and *joy* in English and German based on news texts available via the web archives of newspapers using the search engine Webcorp. However, this study is based on the cognitive framework and focuses on the differences in metaphorical mappings between these two languages. It uses the corpora only to find the instances of metaphor, mentioning nothing about frequency or collocates. This is the typical way most researchers make use of corpora. On the other hand, while the advent of parallel or translational corpora has rapidly revived contrastive linguistics, very few corpus-based contrastive studies deal with meaning or meaning differentiation. Most of the studies are associated with translation or usage.

A corpus-based semantic analysis of emotion items can provide a more accurate description of their meanings and lead to a better understanding of them. Cross-linguistic studies on emotions can also benefit from the corpus-linguistic approach. By looking closely at how emotion items are used in various languages, we can observe both similarities and differences in the use of these emotion items and their equivalents in other languages; we can identify what elements they share with similar expressions from other languages and what elements are specific to their own language. An empirical examination of emotion items in large corpora is likely to give more objective results and to further the discussion, which until now has all too often relied on rather vague introspection or the analysis of interviews with a number of participants that can hardly be considered representative. My work with corpora ensures that my investigation leads to tenable results.

Contrastive lexical semantics

3.1 Lexicalization

One important question that comes up frequently in lexical semantics is that of the motivation for lexicalization. The question is what makes certain sorts of notions or semantic configurations get lexicalized as single words rather than expressed by phrases? In specific terms, when would somebody say *kill* rather than *cause to die*? For Fillmore, 'the act of lexicalising something is to present it as an established category of human thought' (2003: 258). If a lexical item exists in a language, in Fillmore's words, 'it must exist as some part of a frame and must correspond to some part of a schema' (p. 258). His example of the English word *vegetarian* illustrates this point successfully. *Vegetarian* does not merely refer to a person living on vegetarian food, such as fruits, vegetables, grains. It implies that there are many people who eat meat, and by contrast there are people who deliberately do not eat meat. Otherwise, there would be no need for a particular word to represent such a concept and hence such a distinction.

Different languages organize lexical information in different ways. Words from different languages can differ in semantic 'transparency', 'motivation' and 'analyticity' (Fillmore 2003: 274). Ullmann (1958: 680, cited in Fillmore 2003: 274) describes this as the dosage of arbitrary vs motivated words in a language. Fillmore (2003) presents a detailed analysis of this feature. He claims that 'one language might systematically have large repertories of unanalysed words with highly specific meanings; another might have elaborate systems of semantically motivated word-formation principles; a third might depend more on syntactic processes for expressing complex notions. Languages can be seen to differ strikingly in the relative weighting that is given to one or another of these devices' (p. 270). He finds that Chinese month-names are highly motivated, since they have the form '1-month', '2-month', etc., while the English month-names are arbitrary with only slight etymological motivation in September, October, November and December. He makes a study of English verbs in the domain of walking on the basis of a large English-Japanese dictionary and finds that the Japanese translation consists of the word *aruku* (walk) plus a number of adverbs. *Stroll, saunter* and *meander* were all translated as *burabura aruku*; *plod* as *tobotobo aruku*; *totter* as *yochiyochi aruku*; *waddle* as *yoroyoro aruku*; and *lumber* as *doshindoshinto aruku*. His observation is that Japanese tends to combine mimetic adverbs with basic verbs to produce meanings of various 'walking' that are realized in English as single verbs, which share the semantic core of 'walking' and differentiate from each other in manner and attitude. Hence, Japanese and English vary systematically in their lexicalization patterns, with Japanese more analytic in the domain of 'walking'.

Another related issue in contrastive lexical semantics is what Ullmann refers to as 'characteristic tendencies'. Take the expression of motion and location for example. Although all languages seem to decompose motion events into components such as manner, path, the moving figure, etc., they differ both in how they combine these notions into words (Talmy 1985) and in how they categorize spatial relations they distinguish (Bowerman 1989, 1996; Casad and Langacker 1985; Lakoff 1987). For example, Choi and Bowerman's study (1992) shows that English and Korean differ in the way in which they lexicalize the components of motion events. English uses the same verb conflation patterns for both spontaneous motion and caused motion, and path is encoded separately with the same path marker. The former is usually expressed by an intransitive verb and the latter a transitive verb. Korean, by contrast, uses different lexicalization patterns for spontaneous motion and caused motion, and in most cases it uses different path markers for the two kinds of motions.

3.2 The problem of decomposition

It is essential to establish equivalence of lexical items across languages in lexical contrastive semantics. As mentioned earlier, there has been nearly a consensus that equivalent lexical items in different languages can be decomposed into identical sets of features, which are referred to as conceptual primitives or semantic universals. The reduced concepts can thus serve as *tertium comparationis* for establishing cross-linguistic lexical equivalence. However, taking this position poses problems. Krzeszowski (1990) presents a detailed analysis of this difficulty. To illustrate his point, he uses the example involving the words *man, boy, woman* and *girl*, which are usually decomposed into the features [male], [female], [young] and [adult]:

	[male]	[female]
[adult]	man	woman
[young]	boy	girl

He puts forward four reasons for the failure of this sort of framework to serve as *tertium comparationis* and presents strong arguments against decomposition by giving a series of illustrative examples. First, the features obtained from the decomposition analysis are not primitive at all. They can be further decomposed. He exemplifies this point by discussing the feature [young], which, in *The Concise Oxford Dictionary*, is defined as 'that has lived a relatively short time; not mature or fully developed'; *mature* is defined as 'complete in natural development or growth; fully developed in body and mind' and *develop* is defined as 'to grow into a fuller, higher, or maturer condition'. Here there is circularity, which is inherent in dictionary definitions. Features like [young], if they are expressed in natural languages, are problematic as *tertium comparationis*, since the words themselves are polysemous and ambiguous. Apart from being not mature, *young* has other senses, such as 'newly begun or formed; not advanced: The evening is young', 'pertaining to or suggestive of youth or early life: young for her age', 'vigorous or fresh, youthful', etc. The relatedness among its senses does not necessarily lead to the exact correspondence between the lexical items from different languages. For example, *young* is the equivalent to the Polish adjective *mlody* in its sense 'that has lived a relatively short time', but, in the sense 'being in the early period of growth', it is equivalent to *swiezy* in Polish.

Secondly, the features resulting from the decompositional procedure fail to 'reveal accurately the meanings of the analysed lexical items insofar as they leave some area of the meaning unaccounted for' (Krzeszowski 1990: 87). The well-formed *young man* and *young boy* seem to demonstrate that *boy* does not only mean 'young male' and the description is inaccurate. Thirdly, in lexical contrastive studies, the combination of features listed in matrices is insufficient to provide a complete account of the meanings of the lexical items compared. The matching of features [young] and [man] will lead to such items as *boy, lad, youth, urchin* and *master*. A host of other features, especially emotional aspects of meaning of such words, is needed to draw distinctions among them. Fourthly, the componential analysis cannot deal with various fuzzy concepts successfully. 'This procedure cannot be applied to various concepts which have no clear-cut boundaries and which shade into other concepts in a non-discrete way' (p. 88). Krzeszowski uses a set of words expressing non-discrete concepts to illustrate this point: *forest, wood, woodland, grove, copse* and *spinney*. Krzeszowski says that the differences between *spinnery*, *grove* and *wood* in *The American Heritage Dictionary* are 'a matter of degree' (p. 88), and the adjective *small* denotes a relative concept: *spinnery* is glossed as 'a small grove', grove as 'a small wood', while wood as 'a dense growth of trees; forest'. Such features cannot be defined in terms of the classical view of 'sufficient and necessary conditions' on which the componential analysis is based. It is not a yes–no matter, which can be answered simply by finding out whether the defining elements of a certain category are present.

It seems that the establishment of lexical equivalence across languages, by decomposing words into primitive concepts, is more than difficult to achieve because the idea of primitive concept itself is problematic since we have to express it in a natural language, where the great majority of words are polysemous and ambiguous, and traditionally their definitions rely on other words in dictionaries, which will unavoidably lead to circularity. As can be seen, meaning is far more subtle than a component analysis based on discrete features can account for, and far more complex than any print dictionary can describe. Meaning is often fuzzy and difficult to define satisfactorily. James (1980) suggests that, for a cross-linguistic lexical study, a better idea is to start with 'a perceived or assumed similarity' between contrasted items rather than to seek primitive or atomic units. We can only refine the assumed similarity by analysing them thoroughly and by adding explicitness and precision, but we cannot expect to deconstruct them to atomic units and then reconstruct them like building blocks. The human mental world is not as clear and orderly as the physical one. Even if we can deal with satisfactorily lexical items that are related to physical behaviour, such as 'walking' verbs, by decomposing them, we cannot say it applies to all domains of language.

In fact, any aspect of lexical semantics can serve as a basis for cross-linguistic comparison. We thus obtain contrastive studies of various lexical sets such as colours, kinship, modality or vision (see Krzeszowski 1990 for details of these studies). It is true that traditional contrastive studies have, to some extent, yielded some research findings. However, such investigations are incomplete and inadequate because they are not supported by directly observable quantitative data and their descriptions are largely based on individual researchers' introspection, dictionaries or scanty empirical evidence. Due to the inadequacies of the traditional approach, there has been a growing need to employ corpus methods for contrastive lexical semantic studies. This modern methodology arrives at the meaning of a word by focusing on the linguistic behaviour it exhibits in various contexts, namely, concordance lines and collocates, rather than by seeking its semantic primitives. Distinctions of semantically similar lexical items within the same language or across languages can be drawn without decomposing them. The idea is that to know a word does not necessarily mean that you need to decompose it; to understand a foreign word does not mean you need to give up your own language and look for language-independent semantic atoms. What you need to do is to figure out its position in its own language, and then compare it with your own.

Corpus linguistics, parallel corpora and cross-linguistic research

4.1 Corpus linguistics

Corpus-based analyses are 'empirical, utilise a large and principled collection of natural texts, make extensive use of computers for analysis using both automatic and interactive techniques, and depend on both quantitative and qualitative analytical techniques' (Biber *et al.* 1998: 4). When we incorporate corpus linguistics, the only object of analysis will be delimited to directly observable language data. In Sinclair's (1991: 4) words, 'the ability to examine large text corpora in a systematic manner allows access to a quality of evidence that has not been available before'. We can explicitly express the criteria for including texts in a corpus to make a representative sample of the discourse in question, thereby producing replicable corpus evidence. The corpus-based observations and results become transparent and verifiable regardless of the differences in interpretation. Corpus data is 'observed' rather than 'elicited'; it is superior to 'causal citational' data, which is also observed data, in that it is 'systematically and coherently organised' (Ooi 1998: 51).

According to corpus linguistics, the meaning of a word cannot be viewed independently of the contexts in which it occurs. 'Lexical meaning exists solely in the universe of discourse as the complex web tying words to other words via the contexts in which they occur and tying words within their contexts to all other occurrences of these words in all preceding texts' (Teubert 2000: 168). Looking at the context, we will find that it is often a specific co-occurrence pattern that disambiguates different usages or meanings of a word. Words can only be understood in their contexts and collocations. The traditional approach to bilingual lexical semantics is the bilingual dictionary, which consists of lexical items in one language and their equivalents in another, usually based on the linguistic intuitions of lexicographers. The information provided in the dictionary is often not explicit and lexical items are treated in isolation. That is why bilingual dictionaries are always insufficient for matching up lexical items across languages.

4.2 Translation equivalence, parallel corpora and cross-linguistic research

Translation equivalence is an essential issue in contrastive lexical studies. It is:

> ...not something that latently always exists and just has to be discovered. Translation equivalence has to be construed. As with meaning, this construal is a communal activity, only it does not involve a discourse community of a specific language such as English, but the community of bilingual speakers of the two languages involved. One translator will come up with a proposal, which is then negotiated with the other members of that community, until agreement is reached and every translator starts using the same equivalent, or until several equivalents are considered acceptable and translators choose among them.
>
> (Teubert and Cermakova 2004: 146–7)

So translation equivalence as a discourse construct does not exist independently of language use in discourse, i.e. translation process.

The terminology of 'parallel' corpora is a problem as the terms 'parallel' and 'comparable' corpora have been used in quite different ways, the former referring both to translation corpora and to comparable corpora, the latter to monolingual corpora of comparable texts as well as to corpora of comparable texts in different languages. In this book, following Teubert (1996), I use *parallel corpus* to refer to a corpus composed of source texts and their translations in one or more different languages, and *comparable corpus* to one that is composed of L1 data from different languages on the basis of the same sampling techniques.

'Parallel corpora are repositories of the practice of translators' (Teubert and Cermakova 2004: 155). Translators usually know much more about how to translate real texts in use than can be found in any bilingual dictionary; what they rely on for translation is not bilingual dictionaries, but an acquired competence, which is the accumulation of 'experience and interaction with other members of the bilingual discourse community of which they are a part' (Teubert and Cermakova 2004: 155). Parallel corpora can not only tell us how languages differ but also provide insights into the functioning of the languages involved. They can provide more precise information about the co-occurrence patterns and frequency data of the source items as well as of semantically related expressions that are brought into the picture by looking at their translations. The relative frequencies of semantically similar items in the contrasted language pair may relate to their semantic and pragmatic ranges of senses and functions.

In other words, obtaining the quantitative information about semantics and translations is crucial in making sense of the results. The task is by no means simple, as the results at first sight often look 'messy'. But, once the picture starts forming, we can see language in a novel way.

Parallel corpora are viewed as an important resource for contrastive studies. Their usefulness has been amply testified by empirical studies (Aijmer 1998; Altenberg 1999; Santos 1998; Schmied 1998; Xiao *et al.* 2006). For example, Santos's study shows that there is a great difference between English and Portuguese perception verbs in frequency, the way they are used, the kinds of objects they co-occur with and the kind of information that is co-specified with them. Translation data can shed new light on the similarities and differences between the compared language pair. At the same time, the contrastive focus, by revealing what is general and what is language-specific, can give a fuller picture of a given phenomenon in each of the language pair than a mono-linguistic study would do (Aarts 1998; Santos 1998; Viberg 1998). In other words, translation data not only provide a great impetus to contrastive studies, but also offer a fresh perspective on mono-linguistic studies. Further, they 'not only lend themselves to descriptive and applied approaches, but are also suitable for theory-oriented studies' (Aarts 1998: x). The range of linguistic research fields covered by the parallel corpus approach is very broad: semantics, lexis, syntax, discourse, translation process and translation style. Aijmer and Alternberg (1996: 12) outlined some potential uses of multilingual corpora for cross-linguistic research:

- They give new insights into the languages compared—insights that are likely to be unnoticed in studies of monolingual corpora;
- They can be used for a range of comparative purposes and increase our knowledge of language-specific, typological and cultural differences, as well as of universal features;
- They illuminate differences between source texts and translations, and between native and non-native texts;
- They can be used for a number of practical applications, e.g. in lexicography, language teaching and translation.

However, the idea of using parallel corpora for cross-linguistic research is challenged by some linguists due either to the translator's idiosyncrasies, or to 'translationese' (for a detailed discussion of 'translationese', see Gellerstam 1986, 1996), namely the deviance in translated texts induced by the transfer of phenomena from the source to the target language (Johansson and Hofland

1994) (for a detailed discussion of the problems in the use of translation corpora, see Johansson and Oksefjell 1998). For an explanation of translationese, Altenberg and Granger (2002: 17) offer the following:

> Translators transfer texts from one language or culture to another and the translation therefore tends to deviate in various ways from the original. We have already mentioned possible translation effects—traces of the source language or universal translation strategies—and they involve additions, omissions, and various kinds of 'free' renderings that are either called for or motivated by cultural and communicative considerations.

It seems that translationese is inherent in translations (Baker 1993; McEnery and Wilson 2001; McEnery and Xiao 2002; Teubert 1996) since it is 'motivated by cultural and communicative considerations', but it does not follow that translated texts cannot be used for cross-linguistic research (Aston 1999; Baker 1993; Johansson and Hofland 1994; Mauranen 2002; Teubert 1996).

Despite translationese, it is not totally impossible to establish equivalent lexical links across languages by using parallel corpora. Of course, the solution to this problem is not simple. Obviously, we cannot trust all the translations in the corpus as target equivalents. To determine which candidates can be regarded as 'equivalents', one choice is to resort to the procedure of 'back-translation' (Ivir 1987), i.e. to look for those in the target language that can be translated back into their original forms in the source language. This procedure will filter out those unreliable equivalents arising from the translator's style or other translational strategies, but, of course, it requires a bi-directional parallel corpus, i.e. a corpus containing original and translated texts for both directions. Another way is to look for the more recurrent translation equivalents on the basis of quantitative information (Krzeszowski 1990). If the same translation pattern occurs recurrently in a parallel corpus, it obviously increases its potential to be viewed as a translation equivalent. A corpus that contains texts from a variety of translators can be trusted. The third choice would be to combine the above two—back-translation and frequency—to arrive at the 'mutual correspondence' (also referred to as translatability) of two items in a bi-directional parallel corpus (Altenberg 1999). Cross-linguistic equivalence, like any notion of equivalence, is a matter of judgement (Chesterman 1998), so the notion of equivalence is only a relative concept. In practice, 80 per cent will be a high value (see Altenberg 1999). The value obtained often serves as a statistical measure of the degree of correspondence between the compared items (Altenberg 1999).

Dyvik (1998) argues that translation corpora can enrich linguistic semantics not only because they incorporate a multilingual element into this kind of research, but also 'because the activity of translation is one of the very few cases where speakers evaluate meaning relations between expressions without doing so as part of some kind of meta-linguistic, philosophical or theoretical reflection, but as a normal kind of linguistic activity' (p. 51). Teubert claims that 'the common practice of translators for a given language pair reveals the conventions of this bilingual language community. There is no reason to assume that the conventions of a monolingual language community concerning the meanings of text segments differ in principle from those of a community of translators' (1999: 23). This new understanding of translations greatly reduces our worries about translationese, especially when we deal with meaning.

Due to the well-known deficiencies in previous contrastive studies, there has been an increasing awareness that cross-linguistic studies cannot rely on introspection or dictionaries, but must be firmly based on naturally occurring language data. The development of machine-readable corpora and relevant computer technology are well suited to meet these new demands. The corpus-linguistic approach to cross-linguistic research allows us to investigate with more objectivity and greater accuracy how words are used in natural or at least relatively natural contexts. Parallel corpora have been successfully used in a variety of cross-linguistic studies, though most of them are concerned with non-meaning aspects of language.

This book is going to focus specifically on lexical meaning, so large corpora are required to fulfil this purpose. To find what a word means, we will search it in a monolingual corpus and examine the words in its company. A large corpus will yield sufficient citations of the examined word. We can set up its collocation profile, which, coupled with paraphrases and examples, will tell us what it means. The parallel corpus will be used to link the synonymous words from the two languages. After arriving at the meanings of the words in monolingual corpora respectively, we can compare and contrast the semantically equivalent word(s) linked by the parallel corpus.

The corpus-linguistic framework

5.1 Corpus linguistics: Theory or methodology?

It has been a great controversy whether corpus linguistics is only a methodology that can be used in almost any area of linguistic research, or whether it is an independent discipline in its own right in the same sense as cognitive linguistics. It is well acknowledged that corpus linguistics has opened up exciting possibilities that could not have been envisaged without corpora; in other words, the corpus technology has led to new findings that cannot be achieved by intuition alone. But the real strength of corpus linguistics lies in the fact that these findings have shaken the foundations of linguistics (Scott and Tribble 2006). For example, 'Sinclair's (1991) corpus-based questioning of the parts of speech which were so traditionally established, or Francis, Hunston and Manning's (1996) pattern grammar arguing that grammar is much more local than it had seemed' (Scott and Tribble 2006: 4). The wide recognition of pattern grammar suggests that lexis has shaken the dominant position of syntax and grammar in language study and attracted considerable attention (Scott and Tribble 2006). Tognini-Bonelli (2001) proposes that a distinction should be drawn between the corpus-based and corpus-driven approaches. In the former, corpora are used only to 'expound, test or exemplify theories and descriptions that were formulated before large corpora became available to inform language study' (p. 65), while, in the latter, the aim is to 'derive linguistic categories systematically from the recurrent patterns and the frequency distributions that emerge from language in context' (p. 87). 'The distinction between "corpus-based" and "corpus-driven" approaches may be seen to correspond to the "top-down" and "bottom-up" approaches' (Ooi 1998: 52). According to Tognini-Bonelli (2001), only the corpus-driven approach is related to corpus linguistics as a separate discipline.

'When corpus linguistics started off, the main reaction was the excitement about various unexpected findings and technical possibilities. However, the interest in the theoretical consequences of corpus linguistics has been gaining importance' (Mahlberg 2005: 17). Corpus studies have yielded numerous findings on the following topics that existing theories have either failed to explain or totally ignored: (extended) unit of meaning or lexical item (Sinclair 1996, 1998, 2004; Sinclair & Teubert 2004; Stubbs 2009; Teubert 2005), pattern grammar (Francis *et al.* 1996; Hunston and Francis 1998, 1999), collocation, semantic prosody (Bednarek 2008; Hunston 2007; Louw 1993, 2000; O'Halloran 2007; Ooi 1998, 2000, 2008; Partington 2004; Sinclair 1996, 1998; Stewart 2010; Whitsitt 2005; Xiao and McEnery 2006), part of speech (Sinclair 1991), lexis as the core of language (Hoey 2004, 2005; Sinclair 1991, 2004; Teubert 2004a, 2005), the relationship between form and meaning (Hoey 2005; O'Halloran 2007; Sinclair 1985, 1987, 1991; Stubbs 1996; Teubert 2005; Teubert and Cermakova 2004; Tognini-Bonelli 2001; Williams 1998), paraphrase as interpretation of meaning (Teubert 2005, 2010; Teubert and Cermakova 2004). Only corpus-based analyses can discover them. 'The potential of corpus linguistics and its role in linguistics will be seriously underestimated if we regard it as a method only' (Mahlberg 2005: 17). Corpus linguistics is a promising enterprise as it has provided a new philosophical approach to linguistic enquiry (Tognini-Bonelli 2001) and a new look at language (Teubert 2005, 2010), which greatly help reveal the real nature of language.

Both 'corpus-based' and 'corpus-driven' approaches are useful notions. In this study, the corpus-based approach is taken to mean that the notion of 'lexical word' still applies and is not reformulated. Complementing this perspective, the 'corpus-driven' approach uses empirical evidence for reformulating the traditional category of 'lexical word' (which is not taken for granted). Words are polysemous, and so are emotion words. I will focus only on the 'feeling' sense for emotion words. In dealing with the data, this study is more corpus-driven as it is based on the corpus-linguistic framework and takes the data as the centre of the analysis. Despite the corpus-based vs corpus-driven distinction noted earlier, in practice a mixed approach of both is often necessary (Ooi 1998). A more recent notion is 'triangulation', which refers to 'the use of more than one approach to a research problem, including using several research methods or instruments to investigate the same thing, so as to corroborate findings and minimise the possibility of a method distorting the evidence' (Sealey 2010: 64). It seems that the combination of approaches to a research question has become the current trend. We may use corpus data to triangulate our intuitions in order to make a more accurate description of the lexicon.

5.2 The corpus-linguistic view on meaning

5.2.1 Meaning as a social construct

The claim that meaning is a social construct is either articulated or implied in social constructivism (Berger and Luckmann 1966; Lave and Wenger 1991; Vygotsky 1978), focusing on the construction in the individual mind derived from his/her interaction with social structures, and social constructionism (Burr 1995; Gergen 1994, 1999), with the emphasis more on the collaborative construction through social interaction. Corpus linguistics is closer to social constructionism in terms of the collaborative construction of meaning (details will be addressed in Section 5.2.2). Critical discourse analysis (CDA, henceforth) also works along this line. CDA, by describing, interpreting and explaining the situation, recipients, consequences and social responses of the discourse, aims to reveal the underlying ideological bias of the discourse and uncover inequality and social reality (Fairclough 1989). CDA and corpus linguistics differ in their attitude towards the relationship between society and discourse (Teubert 2010). CDA (Fairclough 1989) claims that it is society that determines discourse, while corpus linguistics (Teubert 2010: 121) believes that 'it is the discourse that constructs social structures, not the other way around'. Despite the theoretical difference stated above and CDA's heavy focus on the relation between ideology and inequality in social reality, CDA confirms the claim that meaning is constructed in discourse by language users. It has done much in revealing how meaning/ideology is constructed to maintain the unequal power relations in society. However, there is no standard methodology for critical discourse analysts to follow. Stubbs (1997) raised some practical questions such as how frequency of use relates to naturalization, how the data is selected and whether they are representative. Corpus linguistics opens up a new battlefield to deal with meaning construction in discourse. The corpus-linguistic approach can circumvent CDA's disadvantages noted above because corpus-based analyses are empirical and 'depend on both quantitative and qualitative analytical techniques' (Biber *et al.* 1998: 4).

The corpus-linguistic claims relevant to the negotiation or construction of meaning from Teubert's 25 theoretical theses are listed below (2005: 2–4):

1. The focus of corpus linguistics is on meaning. Meaning is what is being verbally communicated between the members of a discourse community. Corpus linguistics looks at language from a social perspective . . .

3. Every text segment, word, multi-word unit, phrase etc., can be viewed under the aspect of form and the aspect of meaning. The form is what represents the meaning, and there is no meaning without the form by which it is represented ... Normally the members of the language community deal with text segments without being aware what these text segments mean ... Unless there is some (potential) communication disorder, there is no need to discuss meaning within the discourse community.

4. Meaning is in the discourse. Once we ask what a text segment means, we will find the answer only in the discourse, in past text segments which help to interpret this segment, or in new contributions which respond to our question. Meaning does not concern the world outside the discourse. There is no direct link between the discourse and the 'real world'. It is up to each individual to connect the text segment to their first-person experiences, i.e. to some discourse-external ideation or to the 'real world'. How such a connection works is outside the realm of the corpus linguist.

5. For corpus linguistics, the meaning of a text or of a text segment is independent of the intentions of its speaker (its author) ...

7. Corpus linguistics makes general and specific claims about the discourse, based on the analysis of a suitably selected cross-section of it, i.e. the corpus. General claims have to do with rules or with probabilistic expectations. They fall within the field of grammar or variation or language change, and also into the field of lexical meaning insofar as a text segment occurring in a text can be viewed as an instantiation (a token) of a lexical item. Specific claims are interpretations of texts or text segments viewed as unique occurrences.

From the above theses, we can see that, according to Teubert (2005), corpus linguistics focuses on meaning in the collective sense as found in a discourse, not on understanding in the individual sense or intention as found in people's heads. Through the explication of a haiku randomly produced by a computer program, Teubert (2010: 215–40) shows that the meaning of a text is separate from the intention of its author. The general claim in Thesis 7 refers to the meaning in the collective sense, while the specific claim is the interpretation based on the collective sense, regardless of what is intended by its author or speaker. Meaning emerges as social constructs independently of the discourse-external reality; not only meaning, but also our perception of reality is constructed through social interaction and mediated by the use of language. This perspective is very much in line with constructionism (Gergen 1994, 1999).

Numerous corpus studies show that each linguistic form has a certain meaning (Hoey 2005; O'Halloran 2007; Sinclair 1985, 1987, 1991; Stubbs 1996; Tognini-Bonelli 2001; Williams 1998). This seems to suggest that the members of a discourse community tend to attach a certain meaning to a certain linguistic form. Linguistic forms are only linguistic symbols to represent meanings. Form and meaning cannot be separated. The integration of meaning and form is the outcome of social construction. Members in a discourse community take part in the negotiation or clarification of the meaning of a given linguistic unit in progressive discourse. Words or phrases are just social constructs to which discourse members attach meanings in social contexts. They have nothing to do with the discourse-external reality. In a recent interview (Zhang 2009), Teubert (p. 87) exemplifies this view:

> One of the basic units of biology is the species. But today all biologists would admit that what we call a species is not something that exists out there in the real world; what we call a species is the result of never-ending negotiations within the discourse of expert biologists. A species is a discourse concept, nothing more. We can find it useful today and discard it tomorrow, just as the infamous phlogiston has been discarded after it had outlived its usefulness. The idea that science can tell us the truth about natural phenomena is not helpful ... and this 'knowledge' does not refer to 'true' properties of things in the 'real' world out there, they are nothing but agreements accepted by certain discourse communities.

According to Teubert (2005, 2010), meaning is only a social construct and the reality is constructed via discourse; the discourse-external reality is meaningless because it cannot be discussed, exchanged, shared and known; the personal experience will enter the discourse after it is shared and discussed. We come to know the world only through all the texts (written or spoken) exposed to each of us, which vary greatly from person to person. It is impossible to get access to the individual discourse, i.e. all the texts one individual has been exposed to, so we can only try to reveal the linguistic truth based on the public discourse in the form of corpora, which is also incomplete because the great majority of the texts produced by us have been lost. The meaning of a linguistic unit is neither what it refers to out there in some discourse-external reality nor some representation people have in their minds; meaning is usage and paraphrase (Teubert and Cermakova 2004) as we find in discourse.

5.2.2 Meaning as paraphrase

Meaning can be rephrased in different words. Corpus linguistics takes meaning as paraphrases in discourse. Teubert's (2005: 6–7) theses relevant to this claim are shown below:

19. Meaning is paraphrase. Whenever lexical item tokens are the cause of a communication disorder, their meaning will be negotiated, described or explained, replaced by synonyms, and sometimes even 'defined' as in dictionaries or in encyclopaedias. What we find paraphrased in the discourse are text segments that are looked upon intuitively by the members of the discourse community as units of meaning. However, the same lexical item type can be paraphrased in an infinite variety of ways. Therefore, whenever a lexical item token is being paraphrased, we can view it from two perspectives: as an instantiation of the lexical item type, and as a unique occurrence. From a synchronic perspective, the meaning of a lexical item type is a generalization on all the paraphrases we find for the instantiations of this lexical item. But paraphrases are also relevant for specific claims. From a diachronic perspective, it is the history of paraphrases of a recurrent text segment, as evidenced in its intertextual links, that tells us what it means as a unique occurrence.

20. There is no true and no fixed meaning. Everyone can paraphrase a unit of meaning however they like, therefore the meaning of any lexical item type is always provisional. The next paraphrase may already lead to a revision. The members of the discourse community will continue to negotiate, among themselves, what a unit of meaning means. They may agree or not: the issue is not truth, but acceptance. An explanation, a paraphrase that is widely accepted and re-used, is more relevant than a paraphrase that is never repeated, just as texts which are constantly referred to are more relevant than texts that leave no traces in subsequent texts.

21. The discourse is a self-referential system. Natural language is the only codification system in which the functions of its elements are determined not by ascription from outside but by discourse-internal negotiation. This sets natural languages apart from formal calculi, like the code of mathematics.

Before discussing the above quotes, it is helpful to clarify some corpus-linguistic terms. In corpus linguistics, 'lexical items' or 'units of meaning' can be 'single words, compounds, multiword units, phrases, and even idioms' (Teubert 2005: 5). 'They are, in principle, monosemous. This is what distinguishes the concept of a lexical item from the concept of a word' (Teubert 2005: 5). The above theses show that within a discourse individuals each develop their own interpretation of a given lexical item, in which some of them may be quite apart from each other, and this process is ongoing. Whatever is said about a given lexical item within the discourse contributes to the meaning of this lexical item, which is the accumulation of its previous occurrences, including what has been given in dictionaries. It is, from a synchronic perspective, a generalization of all the instantiations of this lexical item or a 'loose consensus', in Sinclair's words (Sinclair and Teubert 2004), we are searching for or can achieve. The meaning of a given lexical item is co-constructed by the members of the discourse community, regardless of whether it is true or not. 'Lexical items and what they stand for are discourse objects (and not objects of the "real world") constructed through the contributions of the members of the discourse community' (Teubert 2005: 7).

Paraphrases are interpretations in the form of explanations, explications or redefinitions. An interpretation can be re-discussed, reinterpreted or further elaborated in the discourse. On this account, the meaning of a lexical item is co-referential within the discourse. Whenever a new lexical item is introduced into the discourse, it will be explained or interpreted in various ways. Its meaning will be argued and negotiated by its discourse members, when it is referred to numerous times later. It is through this negotiation and argument that its meaning is constructed socially and collaboratively within the discourse. A lexical item is a type and each instance of it is a token. The contribution of each instance to its meaning varies considerably. Some instances are real paraphrases, like 'sadness is a less strong feeling', which can make obvious and significant contributions to its meaning, while others may only contain a piece of knowledge concerning the given lexical item that can tell us something about its meaning, and still others may make little contribution. Typical examples can contribute quite a lot to its meaning, so they can be taken as implicit paraphrases. Real paraphrases can be identified and also extracted by using corpus tools. Cheung (forthcoming), based on the analysis of syntactically defined patterns in which paraphrases occur in texts, developed a method to automatically retrieve paraphrases from a corpus. However, the availability of real paraphrases differs greatly. For some words/items, sufficient real paraphrases cannot be identified in the corpus examined due to its limited size, which is seemingly quite big but actually still pretty small compared with the size of the human output. This is particularly the case for Chinese sadness expressions. Another reason for the lack of paraphrases in the CCL corpus might be that it does not include books in psychology in which emotion concepts are extensively discussed (cf.

Section 5.2.3). Therefore, in some cases, we may need to resort to implicit paraphrases, i.e. typical examples, and collocates to analyse and disclose meaning. However, I will illustrate, if paraphrases are available, how they can help make meaning transparent in Section 7.1.1 (pp. 74–76) and Section 7.1.7 (pp. 140–41).

5.2.3 Meaning as usage

According to Teubert and Cermakova (2004), apart from paraphrase, the meaning of a lexical item is also its usage as found in the discourse, such as its frequency, contextual information, collocational profile, etc., which can be established by a computer. Usage is 'something we have to cope with as members of the discourse community' (p. 128). This view is also shared by Hoey (2005: 81) who argues that 'the meanings of a word will have to be interpreted as the outcome of its primings, not the object of the primings'. In other words, the meaning of a word (sense) lies in the colligations, collocations and semantic associations a word is primed for, not elsewhere. Hoey's notion of lexical priming will be addressed in detail in Section 5.3.2.

This book is to explore how meaning can be described, defined, explained, negotiated and elaborated by the members of a discourse community. Based on the principles stated above, I will see how the meaning of a word/item can be arrived at by examining its semantic profile based on all its instances in a corpus and also by investigating its real paraphrases and typical examples. One thing that should be noted is that I will use the principles discussed to guide my research at the macro-level, but I may not use these terms, such as social construct, paraphrase or usage, in my analysis. In presenting the data, I will use the corpus-linguistic structural categories of the lexical models at the micro-level to direct my analysis. While most of the items I am going to examine in this research are lexical words, I will only focus on its sense as a feeling, so it is monosemous in this sense.

5.3 A lexical model: colligation + collocation + semantic association/preference

5.3.1 Sinclair's notion of (extended) unit of meaning and his lexical model

In Firthian and neo-Firthian linguistics, the notion of word as the unit of meaning has been abandoned by most corpus linguists since a common word of a language typically can have several meanings (Sinclair 1991, 1996, 1998, 2004; Sinclair and Teubert 2004; Stubbs 1996; Teubert 2004a, 2005; Tognini-Bonelli 2001). Sinclair points out that a unit of meaning is 'rather a phrasal unit than a word' (Sinclair and Teubert 2004) as the co-occurrence tendencies between words are so strong that 'we must widen our horizons and expect the units of meaning to be much more extensive and varied than is seen in a single word' (Sinclair 2004: 39). He argues that the model of a lexical item, or a unit of meaning, is the only one to facilitate the study of meaning. His classical examples *the naked eye, true feelings* illustrate what could be a unit of meaning. Sinclair focuses more on co-selection between words when he examines this concept. He explores extended units of meaning by trying to incorporate all the constraints around, for example, *the naked eye*, both at the lexico-grammatical and the semantic levels, into the extended unit of meaning, including the semantic preference of 'visibility', realized by strong collocations with words such as *see, visible*, etc. He also argues that a lexical item is prone to variation; the canonical form would be the prototype of a lexical item. For example, *get in touch with* is the canonical form of the lexical item. There are all sorts of other verbs that could be substituted for *get: bring, be, keep, remain*, etc. (2004). For Sinclair, lexical items or units of meaning have a strong tendency to become delexicalized. With regard to this, he states (2004–20):

> The meaning of words chosen together is different from their independent meanings, they are at least partly delexicalised. This is the necessary correlate of co-selection. If you know that selections are not independent, and that one selection depends on another, then there must be a result and effect on the meaning which in each individual choice is a delexicalisation of one kind or another.

This accounts for why a lexical item means different from the phrase which is interpreted according to the *open choice principle*.

Sinclair (1996, 1998, 2004) proposes a lexical model in which four structural categories are combined to describe lexical items—collocation, colligation, semantic preference and semantic prosody. In this model, the category of semantic preference refers to the similar semantic features shared by the item's collocates. Colligation is 'one step more abstract than collocation' (Sinclair 2004: 32) and it has to do with the co-occurrence of grammatical choices. Collocation is defined as 'the occurrence of two or more words within a short space of each other in a text' early in his book *Corpus, Concordance, Collocation* (1991: 170). In his famous article 'The search for units of meaning' (1996, 2004), Sinclair investigates *true feelings*, a common collocation that is not idiomatic in the normal sense, and summarizes the result as follows (2004: 35):

> a semantic prosody of reluctance/inability
> a semantic preference of expression (and a strong colligation of a verb
>   with the semantic preference)
> a colligating possessive adjective
> the core

Sinclair tells us that we choose this particular collocation when we talk about our reluctance to express our genuine emotions. This expression is almost never used in any other way. Many studies have sought to scrutinize the notion of semantic prosody (Louw 1993; Partington 2004; Whitsitt 2005). The usual interpretation of semantic prosody is seen as too restrictive in that it is often associated with only three possibilities: positive, negative and neutral connotation. Sinclair uses this term in a less restrictive sense, i.e. it does not only refer to the above three possibilities, but refers to any attitudinal/pragmatic meaning implied in the lexical item examined. Hunston (2007), taking *budge* for example (Sinclair 2004: 142–7), explicates Sinclair's idea on semantic prosody:

> Sinclair's point is that the sequence '*inability + negative + budge + (something)*' is chosen in contexts where something difficult and important is being attempted, to no avail, and that the sequence '*unwillingness + negative + budge*' is chosen to express disapproval of someone's lack of flexibility. The sense of frustration is a more complex concept than a simple positive or negative evaluation, and it is clear that it belongs to the sequence as a whole, the unit of meaning, rather than just to the word *budge*.

From the above elaboration, it can be seen that semantic prosody, in Sinclair's sense, is used to define the discourse function of the whole (extended) unit of meaning. Sinclair takes semantic prosody in part as connotation (2003: 178) and argues that 'the reason why we choose to express ourselves in one way rather than another is coded in the prosody, which is an obligatory component of a lexical item' (2000: 200).

Similarly, Partington (1998, 2004) takes semantic prosody as an aspect of evaluative meaning, which he considers to be close to expressive connotation (2004: 154). He points out that items like *timely, excessive, flabby* are said to have clearly favourable or unfavourable evaluation, and 'semantic prosody describes the same kind of evaluative meaning but spreads over a unit of language which potentially goes well beyond the single orthographic word' (2004: 131–2).

Partington (2004) groups Sinclair's attitudinal meaning under the category of 'expressive connotation'; however, Whitsitt (2005) treats Sinclair's definition of semantic prosody as a distinct concept as it emphasizes the pragmatic function. Louw (2000: 50) also argues that the force behind semantic prosody is 'more strongly collocational than the schematic aspects of connotation'.

As there has been much confusion and debate over semantic prosody and connotation, Morley and Partington (2009), in a recent article, have revisited this issue and proposed to express them in terms of prototypicality (Rosch 1977). In their discussion, semantic prosody is considered to be an aspect of '(evaluative) connotational meaning', which differs from 'connotation' in relation to single word/item as it is 'defined as expressed over stretches of discourse' (Morley and Partington 2009: 151); connotation is often thought to be more evident and less hidden than semantic prosody, while the latter resides in the 'collocational patterns of items in a text' (p. 150), which may contribute to its nature of being more hidden. This explains why semantic prosody is usually not accessible via introspection alone, and is derived more accurately through a closer inspection of a sufficient number of instances of the lexical item in the concordance. Morley and Partington (p. 151) have borrowed the prototype theory to illustrate the 'obviousness' of evaluative connotation:

> ... where the items closer to the centre are those with the most evident and consistent evaluative connotation, whilst those closer to the outskirts have an evaluative connotation which is less obvious and consistent and which is perhaps more likely to be switched off or overturned when contextual requirements demand.

In their illustration, items such as *good, murder* are in the centre as they seem to express clearly favourable and unfavourable connotation respectively; items like *cause, commit, symptomatic* are somewhere in the middle, while *set in, happen* and *utterly* are on the outskirts as they were totally obscure before corpus data became available; still other items like *chair, tree* are outside the circles as they do not display any statistical tendency even after the corpus data are examined. We may summarize their discussion as follows: connotation in its narrow sense is more consistent, obvious and often discussed in relation to individual word/item, while semantic prosody can be considered a part of connotation in the broad sense and is a product of collocation, which makes it less consistent, hidden in the collocational patterns of items and spreading over stretches of discourse.

Sinclair's lexical model, as stated earlier, is mainly intended for (extended) unit of meaning. He proposes that the major structural categories involved in the model—collocation, colligation, semantic preference and semantic prosody—assume a central rather than a peripheral role in language description. He further argues that 'this model does not exclude single words that are apparently chosen on open-choice principles' (2004: 39) and makes an in-depth analysis of *place* (sense 13) to support his claim. Nevertheless, as discussed above, items, whether single item/word or (extended) unit of meaning, vary in their obviousness of semantic prosody. Although it seems that an (extended) unit of meaning is more likely to have an obvious semantic prosody, this model 'has largely been illustrated by individual case studies, and it remains unclear whether all phrases, or only some, have semantic prosodies' (Stubbs 2009: 12). If there is still difficulty in applying this model to larger (extended) units of meaning, it will pose more problems for single words, as they have a wider range of collocates, which are less likely to be grouped under one single label for communicative purpose. To seek an appropriate lexical model for my analysis of single words, let us look at Hoey's notion of lexical priming.

5.3.2 Hoey's notions of semantic association and lexical priming

In line with Sinclair's claim that grammar exists just because we cannot say everything at once (Sinclair and Teubert 2004), Hoey (2005: 1) proposes a theory of lexicon that 'reverses the role of lexis and grammar, arguing that lexis is complexly and systematically structured and that grammar is an outcome of this lexical structure'. It is a theory of lexis moving from the surface of language product inwards into the psycholinguistic reality. Hoey is trying to illustrate lexicon through collocations, colligations and semantic associations 'that are built up in the individual mind, and harmonised in a collective consciousness of language' (Williams 2006: 327). His theory puts the lexis at the centre of language capacity and claims that grammatical and lexical choices will be governed by lexical primings. Hoey (2005: 2) points out that the problem with the traditional theory is that it 'account[s] only for what is possible in a language and not for what is natural'. Corpus linguistics 'is concerned with how naturalness is achieved and how an explanation of what is natural might impinge on explanations of what is possible' (Hoey 2005). 'A key factor in naturalness, much discussed in recent years, is collocation' (Hoey 2005). He also takes collocation as central to his approach; unlike Sinclair, however, he defines collocation as a psychological association between words.

Hoey's theory 'sets out to outline a new theory of language based on co-occurrence patterns that are stored in the individual's mind' (2005: 15). Some of his claims are not entirely new, but they are expressed from a new psycholinguistic perspective. Chomsky (1986) distinguishes between E-Language (externalized language) and I-Language (internalized language). Cognitive linguistics focuses on the latter, while corpus linguistics examines the former. Hoey's (2005) theory of lexical priming is intended to bridge the gap between the two, with a focus on lexis rather than grammar. 'Priming can be seen as reversing the traditional relationship between grammar as systematic and lexis as loosely organised, amounting to an argument for lexis as systematic and grammar as more loosely organised' (Hoey 2005: 9). Hoey (2005: 13) puts forward a list of psycholinguistic hypotheses using a corpus as evidence, of which those relevant to my research are shown below:

3. Every word is primed to occur with particular semantic sets; these are its semantic associations.

5. Co-hyponyms and synonyms differ with respect to their collocations, semantic associations and colligations.

6. When a word is polysemous, the collocations, semantic associations and colligations of one sense of the word differ from those of its other senses.

We can see that whether from a sociolinguistic, psycholinguistic or purely linguistic perspective, whether taking a corpus as a discourse, a collective mind or a collection of texts, the corpus data tell us the same thing. One of the main differences between Hoey's lexical priming theory and Sinclair's lexical model lies in the notion of semantic association, which replaces Sinclair's semantic preference and semantic prosody. Semantic preference refers to the habitual collocation of lexical items with linguistic expressions that come from certain semantic fields. Semantic associations allow collocates to be grouped into semantic sets. 'These reveal patterns of language that go beyond collocation to form phraseological units with a string of variable elements' (Williams 2006: 328). A simple comparison will reveal that the notion of semantic association is actually a different label of Sinclair's concept of semantic preference (cf. Hoey 2004: 388; Ooi 2008: 312). So the lexical model I will use for my research can be taken as an adapted version of Sinclair's model, with semantic prosody removed as it does not apply to every single word, or as Hoey's model, but from a sociolinguistic perspective, rather than a psycholinguistic one, as what I am discussing is the social construction of meaning. In analysing the corpus data, I will not distinguish them as they both reveal the same thing.

Semantic preference is commonly shared by speakers of a given speech community (Partington 2004; Hoey, 2005). However, it varies in degree or strength (Louw 1993; Partington 2004); it is genre- or register-specific (Hoey 2003, 2005; O'Halloran 2007; Partington 2004). In addition, different word forms of the same lemma may have distinct semantic preferences. For example, O'Halloran (2007) points out that in newspaper texts the verb *erupt* (in the word forms *erupted/erupts*) has a semantic preference for human phenomena, whereas the noun *eruption* (in the word forms *eruption/eruptions*) has a preference for geological phenomena. In my research, I will examine various forms of a derivative family separately to reveal their respective differences in semantic preference.

Hoey's theory, to some extent, bears a similarity to Mel'čuk's Meaning Text Theory and Fillmore's Frame Semantics. Williams (2006: 332) makes the following remarks concerning this:

> The discussion of semantic associations shows an analysis which comes close to the lexical functions of Mel'čuk and the Frame semantics developed by Fillmore, but both theories are overlooked. Meaning Text theory (Mel'čuk 1988) and FrameNet (Fillmore *et al.* 2003) have a cognitive base and do attempt to build on the psychological underpinning of language. While it is true that these theories have not grown out of corpus studies and are largely based on linguistic intuition, they both make use of corpora. These are largely corpus-based, to use the terminology of Tognini-Bonelli (2002[1]), that is to say the corpus is used as a test-bed to verify intuitions, as opposed to Hoey's corpus-driven methodology where the theory grows out of the exploration of the corpus.

In effect, lexical studies using corpus data as evidence to support their theoretical claims are quite numerous (Chang *et al.* 2000; Chief *et al.* 2000; Liu 2002; Liu *et al.* 2000; Tsai *et al.* 1998; Wang 2009). What is common among them is that various non-corpus-linguistic theoretical frameworks, mostly cognitive ones, are applied and corpora are merely used to provide data from which observational tendencies or generalizations can be derived. But collocation, a central concept to corpus linguistics, is hardly mentioned in them. I will base my exploration on a corpus-linguistic framework, where collocations, colligations, semantic associations/ semantic preferences and paraphrases will be put at the centre of the investigation. My findings will grow out of the corpora I use, not elsewhere. My aim is to gain a full understanding of the synonym pairs in the domain of sadness, tease out the subtle nuances of their meanings and differentiate them from each other.

5.4 Summary

This chapter has described the theoretical basis underlying this research, i.e. corpus-linguistic theories on meaning (as a social construct, usage and paraphrase) and a corpus-linguistic lexical model. This model originates from Sinclair's lexical model for (extended) unit of meaning. Hoey replaces semantic preference and semantic prosody with semantic association, a psycholinguistic notion, to adapt it for single words. The corpus analysis in this book is embedded in a corpus-theoretical framework. The idea is that the semantic information of a word/item can be gleaned from the words in its company and its meaning can be teased out of its collocates, paraphrases and examples. If what is obtained from its collocates and paraphrases is not sufficient to reveal its meaning, which usually happens when its occurrence frequency in the corpus is too low, we have to resort to its examples. This research aims to confirm with corpus evidence that, from a corpus-linguistic perspective, (1) meaning is a social construct, the outcome of collaborative construction by the members of a discourse community; (2) understanding in people's heads based on intuition is private and individual and therefore has to be attested by empirical data, and meaning in the collective sense can only be found in discourse; and (3) meaning can be described in terms of usage, namely colligations, collocations and semantic preferences/associations, and paraphrases, both explicit and implicit.

6

Methodology

The present chapter deals with the methodological details for this research. Essential to corpus studies is the selection of the corpora on which generalizations are based and the corpora to be used in the present study are introduced in Section 6.1, in which relevant issues such as comparability, representativeness and annotation are also addressed. Section 6.2 and Section 6.3 give some brief information on the dictionaries and corpus tools. The data processing methods for English data and Chinese data are outlined in Sections 6.4 and 6.5 respectively. In Section 6.5, the existing problems in Chinese POS classification and tagging are also discussed at great length as they are closely related to the method adopted in this book. In addition, some limitations of the methodology for the book are also mentioned. Section 6.6 details the ways in which the English and Chinese data from the corpora are analysed.

6.1 Corpora used

6.1.1 The Bank of English

A comprehensive account of the latest version of the Bank of English (BOE, henceforth) is available in the *Release Notes 2009* at http://wordbanks. harpercollins.co.uk/Docs/WBO/WordBanksOnline_English.html. Details will not be repeated here. What follows is only a brief introduction to some issues relevant to the current research. The BOE is a collection of samples of modern English language since 1960 and the bulk of the corpus ranges from 2001 to 2005. It contains a wide range of texts, both written and spoken, from various sources, including Britain, America, Australia, Canada, India, New Zealand, South Africa and Ireland. Written texts mainly include newspapers, magazines, books, brochures, leaflets, reports and letters, whereas the spoken part comprises transcriptions of everyday casual conversation, radio broadcasts, meetings, interviews and discussions. It covers a wide range of domains, such as news, tv-radio, fiction, lifescience, culture, biology, business, religion, computer, medicine, natural science, lifestyle, leisure and music, etc. The vast majority of texts come from newspapers (51.8%). To be precise, it currently contains 455,039,614 tokens of word forms. The BOE has benefited a lot of corpus research on language, for example, Sinclair (1991), Renouf and Sinclair (1991), Hunston and Francis (1998, 1999), Moon (1998). It has been extensively used for the analysis of vocabulary, grammar and usage of English. This book will show in detail how the BOE could be used wisely to assist with a contrastive lexical analysis.

6.1.2 The CCL Corpus

The Chinese corpus compiled by the Centre for Chinese Linguistics (CCL), Peking University, China, consists of two sub-corpora: Old Chinese and Modern Chinese. I will only use the modern sub-corpus for my research, but, for the sake of convenience, henceforth I will refer to it as the CCL corpus. It contains 307,317,060 Chinese characters[1] (sourced from http://ccl.pku.edu.cn:8080/ccl_corpus/CCL_CC_Sta_Xiandai. pdf, updated on 20 July 2009). It is a collection of samples of Modern Chinese (since 1919, which marks the beginning of Modern Chinese), both written and spoken. The great majority of the corpus ranges from 1993 to 2009, according to its documentation (sourced from http://ccl.pku.edu. cn:8080/ccl_corpus/CCL_Xiandai. pdf). It contains a broad range of texts from Mainland China, Taiwan and Hong Kong, covering a wide range of text types, such as applied writing, literature, TV and movie, internet article, historical biography, newspaper and magazine, and translated work.

Comparability

To make a corpus-based cross-linguistic analysis, the ideal situation is to use two corpora with the same, or at least comparable, size and make-up. However, to the best of my knowledge, there is no sizeable Chinese corpus compiled on the same or similar principles of the BOE. The CCL corpus is the largest general Chinese corpus, which is of roughly comparable size (307 million) with the BOE (455 million). As stated earlier, a large corpus is needed for lexical studies to produce a decent collocational profile, especially for the exploration of less frequent words. Small corpora are likely to show skewing, with too few examples of infrequent words (Moon 2010). This book will look at most, if not all, of the sad expressions in English and Chinese, some of which are not highly frequent. To obtain a decent collocational profile for them, I would give the priority to the size of the corpus. Since absolute comparability cannot be achieved, what we can do is to find the closest to the one with which we want to compare it.

Representativeness

Linked to the issue of comparability is the issue of representativeness. Kennedy (1998: 62) has pointed out that representativeness is a matter of judgement and 'can only be approximate'. Teubert and Cermakova (2004: 117) cast doubts on the notion of representativeness by questioning what a corpus is to represent. They argue as follows:

> In any case, we are only justified in claiming that a given corpus is representative of a discourse, however we have defined it, if we have, at least in principle, access to all the texts the discourse consists of. Only then will we have all the relevant information concerning the parameters mentioned above, and only then can we be sure that the corpus we compile as a sample of this discourse is representative ... But if this utopia came true, we could do without the corpus. We would already have the discourse as a whole and would not sample it ... This is why it does not make much sense to talk about representativeness.

It seems that a corpus is never too big if it can be handled computationally. Even a written corpus of 30 million words is small as compared with the actual written texts produced from which it is sampled (Summers 1991).

The BOE and the CCL corpus are both the largest general corpora available for their own language. Although they were not built based on exactly the same principles, I can assume they are so far the best that can represent English and Chinese, respectively. Since the criteria to build a general corpus are still debatable (Hunston 2002; Kennedy 1998; Teubert 2004a), we cannot say which one is better than the other because they were both designed following their own principles. My research is to examine how sadness expressions are used and interpreted in both languages, what they share and how they differ, and how correspondences between them can be established. I will not discuss their distributions or percentages contrastively since the data come from two corpora not exactly comparable in composition. Instead, I will first look at monolingual data and present semantic profiles within each language, and then compare them in terms of collocations and semantic associations across languages.

6.1.3 The Babel English–Chinese Parallel Corpus of Fiction

The Babel English–Chinese Parallel Corpus of Fiction (BPC, henceforth) is the fiction part of the Babel English–Chinese Parallel Corpus built at the Institute of Computational Linguistics at Peking University by Chang Baobao and colleagues. I also searched for the target emotion words/items in Babel's non-fiction part and found nothing because it does not talk about emotions at all. To ease the searches, I will only use its fiction part for my research and refer to it as the Babel Parallel Corpus henceforth. The Babel Parallel Corpus contains a total of 3,707,397 tokens (1,605,850 English words and 2,101,547 Chinese characters). The texts included in the corpus were produced from the nineteenth century on. All the texts have been aligned at sentence level and all the Chinese texts have been segmented.

6.2 Dictionaries used

A reliance on corpus data does not exclude the use of dictionaries for gathering lexical evidence; rather they are complementary to each other (Ooi 1998; Teubert 2000). I will base my analysis on monolingual and parallel corpus data as well as monolingual and bilingual dictionary glosses. The dictionaries to be used in the analysis include:

Chinese:

> *Hanyu Da Zidian*. Wuhan/Chengdu: Hubei Cishu Chubanshe/Sichuan Cishu Chubanshe.
> *Xiandai Hanyu Cidian: Bilingual Edition* (*A Dictionary of Modern Chinese*). Beijing: Waiyu Jiaoxue Yu Yanjiu Chubanshe.
> *Xiandai Hanyu Cidian* (*A Dictionary of Modern Chinese*). Beijing: Shangwu Yinshu Guan.

English:

> *Collins COBUILD Advanced Learner's English Dictionary* (5th edition). London/Glasgow: HarperCollins.
> *Oxford Advanced Learner's English–Chinese Dictionary* (4th edition). Beijing: Shangwu Yinshu Guan.
> *Longman Dictionary of Contemporary English* (4th edition). Harlow, Essex: Pearson/Longman.
> *Oxford English Dictionary Online*. Oxford: Oxford University Press.

6.3 Software

The WordSmith Tools

The WordSmith Tools (Version 5.0, available at http://www.lexically.net/wordsmith/, WordSmith 5.0 henceforth) is probably the most extensively used software program for corpus-linguistic analysis. It has three major functions, i.e. Concord, WordList and Keyword. My research will mainly use Concord, so the remainder of this section will only introduce this function. Concord does single as well as multi-word searches. It can generate a concordance for the search term, and it also provides the possibility of re-sorting the concordance lines according to the alphabetical order for languages such as English or a certain defined order for languages such as Chinese. A concordance is 'a collection of the occurrences of a word-form, each in its own textual environment' (Sinclair 1991: 32). It is in the form of a concordance that the computer shows us repeated patterns to the right or left of the search term. Another feature of Concord is to generate collocates, clusters and patterns for the search term. Collocation, in Sinclair's words, 'is the occurrence of two or more words within a short space of each other in a text' and '[a] word which occurs in close proximity to a word under investigation is called a collocate of it' (Sinclair 1991: 170). 'A cluster is a *group of words which follow each other in a text*. The term *phrase* is not used here because it has technical senses in linguistics which would imply a grammatical relation between the words in it' (Scott 2009: 289). In other words, clusters may be found repeatedly in each other's company, but they are not necessarily meaningful in syntactic sense like patterns, 'though clusters often do match phrases or idioms' (p. 289). The number of collocates Concord can produce depends on the value settings, such as span and minimum frequency of the word. WordSmith 5.0 works well for many languages, including Chinese. Of course, Chinese needs to be segmented before it can be processed by it. We will talk about this in Section 6.5.2. Figure 6.1 is the collocate display for Chinese 伤心 generated by WordSmith 5.0.

ParaConc

ParaConc is a parallel concordance program via which recurrent patterns in translated texts can be identified. ParaConc can handle up to four parallel texts, which could be an original text with three different translations or four different languages. The translated texts have to be aligned before they can be analysed by ParaConc because no 'language-particular information is encoded within the

N	Word	With/lation	Texts	Total	Left	Right	L5	L4	L3	L2	L1	centre	R1	R2	R3	R4	R5
60	感到	伤心 0.000	1	66	59	7	3	7	10	18	21	0	2	2	3	0	0
61	也	伤心 0.000	1	65	14	51	1	1	6	2	4	0	28	9	8	2	4
62	一个	伤心 0.000	1	64	45	19	11	8	9	6	11	0	2	3	3	6	5
63	死	伤心 0.000	1	63	26	37	9	5	6	4	2	0	11	5	7	7	7
64	把	伤心 0.000	1	63	26	37	7	4	10	2	3	0	1	17	7	6	6
65	她	伤心 0.000	1	63	6	57	1	2	1	1	1	0	16	19	5	12	5
66	叫	伤心 0.000	1	62	52	10	0	4	13	34	1	0	0	5	3	0	2
67	母亲	伤心 0.000	1	62	50	12	6	11	7	8	18	0	1	4	2	3	2
68	土	伤心 0.000	1	61	30	31	9	10	4	2	5	0	1	3	7	11	9
69	眼泪	伤心 0.000	1	60	7	53	3	2	0	1	1	0	5	24	8	10	6
70	话	伤心 0.000	1	59	33	26	13	7	6	6	1	0	6	3	4	6	7
71	着	伤心 0.000	1	59	38	21	4	8	16	8	2	0	2	7	4	4	4
72	太	伤心 0.000	1	58	49	9	3	1	6	3	36	0	1	1	1	1	5
73	对	伤心 0.000	1	57	16	41	6	2	3	5	0	0	4	12	6	15	4
74	别	伤心 0.000	1	57	48	9	1	2	9	10	26	0	1	6	1	1	0
75	大	伤心 0.000	1	56	24	32	9	4	5	3	3	0	3	8	7	10	4
76	和	伤心 0.000	1	56	31	25	9	9	6	5	2	0	9	2	7	4	3
77	现代	伤心 0.000	1	54	2	52	2	0	0	0	0	0	0	23	10	10	9
78	什么	伤心 0.000	1	54	30	24	5	4	5	6	10	0	8	4	3	4	5
79	他们	伤心 0.000	1	52	29	23	1	4	3	8	13	0	2	4	8	4	5
80	读者	伤心 0.000	1	52	1	51	0	1	0	0	0	0	0	0	0	17	34
81	个	伤心 0.000	1	52	30	22	12	6	4	3	5	0	0	2	5	5	10
82	处	伤心 0.000	1	51	4	47	0	2	0	1	1	0	37	5	1	3	1
83	知道	伤心 0.000	1	51	29	22	10	7	7	3	2	0	1	6	3	8	4
84	落泪	伤心 0.000	1	50	3	47	0	1	0	1	1	0	42	4	1	0	0
85	没	伤心 0.000	1	50	20	30	7	8	3	1	1	0	2	8	5	6	9
86	再	伤心 0.000	1	49	23	26	7	3	6	1	6	0	2	3	6	8	7

concordance collocates plot patterns clusters filenames follow up source text notes
716   Type-in 星

Figure 6.1 A screenshot of the collocates of 伤心 by WordSmith 5.0

program' (Barlow 2008: 106) and the search is done in a mechanical manner. 'Alignment is the provision of information on equivalent text segments in the two languages, typically using the sentence unit as the basic alignment segment' (Barlow 2008). Usually, the source and translated texts in the aligned parallel corpus are put in separate files, with the source and target text of each sentence being linked together with a unique identifier. The following sample shows what the English text looks like after the alignment:

>
> <a id='3' no='1'>
> <s id='1'> On his bench in Madison Square Soapy moved uneasily.</s>
> </a>
> <a id='4' no='1'>
> <s id='2'>When wild goose honk high of nights, and when women without sealskin coats grow kind to their husbands, and when Soapy moves uneasily on his bench in the park, you may know that winter is near at hand.</s>
> </a>
>

The sentence number is inserted as the value of an 'id' attribute of the <s> tag. The 'id' is organized in such a way that it will be a unique identifier to link the sentences in Chinese and English:

```
<p id='3'>    paragraph 3
<a id='3' no='1'> alignment pair 3 (consisting of 1 sentence),
<s id='1'> sentence 1
```

The id number for the alignment pair is unique as it is counted throughout the text. Alignment is an essential step in the construction and exploitation of parallel corpora. Its aim is to make it possible to retrieve mechanically corresponding texts from the original and the translation by using a search program. To show how an alignment is done, a sample of aligned texts by using Pasaligner, developed by the Institute of Computational Linguistics at Peking University, is given below:

(1) ••
   ◆ 〖1:1〗
   <s>老师已经表示过, 就算能把它弄到车上, 到了他要去的基督堂[注]那个城市, 他还是不知道拿它怎么办, 因为他初来乍到, 只能临时找个地方住住。 </s>
   <s>The master had remarked that even if he got it into the cart he should not know what to do with it on his arrival at Christminster, the city he was bound for, since he was only going into temporary lodgings just at first.</s>

(2) ••
   ◆ 〖2:1〗
   <s>一个十一岁的男孩子正帮着扎东西, 挺有心事的样子, 这时走到大人这边来, 趁他们摸着下巴颏的时候, 大声说:'姑婆有个好大的柴房哪, 你找到地方放它之前, 也许能寄放在那里头吧。'</s>
   <s>他因为说话声音大, 脸红了。 </s>
   <s>A little boy of eleven, who had been thoughtfully assisting in the packing, joined the group of men, and as they rubbed their chins he spoke up, blushing at the sound of his own voice: 'Aunt have got a great fuel-house, and it could be put there, perhaps, till you've found a place to settle in, sir.'</s>

(3) ••
   ◆ 〖1:2〗
   <s>裘德呀, 你这会儿还不懂我走的道理, 等你再大点, 你就明白啦。'</s>
   <s>You wouldn't understand my reasons, Jude.</s>
   <s>You will, perhaps, when you are older.'</s>

The markup illustrated here is all inserted automatically when the program is run. The markers ••, ◆ used here identify paragraphs and alignment pairs respectively. Angle brackets are used for tags: <> stands for 'start-tags' and </>

for 'end-tags'. <s> 'You will, perhaps, when you are older.'</s> means that this is a single sentence in its original text. 〚1:2〛 in Example 3 shows that a single sentence corresponds to two sentences in the other language. There are also cases where two sentences are aligned with a single in the other language marked by 〚2:1〛, as illustrated in Example 2. In Example 3, the Chinese sentence '裘德呀, 你这会儿还不懂我走的道理, 等你再大点, 你就明白啦' was split into two sentences in English. Texts with quotations are prone to cause errors, as shown below:

(4) ◆ 〚1:1〛
    <s>'我可没那么多钱买。'</s>
    <s>'I cannot afford that,' said Sue.</s>
    ◆ 〚2:1〛
    <s>她说。</s>
    <s>她还的价非常之低, 再没想到, 卖像人居然把拴像的细铜丝解开, 隔着篱梯把它们递过来。</s>
    <s>She offered considerably less, and to her surprise the image-man drew them from their wire stay and handed them over the stile.</s>

The misalignment in Example 4 occurs because 她说 (*said Sue*) is followed by a stop 。, which is a comma in its original text. Of course, the error here is trivial, but sometimes it can lead to a mess. The approach used in this program is a statistical one. It is based on sentence length in terms of words and characters per sentence in Chinese and English.

Compiling a parallel corpus is much more difficult than compiling a monolingual one. First, all automatically aligned texts, however well the program works, need to be manually post-edited to check errors. The post-editing work is usually quite heavy, making alignment a time-consuming task. Besides, the compilation of parallel corpora will be greatly restricted by the availability of translated texts, since the number of source texts that have been translated into another language is limited. Their lesser availability in machine-readable form will make this task even more difficult to accomplish. In addition, there is another issue to consider: the quality of translations, which relates closely to the reliability of the data retrieved from the corpus, as well as to the progress of alignment. Therefore, it seems improper to use the same criterion of representativeness for monolingual corpora to judge parallel corpora. What it looks like after running ParaConc is shown in Figure 6.2.

ParaConc presents the user with '(i) multiple instances of the search term and (ii) a large context for each instance of the search term, thereby allowing a thorough analysis of usage in terms of the equivalences between two languages' (Barlow 2008: 105). The concordance lines can be sorted in alphabetical order

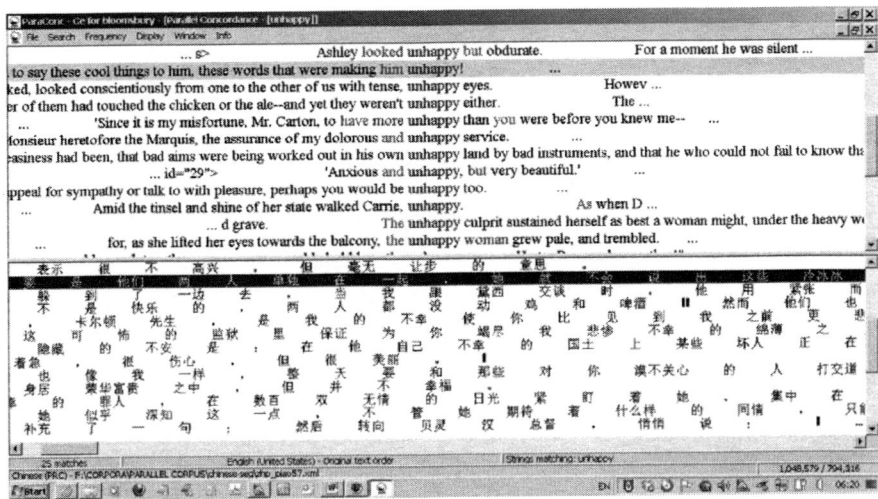

Figure 6.2 A screenshot of searching result by ParaConc

for languages such as English or a certain order defined for other languages such as Chinese (see Michael Barlow's homepage for how to use the software: http://www.michaelbarlow.com/). By using this program, we can obtain some empirical evidence on 'the congruence in particular forms between two languages' (Barlow). For example, drawing on the parallel data retrieved from a bidirectional English–Chinese parallel corpus, we can examine the congruence between the English word *sorrow* and the Chinese word *bēishāng*. How likely is it *sorrow* will be translated by *bēishāng* and how likely that *bēishāng* will be translated by *sorrow*? For more polysemous words such as *unhappy*, a more detailed investigation will be needed to examine the different senses and translations of *unhappy* to identify what Chinese equivalent expression(s) each sense is likely to correspond to. The congruence issue across languages has been greatly complicated by the association of more than one meaning with the same linguistic form, which is inescapable in all human languages.

ParaConc provides a variety of frequency statistics, of which the most relevant kind to my investigation is collocate frequency. By clicking on the COLLOCATE FREQUENCY DATA, it gives the collocates of the search term ranked according to frequency. It offers collocates within the span of −4 to 4. It is difficult for the program to locate translations automatically. The Hot Words function may suggest some possible translations or associated words such as collocates of the search term, but it does not work well for a less morphological language like Chinese. In an investigation concerning Chinese, we have to examine the concordance lines manually to find the candidates of equivalence. Based on their frequency, translation equivalents can be identified. Therefore, all I need from ParaConc for my research is the parallel concordance lines and frequency data of the search term.

The advantage of using parallel data to obtain information on congruence between language pairs is that we do not rely on intuitions, but objective and quantitative information on correspondences, to judge congruence. However, we have to bear in mind that the parallel data will vary according to the corpus used in the investigation, and that the interpretation of corpus data will still involve researchers' intuitions about language, though it is conducted on the basis of quantitative data (Barlow 2008).

In this section, I have briefly introduced a parallel concordancer, *ParaConc*, which is highly useful for contrastive analyses. I have examined some of its important features and the rationale of the program. The frequency data as well as the parallel texts generated by this program can guide our investigations into similarities and differences of lexis or constructions between compared language pairs (Barlow 2008).

6.4 English data

6.4.1 Clean-text policy and annotation

Views differ as to whether corpora should be kept unprocessed or annotated with part of speech (POS) or other codes. Sinclair (1991: 21) strongly favours 'the clean-text policy' for two reasons:

> Firstly, each particular investigation is likely to view the language according to different priorities. Its analytic apparatus may well be valuable and interesting to the next investigator, and even adaptable to the new needs; but not so standardised that it can become an integral part of the corpus. Secondly, although linguists leap effortlessly to abstractions like 'word' (meaning lemma . . .) and beyond, they do not all leap in the same way, and they do not devise precise rules for the abstracting. Hence, even the bedrock of assumptions of linguistics, like the identification of words, assignment of morphological division, and primary word class, are not at all standardised. Each study helps the others, but does not provide a platform on which the others can directly build.

Sinclair thinks the analytical systems derived from traditions of language analysis are problematic, even the traditionally established parts of speech, so we should reject them all and derive some new categories from raw corpora. We have discussed this issue in Section 5.1. Contrary to Sinclair, Leech (1997) argues that annotation can enrich the corpus and therefore facilitate investigations. This opposition is also related to the distinction between corpus-based and corpus-driven approaches to language studies. Sinclair's idea is 'to refrain from imposing analytical categories from the outside until we have had a chance to look very closely at the physical evidence' (1991: 29). It seems that annotation should be used with caution before we are sure about the analytical categories we will assign to the texts. I will come back to this issue when I discuss Chinese POS tagging in Section 6.5.2.

6.4.2 English data processing

For the English data in this investigation, I will draw upon the BOE, which allows the investigator to expand concordance lines to five lines of co-text, so it is possible to examine the wider contexts. It is POS tagged and available online at http://wordbanks.harpercollins.co.uk/. The BOE is accessed and manipulated via the Sketch Engine (http://www.sketchengine.co.uk). The Sketch Engine is a software program that has been developed by Lexical Computing Ltd. More detailed information can be found in Kilgarriff and Tugwell (2001), Kilgarriff and Rundell (2002), Kilgarriff *et al.* (2004), Krek and Kilgarriff (2006) and Kilgarriff (2009). The interface for its concordancing options is shown in Figure 6.3.

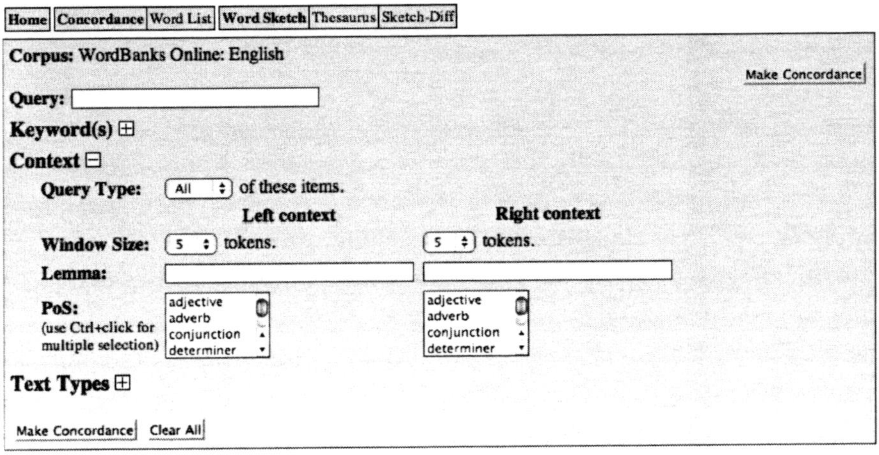

Figure 6.3 The interface of the concordancing options of word sketch

As can be seen from Figure 6.3, the Sketch Engine produces concordances, word lists, thesaurus, word sketches and sketch differences. Word Sketch provides collocates of a given word occurring in its main grammatical relations/patterns according to frequency or statistical salience. The present statistics used is logDice, based on Dice coefficient (see Rychly 2008). Sketch Diff compares the grammatical and collocational behaviour of two semantically related words and shows what they share and how they differ. The Sketch Engine works on lemmatized forms, so all of the grammatical forms of a given word would be considered unless it is set to search for only one form. All collocate searches will be made on the basis of lemma and the span will be set at 5 to the left and 5 to the right for word sketches and sketch differences, and −1 to +1 for the top 50 collocates, unless otherwise stated. In terms of statistic measurement, the top 50 collocates will be based on t-score and the word sketches and sketch differences on salience.

6.5 Chinese data

6.5.1 Chinese data processing

Unlike English or other western languages, Chinese does not delimit words by space, so word segmentation is a prerequisite to Chinese language processing. Chinese words are formed by combination of characters and one character may occur in any position of a word, so segmentation ambiguities may occur in a text, as the following examples show (Goh *et al.* 2005: 382):

不/可以/淡忘/远在/故乡/的/父母/
not/ can/ forget/ far away/ hometown/ DE/ parents/
(Cannot forget parents who are far away at home)
不可/以/营利/为/目的/
cannot/ by/ profit/ be/ intention
(Cannot have the intention to make a profit)

As shown above, the character 可 (*kě*) can combine with 以 (*yǐ*) to form 可以 (*kěyǐ*/can) or combine with 不 (*bù*) to form 不可 (*bùkě*/cannot). Segmentation is done based on the context in each sentence. Many researchers in computational linguistics have been developing various systems to improve the segmentation performance in order to achieve a high accuracy rate.

The CCL corpus will be the main source of my Chinese data. It is a raw corpus, unsegmented and POS untagged. Besides, its online concordancer generates only the concordance of the search item, but no collocates. So I will download all the concordance lines containing the search item and segment them by using FreeICTCLAS (Institute of Computing Technology, Chinese Lexical Analysis System) developed by the Institute of Computing Technology, Chinese Academy of Sciences (for details see http://www.ict.ac.cn/technic/channel/detail3432.asp). According to its official website, its segmentation precision rate is 97.58%. Finally, the segmented texts/lines will be processed by using Wordsmith 5.0 to obtain both collocates and concordances. For the collocates, the span will be set at 5 to the left and 5 to the right.

6.5.2 Chinese part-of-speech classification and tagging

Concepts are encoded as words in language. A given concept may not relate to the same word class in different languages. The classifying criteria for word classes might be particular to each language (Dixon and Aikhenvald 2004). The recognition of word classes in an inflectional language is purely based on its syntactic distribution. For Chinese, there is no simple one-to-one correspondence between word class and syntactic function (Zhu 1985) because it has little inflectional morphology. Since *Mǎshìwéntōng* (马氏文通), the issue of word class classification has been a tricky problem in the field of Chinese grammar, where no agreement about it has been made (Hu 1996). The main reason is due to the fact that a Chinese word with the same meaning may perform different syntactic functions in different contexts. Consider the following examples containing *bēishāng*:

[悲伤] 的 泪水	'sad tears'
装满了个人的烦恼和[悲伤]	'be filled with private worries and sadness'
[悲伤] 地 哭 了	'cried sadly'

The English translations above are all direct ones, from which it is clearly seen that *bēishāng* can function as an adjective, noun or adverb, meaning almost the same. It has been generally agreed that each Chinese word has two properties: semantic property (lexical meaning) and grammatical property (function). The word class recognition in Chinese can be based on meaning or function or both. Syntactic function is not the indisputable criterion in Chinese word classification, and the fuzzy concept of meaning it is involved in, so there is wide disagreement about this issue. Most mainland Chinese scholars focus on meaning or both, while non-mainland scholars, including those from Taiwan, tend to base their classification on syntactic function alone. In the mainland, the mainstream point of view is that an adjective, in some cases, can be used as a noun or adverb, but, if this happens not very frequently, then it is better to say it is only used as another word class, not that it has acquired one more word class membership (Hu 1995). It is still an adjective and just sometimes used as a noun. Such a phenomenon is referred to as *huóyòng* (活用). This idea has originated from Lü Shuxiang (1954, 1984) who proposes that a word should belong to a fixed category and the proportion of multi-category words should be minimized. This idea has become a guiding principle in classifying word classes in Chinese and has been widely accepted by Chinese linguists. Recently, however, it has been challenged by some researchers, such as Gao (2009), who looks at Chinese word classes from a cognitive perspective and claims that, since word classes are symbolic structures that emerge from language use, the proportion of multi-category words should be determined by the empirical data, rather than adhering to *a priori* principle. He argues that Lü's theory is an idealized one that does not conform to the Chinese linguistic facts. He gives some examples, in which the underlined words marked only as adjectives in *Xiandai Hanyu Cidian* (5th edition, the 5th XHC henceforth) are used as nouns (p. 21):

自己富了, 也得设法为国家分担忧愁 (*yōuchóu*)。
他声音里不但充满骄傲 (*jiāoào*), 也充满自信 (*zìxìn*)。
很多人对开刀都很害怕 (*hàipà*), 有的在做一些小手术时都会产生恐惧 (*kǒngjù*)。
酒虽然不能解除任何痛苦 (*tòngkǔ*), 至少总可以使人暂时忘记。
基因工程的发展对人类的贡献是无法估量的, 但也带来了一些烦恼 (*fánnǎo*)。
后来, 梁大爷虽然脱离了危险 (*wēixiǎn*), 但慢慢地瘫痪在床。

Many of the underlined words above are emotion words, such as 忧愁 (worries), 恐惧 (fear), 痛苦 (anguish) and 烦恼 (vexation). In fact, such phenomena are not uncommon in Chinese. Ma (1994) makes a statistical analysis in a one-million-word corpus and finds that many emotion words, such as 烦恼 (vexation), 欢乐 (joy), 苦恼 (distress), 快乐 (gaiety), 痛苦 (anguish), 喜悦 (rejoicing) and 忧虑 (anxiety), are used more frequently as nouns than as adjectives, while for others, such as 悲哀 (mournful, 13:4), 悲伤 (sorrowful, 8:3), 悲痛 (grieved, 10:4), 愤怒 (indignant, 11:4) and 羞愧 (shamed, 7:3), the adjectival use still dominates the picture. He proposes to classify a word according to its main use on a statistical basis. But obviously we cannot be convinced that 痛苦 is a noun but 悲伤 is an adjective, since they all denote feelings.

What makes the issue more complicated is that there is a tradition of saying Chinese does not distinguish verbs and adjectives (Bhat 1994; Schachter 1985; Thompson 1988).[2] Quite a few linguists argue that Chinese adjectives (at least a subset of them) have some grammatical properties in common with verbs. It is really a subtle matter to distinguish verbs and adjectives based on syntactic function alone. Some examples follow:

今儿怪<u>冷</u>的。
价钱很<u>便宜</u>。
他心里<u>空空洞洞的</u>, 什么也不怕。
浑身<u>软绵绵的</u> ...

In the above examples, the underlined words are all adjectives, which function as intransitive predicate in the above sentences. They are similar to verbs in terms of grammatical property. There is another set of adjectives in Chinese, like *jīn* (gold), *yín* (silver), *nán* (male), *nǚ* (female), *mànxíng* (chronic) and *dàxíng* (large-scale), which can only function as attributive modifiers. They are referred to as 'non-predicative adjective' or 'determiner' (Zhu 1982). Some scholars (e.g. Li 1924; Shen 1999; Wang 1955; Zhang and Fang 1996; Zhang 1979) argue that the main function of Chinese adjectives is to serve as attributive modifiers. However, some other scholars, such as Chao (1968), Li and Thompson (1981), Zhu (1982), view adjectives as a sub-class of verbs, on the basis of the belief that Chinese adjectives mainly function as predicates. McCawley's (1992) investigation further supports this viewpoint. He examines Chinese adjectives by using the distinctive features between verbs and adjectives in many other languages and comes to a conclusion that Chinese adjectives are exactly verbs, rather than a subset of them with adjectival properties. From the above discussion, it can be seen that Chinese adjectives are quite different in grammatical properties from the familiar kind of adjectives in English. The debate on their scopes and functions is still going on. I do not see it ending soon.

It is well known that linguistic applications have to depend on the development of linguistic theories. The theoretical disagreement about Chinese word class classification has seriously hindered its application to Chinese lexicography. The great majority of old Chinese dictionaries simply evaded this issue by not marking the word class. The 5th XHC has made an attempt to touch on this issue, but, as mentioned earlier, the result is unsatisfactory.

The controversy over the Chinese word class classification has also posed a problem for automatic POS tagging in corpus linguistics. Since there have been no well-accepted criteria for recognizing word classes in Chinese, different POS tagging tools may adopt different tagsets to accomplish their tasks. Xia (2000: 4) makes the following comments on this issue:

> The central issue in Part-of-Speech (POS) tagging is whether the POS tagging should be based on meaning or on syntactic distribution. This issue has been debated since the 1950s (Gong 1997)[3] and there are still two different viewpoints. For example, a word such as 毁灭 in Chinese can be translated into *destroy/destroys/destroyed/destroying/destruction* in English and it is used roughly the same way as its counterparts in English. According to the first view, POS tags should be based solely on meaning. Because the meaning of the word remains roughly the same across all of these usages, it should always be tagged as a verb. The second view says that POS tags should be determined by the syntactic distribution of the word. When 毁灭 is the head of a noun phrase, it should be tagged as a noun in that context; when it is the head of a verb phrase, it should be tagged as a verb.

Most projects outside the mainland of China, such as Sinica Corpus (Academia Sinica Balanced Corpus of Mandarin Chinese, in Taiwan) (http://rocling.iis. sinica.edu.tw/CKIP/paper/wordsegment_standard.pdf) and CTB (Penn Chinese Treebank), choose syntactic distribution as the main criterion for their POS tagging because it 'complies with the principles adopted in contemporary linguistics theories, such as the notion of head projections in the X-bar theory and the GB theory' (p. 5). Some linguists tend to apply western linguistic theories to explain all Chinese linguistic facts. For some phenomena, it is true that they do; however, for some others, they do not work well. For example, 政治 (politics) is a noun, but it is tagged as an adverb in '只[only)] 能[can] 政治 [politically]/ AD 解决 [resolve]/VV 这个 [this]/M 问题 [problem] <This problem can only be resolved through political means>' in CTB (Xia 2000: 17). It is hard to accept that 政治 has become an adverb just because it is used in a sentence with omission. Look at another example:

去	行,	不	去	也	行
qu	xing	bu	qu	ye	xing
go	ok	not	go	also	ok

If solely based on function as *politically* was treated in that sentence, it seems that *qu* (go) in this example should be tagged as a noun. However, few Chinese scholars would agree that *qu* is a noun.

ICTCLAS bases its tagging on both meaning and function. For example, it divides adjectives into four subclasses: ad/副形词 (both adverb and adjective), an/名形词 (both adjective and noun), ag/形容词性语素 (adjectival morpheme) and al/形容词性惯用语 (adjectival idioms). Taking meaning into consideration, ICTCLAS is rather conservative about POS tagging, trying to achieve the highest accuracy and not to overgeneralize about POS classification. For example, the team makes reference to CTB, and assigns specific tags to '是'/be, but they do not use the tag of 'copula' because they are aware that '是' has many functions, of which copula is only one. It is extremely difficult to distinguish these functions on the basis of the existing technology. If you do it reluctantly, it will lead to a decline of accuracy. To ensure a high accuracy, they choose not to go further now (http://www.ictclas.org/hottopic_010.html). Of course, the result of conservatism is that emotion words, like *bēishāng, kuàilè*, are marked as *an*, which means they can be used as both an adjective and noun. The adverbial use is not considered, probably because they do not think they are also adverbs, but just *huóyòng* (used in a flexible way) as adverbs sometimes. The disambiguation of multi-category words is one of the difficulties in part-of-speech tagging. Generally speaking, Chinese words are more difficult to disambiguate in terms of POS than English (Huang *et al.* 2007). Tseng *et al.* (2005) observe that, in comparison to 19.8 per cent of the English words in WSJ (*Wall Street Journal*), 29.9 per cent of the words in CTB have more than one POS possibilities. According to Huang *et al.* (2007), the highest accuracy for English has reached 97 per cent using various models (Brants 2000; Ratnaparkhi 1996; Thede and Harper 1999), while their re-ranking model using n-gram and morphological features for Chinese has only achieved an accuracy of 94.16 per cent.

As noted earlier, the Chinese corpus I am using for this research is not POS tagged. Currently, the only publicly available POS tagging tool is ICTCLAS. Since it does not distinguish adjectival, nominal and adverbial uses of emotion words, there is no point in POS tagging my Chinese data in this study. Besides, Sinclair's clean-text policy suggests that it is better to defer the use of POS categories to 'refrain from imposing analytical categories from the outside' (1991: 29). Analysing untagged Chinese data will lead to less correspondence between the methodological details for English and Chinese. For English, I will search for all the relevant forms of the same concept separately, for example, *sorrow, sorrowful, sorrowfully*, because they have totally distinct collocates. For Chinese, I will search for only one form, e.g. 悲伤 (*bēishāng*). In doing so, one main disadvantage would be, for the Chinese sadness expressions, I will not be able to present a detailed quantitative analysis of their colligational patterns. Instead, I will focus on some main colligational features and compare them with their English counterparts. Due to the constraints on the development of Chinese

POS classification and therefore the tagging technology, I will compare them as a whole across languages, whether as an adjective, noun or verb, or whether functioning as attribute, subject, object, predicate or adverbial. Since the focus of my research is on the exploration of sadness concepts across cultures, the findings will not be considerably affected.

6.6 Data analysis

For each group of words, the analysis will start with the discussion of the English expressions. Before analysing the corpus data, their definitions from the three corpus-based dictionaries will be examined: *Collins COBUILD Advanced Learner's English Dictionary* (COBUILD, henceforth), *Oxford Advanced Learner's English–Chinese Dictionary* (OALECD, henceforth) and *Longman Dictionary of Contemporary English* (LDCE, henceforth). The *Oxford English Dictionary Online* (OED, henceforth) will also be consulted when more information is needed. For corpus data, I will figure out their colligations and semantic associations/preferences by examining their collocates.

As stated in Section 5.2.3, colligations also contribute to the building up of a word/item's collocational and semantic profile, and thus to the construction of its meaning. For cross-linguistic comparison of colligational properties, the synonyms from two typologically different languages like English and Chinese might favour distinct syntactic patterns. So a comparison across languages can be made to disclose their semantic as well as typological differences. But, within each language, the synonyms from the same word class are strikingly similar in their favoured syntactic environments. In such a case, attention will be given only to those prominent distinctions in colligations between them. In English, as the members of the same derivational family have quite distinct colligational properties, especially in terms of prepositions, I will list them separately. For Chinese, however, as I do not distinguish word classes, I will only outline them by highlighting the differences across languages in the summary of the analysis (see Section 7.3). The colligational differences are closely related to the usage of words/items and thus the focus of second or foreign language learning. This book centres upon meaning comparison and differentiation between/among similar concepts of sadness within the same language and across languages, so it will devote much of its analysis to the contrast and comparison of collocations and semantic associations/preferences.

Collocates can be identified automatically by the software. Based on collocates, colligations are not difficult to identify, since they are quite objective. Semantic preference/association is mainly concerned with tendency and probability. In this research, I will focus only on emotion-related collocates and classify them into various groups and assign them labels to indicate their semantic preferences/ associations. The establishment of the lexical links across languages will be made mainly on the basis of the data obtained from the parallel corpus. The Chinese significant collocates will be categorized according to *introversion/extroversion, modifier, feeling* and *others*, which include the words helpful for uncovering the meaning. The Chinese collocates will be selected on the basis of raw frequency because the calculation of t-score by Wordsmith 5.0 requires the whole corpus. What I have for Wordsmith 5.0 to process is only the concordance lines extracted from the CCL corpus. Obviously, my methodology for this research is greatly limited by the availability of corpora and the current technology. Nevertheless, the selection of Chinese collocates according to the raw frequency will not significantly affect the findings because I will not compare the collocate frequencies of semantically similar expressions across corpora because they are statistically incomparable. For example, in Chinese, *gǎnjué, gǎndào, juéde* and *jué* are frequent collocates of *nánguò*, all meaning 'feel'. If we make a quantitative comparison of their frequencies or t-scores or whatever between *nánguò* and its English equivalent(s), should they be counted as one word or four in actual counting or statistic calculation? It appears that a precise or statistical comparison across languages is problematic before we provide an answer to the question of equivalence between languages. Basically, I will rank their collocates separately, present the significant ones based on t-score or raw frequency and obtain a collocational profile of their own. I may compare synonyms based on the same measurement within the same language. The rationale of the analysis is to examine a lexical item or compare synonyms within each language and tease out the distinctiveness of their own and then contrast it/them qualitatively with its/ their equivalents in another language. The idea is that by inspecting the collocates we can get abundant semantic information about the examined item. In addition to collocates, I will also look for explicit and implicit paraphrases, i.e. real paraphrases and typical examples, in the corpus. After obtaining the semantic profiles for sadness expressions in the two languages, a cross-linguistic qualitative comparison will be made based on their colligations, collocations, semantic references/associations and other features implied in their collocates and examples/paraphrases. Finally, a summary of the research findings will be presented.

7

Contrastive analysis of sadness expressions in English and Chinese

Psychologists tend to believe that there exist some innate and universal 'basic' human emotions like *happiness, sadness, anger, fear, disgust* and *surprise*, which are linguistically recognized in all languages (e.g. Ekman 1973, 1993, 1994). Psychological matching experiments are often taken as proof that all languages have words for the basic emotions. Other techniques used by anthropologists and cross-cultural psychologists include similarity judgement tasks, sorting tasks, listing tasks and rating tasks. All of these experiments face the problem of translation, since they all depend on elicitation and/or interpretation in natural language. The practice of taking English emotion terms like *sadness, unhappiness, anger* and *fear* as labels for universal psychological states has been argued to be ethnocentric and problematic (Wierzbicka 1986, 1992b, 1999). Even the traditional psychological categories, such as 'emotion', 'sensation' and 'cognition', have been claimed to be only cultural artefacts of western societies (Harre 1986; Lutz 1988; Wierzbicka 1999). Psychology has been working within the circle of shallow ethnocentrism. However, linguists favour the view that different languages divide emotions into different categories and put different labels on them. Language-specific emotion words might overlap, but they do not exactly map onto each other across languages. Analysis of the emotion lexicon of a language helps reveal the way in which its speakers cut the emotional world. A cross-linguistic comparison of the emotion lexicon can therefore disclose similarities and differences in the conceptualization of emotion across cultures.

This chapter aims to focus on the question of whether the concept of sadness is universal by comparing and contrasting English sadness expressions and their Chinese counterparts in terms of certain structural categories proposed in the field of corpus linguistics. It bases its claims mainly on colligations, collocations, semantic associations and paraphrases, focusing on identifying what elements are common to both languages and what elements are specific to English or Chinese. Throughout this chapter, I will engage with the corpus-based analysis of English sadness expressions and their closest counterparts in Chinese. Some of them will be discussed in pairs due to their close similarity in meaning. Each or each pair of the terms is the subject of an individual study, and an exercise in multifaceted cross-cultural analysis, within a corpus-based methodological framework. During the discussion, the cultural underpinnings for language- or culture-specific categorizations will also be explored. This chapter makes an attempt at a systematic account of English sadness expressions and their Chinese counterparts. I consulted different dictionaries and thesauri to produce a list of English emotion expressions to be included in the analysis, and some of them were excluded after careful scrutiny for some reasons, such as low frequency in the corpus. Their Chinese equivalents are determined basically based on the search results in the parallel corpus. Because the parallel corpus used for this research is a uni-directional one, i.e., from English to Chinese, the Chinese list yielded is longer than the English one. While it is not an exhaustive discussion of all the sadness expressions in the two languages, it does cover most of the frequent sadness expressions, totalling almost 100 including their derivational forms and Chinese equivalents, which constitute the core of the English and Chinese sadness lexicons.

7.1 Contrastive analysis of sadness expressions in English and Chinese

7.1.1 *Sorrow* & grief** and their Chinese equivalents[1]

Sorrow & grief**

Sorrow and *grief* are two common English emotion terms usually taken as synonyms. However, in the following sentences, *grief* and *sorrow* cannot be substituted for each other (Teubert 2004a: 82):

(1) **Grief** gave way to a guilt that gnawed at him.
(2) A magic harp music made its listeners forget **sorrow**.

So they are not synonyms in a strict sense. Native speakers of English may have no difficulties in understanding their meanings, but they are 'less competent in describing' them (Teubert 2004a: 93); in other words, they may find that it is not an easy job to tell clearly what emotion concepts *sorrow* and *grief* are associated with respectively, and in what cases one cannot be replaced by the other. To answer these questions, I drew on the three corpus-based dictionaries: LDCE, OALECD and COBUILD, where I found the following entries, with appropriate omissions of idioms, examples, etc. (henceforth):

LDCE:

sorrow   1. a feeling of great sadness, usually because someone has died or because something terrible has happened to you 2. an event or situation that makes you feel great sadness

grief   1. extreme sadness, especially because someone you love has died 2. something that makes you feel extremely sad 6. *Informal* trouble or problems

OALECD:

sorrow   1. feeling of sadness or distress caused esp by loss, disappointment or regret; grief 悲伤；悲痛；懊丧；悔恨 2. particular cause of this feeling; misfortune 悲伤的原因；懊丧的原因；不幸

grief   1. deep or violent sorrow 忧伤；悲伤 2. event causing such feelings 引起忧伤、悲伤的事；伤心事

COBUILD:

Sorrow is a feeling of deep sadness or regret.

Grief is a feeling of extreme sadness.

According to these dictionaries, it seems obvious that *sadness* is the hypernym of *sorrow* and *grief*, and *grief* is a more intense feeling of *sadness* than *sorrow*, though both of them can be caused by someone's death. A close inspection of the definitions above shows that both *sorrow* and *grief* basically refer to a sad feeling or an event/situation that causes such a feeling. The only exception is that *grief* is also used informally in the sense of 'trouble or problems' (LDCE), which is an extension of its second sense 'something that makes you feel extremely sad'. Since it is not used very frequently as neither OALECD nor COBUILD lists this as a separate sense, we can regard it as peripheral. Our discussion will focus on how to differentiate *sorrow* and *grief* from each other, in the sense of feeling sad. Do they differ only in intensity? Why in the sentences mentioned earlier can they not be substituted for each other? If we want to know their subtle nuances of meaning and differentiate them from each other, we need to draw on corpus data.

To find the colligational patterns of an English sadness expression, I mainly look at its collocates (examined as lemma) within the span of −1 and +1. I am fully aware that the restriction of collocate search to such a short span will result in some perplexing lacunae, but the extension of the search span will unavoidably lead to some inaccuracies. Besides, I inspect its concordance, especially the words immediately before and after the search word, to filter out those irrelevant collocates. I also use word sketch and my intuition to complement this kind of search to get a fuller semantic profile of the search word. This procedure will be followed for searching for colligation properties throughout the chapter, unless otherwise stated. For the sake of space, I will not present all the tables and offer a step-by-step analysis, but only summarize the search findings in most cases. For *sorrow* and *grief*, the BOE yields 3,469 and 8,183 hits (as a noun and lemma, retrieved on 1 September 2010[2]) respectively. According to the corpus data, *sorrow* has strong colligations with prepositions, typically *of (546), in (243), for (169), with (155), at (108), over (64)*; verbs, predominantly *express (49), feel (37), experience (16), bring (11), drown (8)*; modifying adjectives, principally *great (100), deep (77), profound (26), sweet (16), heartfelt (11), genuine (11), real (11), personal (9)*; and possessive adjectives, such as *his (190), their (148), your (103), her (96), my (74), our (69), own (11)*.

For *grief*, similar colligational patterns are found: prepositions, typically *of (1,352), with (490), in (434), for (289), over (155), to (418), at (189), about (57), into (48)*; modifying adjectives, like *good (262), private (70), great (44), personal (36), public (26), deep (22), terrible (20), unresolved (19)*; verbs, mainly *express (35), cause (33), feel (35)*; and possessive adjectives, such as *their (369), her (307), his (261), our (131), my (128), your (91), own (73)*. 262 hits of *good* are found in its collocates because 'good grief' is a fixed phrase used 'when you are slightly surprised or annoyed'. It also frequently collocates with *counselor(47)/counsellor(25)/counsel(24)*, suggesting that in modern society *grief* has increased to be a problem and needs to be handled with professional help.

To find the differences between *sorrow* and *grief* in semantic associations, I looked at their sketch difference. Their collocates in the 'and/or' pattern are shown in Table 7.1 (the first two groups of figures show the frequencies for *sorrow* and *grief* respectively and the figures in the last two columns indicate the salience, henceforth).

From Table 7.1, it can be seen that there is a significant difference in salience (above 2) in *joy (7.7/5.6), shock (4.6/6.7)* and *loss (3.1/5.2)*, which shows that, although they occur in the *and/or* pattern of both *sorrow* and *grief*, *grief* is much more associated with *shock* and *loss*, and *sorrow* is much more significant in its co-occurrence with *joy*. The high frequency of co-occurrence of *shock (98)* with *grief* might imply that the trigger of the *grief* feeling may well be an unexpected event, leading to a sudden violent disturbance of the mind or emotions. We might assume that one's initial response to an immediate cause, a recent loss, often the death of a close person would be numbness and disbelief as one would feel it hard to accept the extremely unpleasant fact. From the statistics in Table 7.1, it can be argued that the principal determinant of *grief* is *loss (115)*,

Table 7.1 The common pattern of *sorrow* and *grief* in the BOE: and/or

and/or	1180 s	1971 g	5.6 s	4.1 g	and/or	1180 s	1971 g	5.6 s	4.1 g
lamentation	9	4	7.8	5.9	heartache	6	6	6.4	6.0
anger	55	151	6.3	7.7	pain	76	126	5.4	6.1
joy	**106**	**27**	**7.7**	**5.6**	suffering	22	20	5.8	5.6
sadness	27	41	7.1	7.5	shame	10	22	4.7	5.7
guilt	23	52	6.1	7.2	disappointment	6	18	3.9	5.4
grief	41	12	7.1	5.2	confusion	5	19	3.5	5.4
regret	28	8	7.0	5.0	happiness	14	4	5.4	3.5
anguish	5	19	5.3	7.0	misery	6	10	4.6	5.2
rage	18	44	5.6	6.8	sympathy	6	15	4.0	5.2
remorse	11	8	6.8	6.0	distress	7	10	4.8	5.2
despair	10	30	5.3	6.8	**loss**	**27**	**115**	**3.1**	**5.2**
shock	**23**	**98**	**4.6**	**6.7**	frustration	11	14	4.8	5.1
loneliness	6	15	5.6	6.6					

which is well in line with psychological findings. The loss may be temporary (separation) or permanent (death), real or imagined, physical or psychological. The loss of a loved person often results in the experience of *grief*; losing a loved one also means the loss of strong bonds of friendship, companionship or love (Izard 1991). From a psychological perspective, people who experience *grief* may come to blame themselves for the loss (*guilt, 52*); *anger (151)* and *despair (30)* may also occur as a result of blaming someone else for the separation or as a result of feeling left alone or deserted (Izard 1977).

Table 7.1 reveals that both *sorrow* and *grief* semantically prefer words denoting emotions, such as *anger/rage, pain, guilt/remorse/regret, anguish/distress, sadness, despair, loneliness, shame, disappointment/frustration* and *sympathy*. One reason for this would be that people's emotions are often complex. Take *grief* for example, the complexities of feelings that can be invoked in *grief*-contexts are clearly exhibited in the following examples from the BOE:

(3) Instead, the families had to spend a long night of fear, worry, **grief** and total despair.

(4) ... and you have an almost intolerable mix of **grief** and regret, tinged with worry about what you might have done ...

(5) I ate them stolidly, full of hate and **grief**, and I didn't look at Art once.

It appears that the discussion of various feelings together in the discourse is quite common, as exemplified below:

(6) Sadness, loneliness, **grief** and disappointments are normal reactions to life's struggles.

In other patterns of their sketch difference, significant differences in salience are also found. It shows that *private (70/7, 4.8/1.5)*, *own (81/12, 3.4/0.6)* and *share (38/7, 4.6/2.2)* occur much more frequently with *grief* than *sorrow*. It seems that *grief* is often a private matter, but it could also be a public and social one. *Sorrow* hardly co-occurs with *public* probably because it is more introverted and introversion implies being private. In the 'grief' only patterns, we find *shared (7)* in the 'a_modifier' pattern, *mother (16)*, *family (27)* and *father (6)* in the 'possessor' pattern, and *overcome (6)* in the 'object_of' pattern. This might suggest that *grief* is a feeling elicited by a misfortune, which may be overcome by sharing it with others. For example, at a time of death, a family comes together to mourn, and, although it is death that brings about this closeness, there is a sense of affectionate ties with other members of the family. Shared *grief* over the loss of a loved one can thus reunite a family and facilitate cohesiveness (Izard 1991). *Grief* is a strong feeling that is usually expressed publicly. *Outpouring (86, −5, +5)*[3] of *grief* provides 'some relief and a sense of release' (Wellenkamp 1988: 495). Expressions of *grief* can also elicit empathy and strengthen bonds among all those who are bereaved (Izard 1977). *Mourning (58, inclusive of mourn, −5, +5)* is a typical context for *grief*. Its close association with *grief*, but not *sorrow*, indicates that *grief* is more a communal, ritualized, culturally mediated and extroverted response to a bad event, in particular, someone's death.

I have searched for *grief is* in the BOE and got some of its paraphrases:

(7) ... but the purpose of **grief is** to cope with the unacceptable, and drastic reactions are both necessary and healthy. If you care for someone in any way, you become attached to them. If you care for someone who dies, then you continue to love them – but there is no longer a person for you to love. We cannot alter our feelings as quickly as life and death can change the world. You may begin to feel foolish about your love for a 'no one', although it is unavoidable. The major grief feeling is LOSS. As Ann Carpenter and Geoffrey Johnson's book makes clear, we can sense this about absolutely anything that matters. We grieve in some way, often the same way, whether someone dies, or is taken from us by divorce. Or when

we lose our pet cat, or move house, change schools, lose a favourite teacher or a 'best' possession. But of course the most severe loss occurs when we are bereaved by the death of someone close to us. Naturally, the first grief feeling to hit when you get bad news is SHOCK and numbness.

(8) When someone we love dies, ***grief is*** a natural consequence. It is a very strong emotion which can sweep us away so that our normal states of mind are eclipsed.

(9) For most people, ***grief is*** not a chain-reaction in which we go smoothly from one state of mind to the next, but rather a switchback ride of feelings, often swinging rapidly from one state to another.

(10) If ***grief is*** repressed or pushed down ('isn't she brave; she's behaving so normally') it may emerge later as physical or depressive illness.

(11) It is essential to be able to talk to each other and not bottle it in. Talking to other women who have miscarried is also very helpful, particularly if they have since succeeded in having a baby. This is also where Mum comes in. She can be your biggest comforter of all. If you do not talk to anyone or communicate, the ***grief is*** closely followed by anger, at yourself, at each other, and at the doctors who didn't explain; 'Surely they could have done something to stop me from miscarrying, although I know that it was ...'

(12) At one level, ***grief is*** or can be shared – the level of support and understanding.

(13) ***grief is*** a selfish emotion ...

(14) At a time when people feel isolated, with few common experiences to unite them, these expressions of grief can give them a sense of belonging, however momentary. So through these collective displays of emotion – showing the world how upset you are and connecting with others who feel the same way – an otherwise fragmented society is able to achieve a sense of collectivity. This can only ever be a temporary phenomenon – the ***grief is*** necessarily transient because, in a sense, it is not real. People may feel genuinely upset, but it is not authentic grief. Grief is the emotional expression of a profound sense of personal loss. So just as soon as today's public mourning springs up, it starts breaking up and disappears.

The above paraphrases give us almost the same information on *grief* as we get from its collocates. As *grief* is a much-talked-about and well-researched topic in written discourse, we can get a good many paraphrases from the BOE, which contains a multitude of books of life science. For other emotion expressions, it is not quite the case. But the case of *grief* shows that, as long as we can collect sufficient paraphrases of a given lexical item, its meaning will become transparent.

So far, the discussion has focused on *grief* as a feeling. The following examples illustrate *grief* in its sense of 'something that causes great unhappiness', which accounts for only a tiny part of the total occurrences:

(15)   And it is an astounding **grief** to me that we've deprived ourselves of this knowledge of architecture . . .

(16)   . . . in the fourth month, and I did not conceive again. This was a **grief** to us . . .

Grief is conceived of as an emotion prototypically linked with death, so the death of someone who is special to a particular group might come as a *grief*. However, it can also be extended to other situations where one will suffer to a similar degree as a consequence of other highly unpleasant events. Their having been deprived of the knowledge of architecture in Example (15) and her not being able to conceive in Example (16) are good illustrative examples of such events.

The following examples show what a *sorrow* in the sense of 'something that causes great unhappiness' could be (like *grief*, this sense accounts for only a tiny part of its total occurrences in the corpus):

(17)   . . . it is a very real **sorrow** for me to have the association end.

(18)   For him personally, he continued, it was a great **sorrow** to be parted from a colleague and a friend . . .

(19)   . . . we have laid to rest young men and women who died in distant lands. For their families, this is a terrible **sorrow**, and we pray for their comfort. For the Nation, there is a feeling of loss, and we remember and we honour every name.

(20)   . . . I think I would have been between four and seven. At that age, I had not yet known anything you could call a great **sorrow**.

Examples (17)–(19) show that a *sorrow* could be the ending of a former association, or the parting with one's colleague or friend, or the death of one's family member. Example (20) tells us that due to the cognitive constraint a young child seems not to know what a great sorrow could be like.

As pointed out earlier, the emotional responses towards an unpleasant event or situation might be complex. The reactions may go through several phases: the first response would be the awareness of the loss; then one might think about the cause, the circumstance or the changes it may bring about, etc., so the emotion would be transformed into a combination of *sorrow* with other feelings, such as *fear, guilt, despair* or *anger*. Example (21) is an example of the mixture of feelings:

(21) 'I wouldn't wish what Todd has to go through on my worst enemy. He feels **guilt, sorrow, anger** and **despair**. He knows the Platts don't want him there, but he must see Billy being buried.'

Or the emotion might alternate between such feelings, as revealed in Example (22) below:

(22) I keep going back and forth between **sorrow** and **anger** and **guilt** that we didn't ask more questions.

Sorrow and *anger* often co-exist also due to the prefabricated phrase *more in sorrow than in anger*, inclusive of its variant:

(23) Mr Hurd reacted to this turn of events more in **sorrow** than in **anger**. He insisted he had been misquoted.

(24) On January 12, an emotional congressional debate ended with the House of Representatives authorizing the use of force by a vote of 250 to 183; the Senate concurred, 52 to 47. More in **sorrow** than in **anger**, the nation steeled itself for combat.

If one deals with something more in *sorrow* than in *anger*, it probably means that one has given the whole matter careful thought and come to the conclusion that he or she is very sad or disappointed rather than angry about it. In Example (23), the speaker was extremely disappointed about the turn of the events due to the misquotation from him, and, in Example (24), the nation was very sad that it had to prepare itself for the coming war. Such conclusions require more thinking about what has happened. *Sorrow* seems to involve a deeper thinking about everything around what has happened. Unlike *anger* or *grief*, it is not a simple perceptual or emotional reaction to an unpleasant event; instead, it is a more rational and advanced emotion involving 'higher' thinking processes.

Sorrow is a 'feeling of sadness or distress caused esp. by loss, disappointment or regret' (OALECD). It implies that the experiencer considers the situation as uncontrollable and thus is not likely to attempt to do something about it. In other words, it is the awareness of powerlessness that is salient for *sorrow*. It suggests a degree of resignation ('I can't do anything about it'); it implies a 'semi-accepting' or 'semi-resigned' attitude towards what has happened (Wierzbicka 1999: 66). The pain comes not only from the irreparable loss, but also from what has been obtained from a rational analysis of the whole matter. This explains why people will be more in sorrow than in anger when they clearly know that the outbursts of anger will not help. The most typical collocate of *sorrow* is *drown (221)*, which can be explained by the idiomatic expression 'drown one's *sorrows*'. Look at more examples from the corpus:

(25)   He ploughed into the pedestrian as he drove home after drowning his **sorrows** with pals over his split from wife Christine.

(26)   ... a cast of characters who drank in the same pub in a vain attempt to drown their **sorrows**.

(27)   ... poor Dalek has been humiliated – no wonder he's drowning his **sorrows**.

As shown in the examples above, the phrase basically means one drinks a lot of alcohol in order to forget one's troubles or problems, which could be the split with one's wife in Example (25), the humiliation in Example (27) or something else. *A vain attempt* in Example (26) seems to show that it is not so easy, as they wish, to forget the problems by getting drunk. 'In the case of *grief* and *grieving* the experience intentionally focuses on the painful subject ("I want to think about this"), whereas in the case of *sorrow* there is rather, an inability to forget ("I can't not think about this")' (Wierzbicka 1999: 67). *Sorrow* is a long-term suffering, which cannot be forgotten easily because there is always a conflict between the consciousness of powerlessness and the reluctance to accept the unpleasant reality. *Grief* implies 'poignant suffering for an immediate cause, a recent loss' (Santangelo 2003: 389). '*Sorrow* may have its roots in the past, but the stress is on the on-going, long-term state' (Wierzbicka 1999: 66). So it is likely that one still feels *sorrow*, which is less intense than *grief*, after even several years of the death of a close person. Example (20) seems to suggest that a young child does not know what a *sorrow* is because s/he never gives a special thought to a sad matter due to the cognitive constraints.

Next let us look at *sorrowful* and *sorrowfully* in the corpus. The BOE contains 342 occurrences of *sorrowful*. By inspection of its word sketch, it is clear that *sorrowful* is often modified by *deeply (7), particularly (3)*, and that it is semantically associated with things showing *sorrow*, such as *voice (4), eye (5), face (4), wail (2), look (3), sigh (3), glance (2), tear (2), sound (2), note (2)*, or things causing *sorrow*, like *mystery (6), tale (4), sight (3), memory (2)*. For *sorrowfully (82)*, it seems that the pattern 'shook (shaking) one's head *sorrowfully*' dominates the picture. So, unlike *sorrow*, both *sorrowful* and *sorrowfully* are principally associated with external manifestations, namely more extroverted.

Now let us proceed to examine *grieve*. Its definitions are shown below:

LDCE: 1. to feel extremely sad, especially because someone you love has died. 2. if something grieves you, it makes you feel very unhappy

OALECD: (*fml*) 1. cause great sorrow to (sb) 使（某人）极为悲伤 2. (a) feel a deep sorrow because of loss (因失去而) 感到悲痛: (b) feel deep regret (about sth) (对某事) 感到非常後悔、懊悔

COBUILD: 1. If you *grieve over* something, especially someone's death, you feel very sad about it. 2. If you *are grieved by* something, it makes you unhappy or upset.

A simple glance of the definitions above shows that, basically, *grieve* means 'feel sorrow' and 'cause sorrow'. Unlike the other two dictionaries, OALECD lists its sense of 'feel deep regret (about sth)' as a separate one. Its collocate data (3,675 hits) from the BOE show that its colligational items include prepositions, typically *for (488)*, *to (498)*, *over (130)*, *at (51)*, *by (43)*, and modifiers, predominantly *deeply (31)*, *properly (23)*. Its top collocates also reveal that it is semantically associated with words indicating people involved in a grieving event (mostly someone one is very close to) such as *family (235)*, *relative (105)*, *parent (85)*, *mother (65)*, *widow (60)*, *father (38)*, *friend (27)*, *husband (23)*, *people (29)*, *dad (16)*, *woman (18)*, *daughter (12)*, *wife (12)*, *brother (11)*. Further, what can be seen from its top collocates is that it, in the form of *grieving*, prefers words related to a length or portion of time, like *process (139)* and *period (18)*, which are all relevant to someone's death. From its word sketch, I find *loss (20)*, *death (7)*, *baby (8)*, *son (7)* and *victim (6)* in the 'pp_for-p' pattern, and *privately (6)*, *openly (5)*, *alone (10)* and *together (20)* in the 'modifier' pattern. The former indicates that *grieving* usually happens due to someone's death, while the latter seems to show that *grieving* is an emotion characterized by both extroversion and introversion.

In sum, *grief* and *grieve* are more semantically associated with words indicating family members or someone with whom one has a very close relationship, words relevant to social rituals, public ceremonies, etc., while *sorrow* more semantically prefers a word describing whether the feeling is deep or sincere, such as *heartfelt*, *genuine*, *real*. The analysis seems to support Teubert's claim (2000) that *sorrow* is a feeling that is deeper, longer lasting, more introverted, more individual, more voluntary, more personal but less intense than *grief*; in contrast, *grief* is more extroverted, more communal, more ritualized and more culturally mediated than *sorrow*. To find out whether the distinction between *sorrow* and *grief* is shared by Chinese, we need to examine their equivalents in Chinese texts.

Chinese equivalents of sorrow* and grief*

Queries of *sorrow** and *grief** are carried out in the BPC and the results are shown in Table 7.2.

Table 7.2 Chinese equivalents for *sorrow** and *grief** in the BPC

	sorrow / 91 hits	*grief* / 72 hits
bēishāng	27	23
yōu/chóu[#]	9	–
shāngxīn	9	10
nánguò	6	–
bēiāi	–	8
bēitòng	–	7

Notes:
– Less frequent in the parallel corpus
[#] The *yōu/chóu* (worry) concept is realized by different Chinese words

Table 7.2 shows that their Chinese equivalents include *bēishāng, shāngxīn, nánguò, bēiāi* and *bēitòng*, excluding *yōu/chóu*. In fact, *shāngxīn* and *nánguò* describe less intense sad feelings. They were used as translations of *sorrow* or *grief* due to the simplification in translating (cf. Baker 1995). I will discuss them in Section 7.1.3. The concept of *yōu/chóu* focuses on worry, which is not my focus, so here I will only discuss *bēishāng, bēitòng* and *bēiāi*, all of which start with *bēi* and form a *bēi* set. Before analysing them, let us look at their definitions in XHCBL, which are shown in Table 7.3.

Table 7.3 Definitions of *bēishāng, bēitòng* and *bēiāi* in XHCBL

	Chinese definition	**English definition**
bēishāng	*shāngxīn; nánguò*	*sad; sorrowful; mournful*
bēitòng	*shāngxīn*	*sorrowful; grieved*
bēiāi	*shāngxīn*	*sad; sorrow; grief*

Table 7.3 seems to suggest that *shāngxīn* is a generic word to denote a sad feeling, but it tells us nothing about their distinctions. Before examining these terms further, let us take a look at the Chinese system of lexicon. Modern Chinese words (polysyllabic *cí*) have evolved from old Chinese characters (monosyllabic

zì), each of which has its own self-contained semantic meaning, such as *bēi, āi, tòng, shāng.* The vast majority of Modern Chinese words are formed by two or more old characters and have developed their new denotations and connotations over time, but there is still a close link between the new meaning of the modern word and the old meanings of its constituents, especially in idioms and conventionalized phrases. Yip (2000: 90) provides a clear account of the structure of Chinese lexicon:

> Chinese is not a language totally deprived of morphological derivations . . . instead of being composed of 'base + affix', a Chinese di- (or poly-) syllabic lexeme will, in the majority of cases, assume the look of a compound, that is, with the two (or more) constituent mononyms contracting a kind of quasi-syntactic relationship with each other, which makes it possible to analyse the internal composition of a Chinese word in syntactic terms.

One of the syntactic structures found in disyllabic lexemes is juxtapositional type: either 'juxtaposer + juxtaposed' or 'juxtaposed + juxtaposer', in which two mononyms of syntactic category and similar orientation form a word. The primary motivation for such a structure might be to comply with the overall disyllabification tendency of the modern Chinese lexicon. In such a structure,

> the juxtaposer is usually the one which occurs more frequently or enjoys greater combinatory power and therefore defines and charts the general semantic orientation of the set, whereas the juxtaposed is the one which tends to make more minute differentiations of meaning within the same general semantic orientation set down by the juxtaposer or determine the syntagmatic potentiality of the resultant combination.
>
> (Yip 2000: 95)

In the case of the *bēi* set mentioned above, obviously, *bēi* is the juxtaposer, which sets the tone for the whole set, and the other three mononyms are the juxtaposed, which fine-tunes the meaning of the juxtaposer. I will try to tease out the semantic differences between this lexical set. As noted earlier, Chinese feeling-denoting words are usually seen and glossed as adjectives, but they can also be used as nouns and adverbs. The present Chinese POS tagging software cannot annotate their word classes with sufficient accuracy, so I chose not to tag them at all. My analysis will focus on the semantic content, i.e. the concept, so I will discuss them together.

Bēitòng

The significant collocates of *bēitòng* (2,677[4] hits) are shown in Table 7.4, from which we can find that *(shēn)gǎn* (deeply + feel) and *(shēn)biǎo* (deeply + express) are segmented as one word by ICTCLAS. They occur very frequently, but they are only recurrent patterns rather than single words. We will ignore this inaccuracy of word segmentation, and focus our analysis on meaning. The first column lists the words pointing to its introversion, such as *gǎndào/(shēn) gǎn* (feel), *xīnqíng* (frame of mind), *xīnlǐ/xīnzhōng* (in the heart), *nèixīn/xīn* (inner heart/heart), and words showing its feature of extroversion, like *biǎoshì/(shēn) biǎo* (express), *kū/kūqì* (cry/weep), *shēngyīn* (voice), *yǎnlèi/lèishuǐ* (tears). English emotion words also frequently collocate with *feel*, but hardly with *in the (inner) heart*; Chinese tends to use *xīnlǐ/xīnzhōng* or *nèixīn* to emphasize that what is talked about is an inner feeling. I will address the cultural reason for this striking difference in detail in Section 7.1.2. Column 2 shows the causes for *bēitòng*: *sǐ/shìshì/qùshì* (die/death), *bìngshì* (die of disease), *xīshēng* (give one's life for/die a martyr's death), *yùnàn* (be killed in a disaster), *èhào* (news about the death of a beloved person), *shīqù* (loss/lose) and *búxìng* (misfortune). *Búxìng* is typically related to death when it is associated with *bēitòng*. Hence, it may be said that the predominant trigger for *bēitòng* is someone's death. Since Chinese emotion words can be used as a noun, an adjective or an adverb, we find two classes of modifiers in the third column, i.e. adjectival, like *jùdà*

Table 7.4 Significant collocates of *bēitòng* in the CCL corpus

Introversion/ extroversion	Cause	Modifier	People involved	Others
gǎndào 121	*sǐ 75*	*wànfēn 117*	*mǔqīn 55*	*lìng rén 20*
(shēn)gǎn 55	*shìshì 54*	*jùdà 99*	*fùqīn 27*	*rén 92 (qiángrén 52)*
xīnqíng 79	*qùshì 41*	*jídù 42*	*fùmǔ 23*	*chénjìn 69*
xīnlǐ/xīnzhōng 36/33	*bìngshì 19*	*shífēn 74*	*qīnrén 21*	*xiànrù 24*
nèixīn 31 xīn 28	*xīshēng 21*	*hěn 69*	*qīnshǔ 22*	*chōngmǎn 19*
biǎoshì 55	*yùnàn 42*	*fēicháng 63*	*jiāshǔ 17*	*zhènjīng 39*
shēnbiǎo 21	*èhào 32*	*shēnshēn 22*	*zhàngfū 22*	*xiāoxī 42*
kū/kūqì 46/19	*shīqù 57*	*wúxiàn 30*	*qīzi 18*	*fènnù 37*
shēngyīn 19	*búxìng 38*	*bùyǐ 29*	*érzi 20*	*juéwàng 24*
lèishuǐ/yǎnlèi 24/19		*wúbǐ 17*		

(enormous), and adverbial, such as *wànfēn/jídù/wúbǐ* (extremely), *shífēn/hěn/ fēicháng/* (very), *shēn(shēn)* (deeply), *wúxiàn/búyǐ* (endlessly). According to the fourth column, the people involved in the feeling of *bēitòng* include *mǔqīn* (mother), *fùqīn* (father), *fùmǔ* (parents), *qīnrén/qīnshǔ/jiāshǔ* (family), *qīzi* (wife), *zhàngfū* (husband) and *érzi* (son), who are either the object or the experiencier of *bēitòng*.

The last column lists its other collocates, which might contribute to the unravelling of its meaning. In Chinese, in most cases, emotion words have to be preceded by 'lìng rén/jiào rén/rang rén/shǐ rén' (make/cause) to express a causative meaning. For instance, if you want to talk about sad news that makes people *bēitòng*, you have to say 'lìngrén bēitòng de xiāoxī (news)'. For the same complex concept, English uses a single word to express it, but Chinese uses a phrase instead. The former is referred to as 'synthetic expression' and the latter 'analytic expression' (Banczerowski 1980: 336). We will return to this issue in Section 7.3. *Rěn* (control) might suggest people sometimes control their feelings and prevent them from exploding. Fifty-two occurrences of *qiángrěn* (try very hard to suppress) reveal that, in most cases, people try very hard to do so. *Bēitòng* also collocates with strong negative feelings, such as *fènnù* (indignation), *juéwàng* (despair). *Chénjìn* (be immersed in) and *chōngmǎn* (be filled with) might show that *bēitòng*, in Chinese, is metaphorically conceptualized in terms of fluid. The association of a strong emotion with the state of 'be immersed in' is specific to Chinese. We will come back to this issue in Sections 7.1.7 and 7.2.

From its collocates *zhènjīng* (shock), *xiāoxī* (news) and *èhào* (news about the death of a beloved person), we can see that *bēitòng* is more an overwhelming emotional eruption, invoked by something extremely bad and unexpected you are hardly able to face or accept, prototypically the death of a close person. It is an intense but transient feeling, which is usually accompanied by crying/weeping and tears. Two hundred and sixty-two hits of *bēitòngyùjué* (*bēitòng* + on the point of + stopping breathing), a four-character idiom meaning 'so *bēitòng* that one has come to the end of life', are found in the CCL corpus. This idiom tells us how intense *bēitòng* is. *Bēitòng* may come suddenly and fade away over time. It comes from the bottom of the heart but is often shown outwardly. From the above discussion, we can argue that *bēitòng* is more individual than communal, more voluntary than ritualized, and more personal than culturally mediated. It is similar to *sorrow* in terms of these three dimensions, but to *grief* in terms of extroversion, intensity and length.

Table 7.5 Significant collocates of *bēiāi* in the CCL corpus

Introversion	Extroversion	Modifier	Feeling	Others
gǎndào 248	kūqì 26	fēicháng 33	tòngkǔ 100	lìng 46
juéde 51	kū 39	zhēn 33	fènnù 58	sǐ 43
nèixīn 21	yǎnjing 28	shífēn 25	shīwàng 33	shīqù 27
xīnlǐ 49	yǎnlèi 25	shēn(shēn) 42	juéwàng 30	búxìng 19
xīnzhōng 36	liǎn(shàng) 24	jùdà 20	jìmò 27	chōngmǎn 43
	shēngyīn 37	mòdà 20	gūdú 21	yīzhèn 29
	biǎoqíng 18	wúxiàn 18	kǒngjù 26	mínzú 29
	shénqíng 18	yīdiǎn 29	huānlè 42	
		xiē/sī 25/20	kuàilè 24	

Bēiāi

The top collocates of *bēiāi* (3,281 hits) are shown in Table 7.5, from which it can be seen that *bēiāi* is not only a mental state of emotion, as indicated by *gǎndào/juéde* (feel), *nèixīn* (inner heart) and *xīnlǐ/xīnzhōng* (in the heart), but is also characterized by outward expression, as revealed in *kūqì/kū* (cry/weep), *yǎnjing* (eyes), *yǎnlèi* (tears), *shēngyīn* (voice), *biǎoqíng/ shénqíng* (facial expression) and *liǎn(shàng)* (on the face). Its frequent modifiers are *fēicháng/ shífēn* (very), *zhēn* (really), *shēn(shēn)* (deeply), *jùdà* (enormous), *mòdà* (utmost) and *yīdiǎn/xiē/sī* (a little). The feelings in its company include *tòngkǔ* (anguish), *fènnù* (indignation), *shīwàng* (disappointment), *juéwàng* (despair), *kǒngjù* (fear), *jìmò/gūdú* (loneliness), as well as some positive feelings, like *huānlè* (joy) and *kuàilè* (gaiety). *Lìng* (cause) occurs in *bēiāi*'s collocates for the same reason for *bēitòng*. *Chōngmǎn* (be filled with) *bēiāi* is also very common. *Yīzhèn* (lasting for a short time) seems to show that *bēiāi* may come suddenly but strongly and disappear after a very short time. *Sǐ* (death), *búxìng* (misfortune) and *shīqù* (loss) may cause *bēiāi*, but unlike *bēitòng*, they are not predominant triggers. In addition, I found quite a few hits of *mínzú* (nation) *de bēiāi*, *rénshēng* (life) *de bēiāi*, *rénlèi* (human kind) *de bēiāi*. The concordance listing for *mínzú de bēiāi* generated from the CCL corpus is presented in Figure 7.1.

Figure 7.1 shows that it is seen as *mínzú de bēiāi* if its culture has been treated lightly, if its people only read picture-storybooks and cannot understand *Hongloumeng*, if indifference has become prevalent in that nation, if scientific and educational films are given the cold shoulder, if abnormal immoral

Figure 7.1 Concordance listing of *mínzú de bēiāi*

phenomena have become normal, etc. *Bēiāi* in *mínzú de bēiā* seems to have developed a new sense that is not associated with great sadness caused by someone's death or a calamity, and it is used as a noun meaning 'an event that makes one *bēiāi*', which is unique in the *bēi* set. Example (28) tells us that this new sense is not totally new:

(28) 无心或心灰意懒是人生中最大的悲哀 (*bēiāi*), 因而庄子说过, 哀(*āi*)莫大于心死。

Zhuangzi has said, as shown in (28), 'the utmost *āi* is *xīnsǐ* (lit. dead heart/broken spirit)'; in other words, the greatest *bēiāi* for one's life is that one feels disheartened and has lost the interest to do anything. Example (29) shows us that the loss of one's son at an old age is one of the greatest *bēiāi* in one's life:

(29) 晚年丧子是人生的一大悲哀 (*bēiāi*)

For its modern sense, look at more examples from the CCL corpus:

(30) 但是如果教育工作者的岗位不在教学和科研上, 而是在股市上或商海里, 这当时是教育和教育者的悲哀 (*bēiāi*)

(31) 为了爱, 反而剥夺了所爱者的生命, 这才是莫大的悲哀 (*bēiāi*)

(32) 仿佛爱情也是一种消费。每当他喊小姐买单的时候, 他特别神气, 伊琳却感到悲哀 (*bēiāi*)

(33) 这是"穷教育"的悲哀 (*bēiāi*)

(34) 有文化而又缺乏爱心甚至爱心泯灭之人, 是我们这社会的最大悲哀 (*bēiāi*) 和污点

(35) 解救一个在风雨中呻吟的病人, 是任何有道德感的人应该做的, 而一个 出租车司机却冷漠地说"不", 我为此感到莫大的悲哀 (*bēiāi*)

(36) 他越来越为中国人的苦难感到悲哀 (*bēiāi*) : 先是"左"的冲击, 物质匮乏; 后之开放国门, 引进西方先进的科技, 暴露了现代文明的各种弊端, 波 及整个民族的困惑, 等等

(37) 可几乎所有的朋友都问过一个问题: 这花了近40块人民币从德国买来 的水泥块, 真的是柏林墙上的一块吗?会不会是假的?我感到 悲哀 (*bēiāi*)。悲哀 (*bēiāi*) 的是只有我的同胞才会提出这样的问题。我们被 自己席卷全国、无孔不入的造假吓坏了。

Examples (30)–(37) illustrate what *bēiāi* is in its modern sense: it is a *bēiāi* thing if the educational staff do not devote themselves to teaching or research, but to stock market and business, if one takes someone else's life just because of love, if one takes love as a consumption, if a nation does not allocate sufficient funds for education, if people are well educated but lack the capability to love and care for others, and if a taxi driver coldly refuses to take to the hospital a patient who is groaning in a mighty storm. It is a *bēiāi de* situation for the Chinese people: first we were suffering material deprivation due to the strong influence of the 'left', and then after introducing advanced sciences and technologies from the West we are in a national bewilderment as to how to deal with various side-effects of the modern civilization. One of the side-effects of the market economy in China due to its lack of adequate supervision is that fraud is pervasive nation-wide. One has been asked by almost all of his friends whether the cement lump he bought at the cost of almost RMB 40 in Germany is a real one from the Berlin Wall. It is a *bēiāi de* thing because only the Chinese people who have experienced and seen too many frauds would ask such a question.

It seems that, in modern texts, *bēiāi* is used to describe something that is sad, disappointing but we can do nothing about, something that should not have happened, something that will lead to very bad consequences if it continues to be ignored, especially when people are not aware of its seriousness at all, and something that we often desire to get better. The concept of *bēiāi* has gone beyond its original circle and been extended to situations connected with a wider range of unfortunate events happening to people, nations, life, human beings or even the whole world (unfortunately, the description of its modern sense is completely missing in the Chinese dictionaries). *Bēiāi* in this sense is more caused by regret, sympathy, pity and disappointment but often with a wish for it to get better.

Consider more examples from the BPC:

(38) 许多东西会在她心里引起悲哀 (*bēiāi*) –那些弱者,那些凄苦无依的人,概激起她的伤心。

      Sorrow in her was aroused by many a spectacle – an uncritical upwelling of grief for the weak and the helpless.

(39) 在餐室里,她那么平静而又拘谨,而现在,她脸上一切伪装的悲哀 (*bēiāi*) 都已烟消云散 ...

      In the dining-room she had been demure and discreet. Now all pretence of *grief* had passed away from her.

(40) 趣味要高尚一点,不要用那条纱巾来表现自己实际上从来没有过的悲哀 (*bēiāi*)。

      And better taste than to wear that veil to advertise a *grief* I'm sure you never felt.

In (38), *the weak and the helpless* points to the altruistic and compassionate aspects of *bēiāi*, and *arouse* to its voluntary aspect. *All pretence of* in (39) and *advertise* in (40) allude to its communal and extroverted aspects, and *that veil* in (40) probably to its ritualized one. *Bēiāi* is more altruistic than personal, for its focus is on other people rather than the experiencer. The person who has just died is the focus, so it is a communal reaction to feel *bēiāi* over someone's death. And the veil in (40) is probably a required accessory to advertise one's *bēiāi*. *Bēiāi* tells us more about what the experiencer thinks about a particular sad event. It implies 'sympathy, compassion or even love, revealing a wish for bad things not to happen to the other person and a desire to do something good for the unfortunate' (Ye 2001: 375). This also explains how its modern sense has developed, for it is also altruistic, compassionate, sympathetic, wishing for an unpleasant event not to have happened and a better situation to come. To sum up, *bēiāi* is an altruistic, compassionate, voluntary and introverted concept. However, it might also be communal, ritualized and extroverted, in terms of which it bears a resemblance to *grief*; it is often associated with regret, pity, sympathy or compassion, in which sense it is more equivalent to *sorrow*, as revealed in Example (38).

Bēishāng

Bēishāng shares the common semantic core with both *sorrow* and *grief* since 27 out of 91 occurrences of *sorrow* and 23 out of 72 occurrences of *grief* have been

Table 7.6 Significant collocates of *bēishāng* in the CCL corpus

Introversion	Extroversion	Modifier and quantifier	Feeling	Others
gǎndào 102	*liǎn 20*	*hěn 91*	*tòngkǔ 117*	*lìng 34*
juéde 30	*liǎnshàng 25*	*fēicháng 30*	*fènnù 54*	*ràng 29*
gǎnjué 17	*yǎnjing 38*	*shífēn 29*	*juéwàng 29*	*chōngmǎn 55*
xīnzhōng 35	*yǎnlèi 35*	*jídù 27*	*kǒngjù 21*	*sī 50*
xīnlǐ 30	*lèi 18*	*bùyǐ 26*	*fánnǎo 19*	*tànxī 21*
nèixīn 20	*shénqíng 25*	*wúxiàn 21*	*yōuyù 19*	*mǔqīn 38*
xīn 39	*biǎoqíng 22*	*guòdù 38*	*yōuchóu 18*	*fùqīn 18*
qíngxù 28	*yàngzi 21*	*yīdiǎn 18*	*shīwàng 18*	
xīnqíng 18	*xiǎnde 20*		*xīwàng 20*	
gǎnqíng 20	*kū 47*		*xǐyuè 17*	
	kūqì 25		*huānlè 29*	
	shēngyīn 21		*kuàilè 32*	
			gāoxìng 17	

translated as *bēishāng*. In the CCL corpus, 2,603 hits of *bēishāng* are found. Its significant collocates are presented in Table 7.6.

A simple glance at Table 7.6 reveals that *bēishāng* shares most of its collocates with *bēiāi*. Like *bēitòng* and *bēiāi*, *bēishāng* is also conceptualized as fluid or gas because it frequently collocates with *chōngmǎn* (be filled with). The main differences lie in *bēishāng*'s unique collocations with *guòdù* (excessively), as found in the pattern '*bēishāng guòdù/guòdù bēishāng*', and with *fánnǎo* (vexation), *yōuyù* (melancholy), *yōuchóu* (worries) and *tànxī* (sigh). *Tànxī* and *wúkěnàihé* (powerless/helpless) *de bēishāng* (7 hits) seem to suggest that *bēishāng* involves 'the powerlessness and resignation on the part of the experiencer' (Ye 2001: 366), and it implies that the experiencer has no other choice but to accept what has happened, however bad it is. It highlights the experiencer's suffering caused by what has happened. In the CCL corpus, it is more related to *mǔqīn* (mother) probably because Chinese mothers tend to be *bēishāng* when they feel powerless.

Bēishāng is more a sentimental concept, which highlights the sense of powerlessness and helplessness due to the laws of nature and society. It is often related to the attitude towards life and the world, more fatalistic, more a result of accumulation of the past unfortunate events or something heavy that settles at the bottom of the heart after the misfortunes. If it is elicited by the death of a close relative or a friend or even a national leader, it is not as explosive and violent as *bēitòng*, which might fade over time and become *bēishāng*. *Bēishāng* is also a feeling triggered by parting or loneliness, which is something people do not want to face but have no choice. You may feel *bēishāng* if you find there will be no chance to make your dream come true, if you have just been jilted by your lover, if you leave your homeland and will never come back, if you realize in your forties that your future will never look any better, or if you are going to retire from playing tennis after doing it for 28 years.

The following examples from the CCL seem to support the claim that *bēishāng* is a long lingering thought left after a sad experience:

(41) 她在丈夫艾伯特逝世后 3 年还沉浸在悲伤 (*bēishāng*) 之中 . . .
      'She was still immersed in *bēishāng* three years after her husband Albert's death.'

(42) 悲伤 (*bēishāng*) 是不能够匆匆而过的 . . .
      '*Bēishāng* is not a fleeting experience'

Example (42) is a paraphrase that helps to explain the meaning of *bēishāng*, which may dominate somebody's feeling for as long as three years as shown in Example (41). *Bēishāng* may return repeatedly to someone's mind or be buried and hidden at the bottom of their heart but stirred again by any possible trigger. It involves a reflection quality, so cognitive development is required. Consider the following examples from the parallel corpus:

(43) 思嘉发现他眼中充满了悲伤 (*bēishāng*), 同时也含有厌恶和轻蔑之情, 这使她惊慌的心里顿时涌起满怀内疚. . .
      '. . .she saw that there was **grief** in his eyes and also dislike and contempt that flooded her frightened heart with guilt . . .'

(44) 他耐心地、冷漠地等着, 等到后来, 苔丝把满腹的悲伤, (*bēishāng*) 发泄完了, 泪如涌泉的痛苦减弱了, 变成了一阵阵抽泣。
      He waited patiently, apathetically, till the violence of her **grief** had worn itself out, and her rush of weeping had lessened to a catching gasp at intervals.

(45) 她一路走到这个地方, 一直把悲伤 (*bēishāng*) 压在心里, 因而心情十分沉重。
      All the way along to this point her heart had been heavy with an inactive **sorrow**.

In (43), Rhett's explosive *bēitòng* towards his daughter's death has developed into long lingering *bēishāng*. It takes much longer to overcome *bēishāng* than *bēitòng*. *Grief in his eyes* seems to suggest that *bēishāng* is something introverted you need to read from one's eyes. In (44), the *violence of grief* has also been translated as *bēishāng*, but this *bēishāng* is different from the *bēishāng* in (45). They are not distinguished in the Chinese lexicon. The former is a fading version of *bēitòng* over time, emphasizing more the missing element, and the latter is a less intense sadness than *bēitòng*. *Grief* was used because the author intended to describe Tess's poignant suffering for the immediate trouble she was facing. In (45), it seems that *sorrow* was used to depict an ongoing stress that has its roots in the past. The Chinese lexicon does not differentiate these two kinds of sadness; in most cases, personal and voluntary great-sadness can be classified into the category of *bēishāng* as long as it is less intense than *bēitòng*, which is so violent and intense that it is usually used in death or calamity-related situations.

Comparison

Drawing on the statistical data and typical examples from the corpora, an in-depth contrastive-semantic analysis of *sorrow* & *grief* as well as their Chinese equivalents—*bēishāng*, *bēiāi* and *bēitòng*—has been made. The analysis has focused on the distinctions between these emotion concepts in terms of cause, intensity, length and accompanying behaviour, etc. *Bēitòng* is an explosive intense sadness typically associated with someone's death. *Bēiāi* is an altruistic, sympathetic and compassionate feeling focusing on other people rather than the experiencer. *Bēishāng* could be a less intense sadness than *bēitòng* or a long lingering haunting thought as a result of accumulation of unfortunate experiences, often related to a fatalistic outlook. The *bēi* set shares basically the same semantic core but each focuses on different elements. Table 7.7 summarizes their features based on the previous discussions.

Table 7.7 Contrastive analysis: *sorrow* & *grief* vs *bēitòng*, *bēishāng* & *bēiāi*

	Extroverted	Communal	Altruistic	Explosive	Intense
bēishāng					less
bēiāi	√	√	√		less
bēitòng	√			√	√
sorrow					less
grief	√	√		√	√

Different cultures and languages categorize emotion concepts in different ways. As Table 7.7 shows, Chinese distinguishes sadness between the following dimensions: extroverted vs introverted, voluntary vs ritualized, altruistic (TO OTHERS) vs personal (TO ME), long lingering vs explosive, and intense vs less intense; however, English lacks the dimension of being altruistic or personal. The feature of being altruistic is Chinese-specific in the domain of emotion. As revealed in Table 7.3, three distinct Chinese sadness concepts (*bēishāng*, *bēiāi* and *bēitòng*) are encoded in the same word *grief* in English and there is no exact Chinese equivalent to it. *Grief* overlaps much with *bēitòng* for their both being extroverted, personal, explosive and intense; in translating, if it was associated with someone's death, and an explosive and intense feeling was described, *bēitòng* was the good choice. *Bēiāi* was selected by the translators to express the concept of *grief* because both are extroverted and communal. When the altruistic, communal or extroverted elements were emphasized, and the feeling described was less intense, *bēiāi* was the only choice. *Bēishāng* is inferior to *bēitòng* in intensity, so it was used to express the concept of *grief* under the 'personal' subcategory when its intensity is less violent. The fading version of *bēitòng* over time falls into this category, though it is unique in its missing element. In selecting the appropriate word to translate *grief*, sometimes not all the elements matched, only the sailent elements were considered.

Table 7.2 shows that *bēishāng* is shared by *sorrow* and *grief*. As discussed earlier, *bēishāng* is less intense than *bēitòng*, and more introverted, more personal and more individual than *bēiāi*. *Bēishāng* covers a wide range of introverted, personal and voluntary sadness from 'less violent' to 'great'. It is similar to *sorrow* in terms of being more introverted, individual, voluntary and less intense. They also share the deeper cognitive involvement characterized by the advanced thinking about or the evaluation of the situation, the subsequent awareness of powerlessness and the final resignation. They differ in the different elements involved in their thinking processes: *bēishāng* may contain the 'fatalistic' elements that are associated with the fatalism in the traditional Chinese culture, but it has separated the 'sympathetic, compassionate and altruistic' element from it, while *sorrow* lacks such an adding and exclusion. In most of the cases, *bēishāng* was used to translate *sorrow*; however, when other people rather than the experiencer were focused on, e.g. when the sadness is mixed with sympathy and compassion, *bēiāi* was chosen instead.

7.1.2 *Unhappy** and their Chinese equivalents

*Unhappy**

Before discussing *unhappy*, we need to look at what is *happy*. COBUILD says that 'someone who is happy has feelings of pleasure, usually because something nice has happened or because they feel satisfied with their life', and that 'a happy time, place, or relationship is full of happy feelings and pleasant experiences, or has an atmosphere in which people feel happy'. So *happy* in English is used to talk about someone's pleasant feeling or something that can lead people to such a feeling. Now we have a basic idea about what *happy* is, but an antonym with a negative prefix is not necessarily the exactly opposite to its stem in meaning. Let us look at how *unhappy* is defined in the three dictionaries:

> LDCE: 1. not happy 2. feeling worried or annoyed because you do not like what is happening in a particular situation 3. *formal* an unhappy remark, situation etc is not suitable, lucky, or desirable

> OALECD: 1. (a) sad or miserable; not happy 悲伤的; 难过的; 不幸福的; 不愉快的 (b) anxious or dissatisfied 忧虑的; 发愁的; 不满意的 2. unfortunate or unlucky; regrettable 不幸的; 不走运的; 令人遗憾的 3. (*fml*) not suitable or appropriate 不合适的; 不恰当的

> COBUILD: 1. If you are *unhappy*, you are sad and depressed. 2. If you are *unhappy* about something, you are not pleased about it or not satisfied with it. 3. An *unhappy* situation or choice is not satisfactory or desirable.

A simple glance at the senses of *unhappy* reveals that an *unhappy* person feels no pleasure and an *unhappy* thing gives no pleasure. Its meaning of 'feeling worried or annoyed' is reflected in the first two dictionaries but defined in different ways. COBUILD does not list its sense of 'unfortunate or unlucky' as a separate one probably because this sense is not frequent in contemporary discourse. One can be *unhappy* about many things, but in real language use it has its own preferences to modify. To find out which words it prefers, we need to look at its corpus data.

Unhappy occurs 9,611 times in the BOE and its top 50 collocates tell us that *unhappy* often precedes *marriage (146), people (121), childhood (75), memory (65), experience (45), man (57), family (38), customer (37), life (37), relationship (33), player (33)* and *ending (31)*. *Marriage* is the most frequent noun modified by *unhappy* probably because marriage is closely related to one's *happiness* or *unhappiness* and an *unhappy* marriage is more likely to be the topic of the discourse. *Unhappy* has colligations with the article-determiner *an (760)*, link verbs, mainly *be* (inclusive of its various forms, henceforth), *feel (81)*, *look (67)*, *become (39)*, prepositions, typically *with (1892)*, *about (765)*, *at (424)*. *Look* seems to indicate that an *unhappy* feeling is often shown outwardly via external manifestations. Its word sketch shows that *unhappy* is often intensified by amplifiers, like *very (487)*, *deeply (111)*, *increasingly (57)*, *desperately (54)*, *extremely (39)* and the emphasizer *really (51)*, but less readily combinable with downtoners like *little (14)* or *slightly (1)* because it 'implies a more "intense" feeling and a "stronger" negative evaluation' (Wierzbicka 1999: 63). The nouns used in the 'pp_with-p' pattern include *result (26)*, *situation (23)*, *decision (23)*, *life (20)*, *outcome (16)*, *performance (14)*, *plan (14)*, *idea (13)*, etc., suggesting a semantic component of dissatisfaction. This reveals that the typical cognitive scenario of 'unhappy' is that you are not satisfied with what has happened or is happening in a particular situation.

What can be found for *unhappily* in OALECD is: *1. sadly* 可悲地; 难过地. *2. unfortunately* 不幸地; 不走运地; 遗憾地. From the above definitions, we can see that *unhappily* can translate as *nánguò de, kěbēi de, búxìng de, bù zǒuyùn de, yíhàn de*. Let us look at *unhappily* (535 hits) in the BOE. Its top collocates show a number of verbs modified by *unhappily*: *marry (56)*, *say (32)*, *end (19)*, *think (13)*, *look (7)*, *stare (6)* and *sit (5)*. If *unhappily* is used to modify a verb of action, it usually means 'sadly'. If we say someone lives or dies *unhappily*, it probably means his life or death is an unfortunate thing. It is noteworthy that *unhappily*, apart from action verbs, is semantically associated with marriage or the ending of it.

From the 1,422 hits of *unhappiness* found in the corpus, an inspection of its top 50 collocates reveals that it has colligations with prepositions, typically *of (198)*, *with (154)*, *at (62)*, *in (64)*, *about (31)*, *over (24)*, possessive adjectives, such as *his (96)*, *their (79)*, *her (78)*, *my (24)*, *your (22)*, *own (19)*, amplifiers, predominantly *deep (23)*, *great (17)*, quality adjectives, like *personal (16)*, *public (11)*, *human (7)*, *marital (5)*, and verbs, mainly *express (11)*, *cause (11)*, *grow (10)*, *bring (7)*. The close association of the 'unhappy' concept with marriage is once more supported by *marital*; *personal, own, public* and *express* seem to suggest that *unhappiness* is both extroverted and introverted. *Cause* and *bring* appear to indicate that *unhappiness* has a definite cause.

Chinese equivalents of unhappy

Next let us move on to the discussion of their Chinese counterparts. *Unhappy** occurs 55 times in the BPC and its most frequent Chinese equivalents are presented in Table 7.8.

Table 7.8 The most frequent Chinese equivalents of *unhappy** in the BPC

Chinese equivalent	Frequency
búxìng	24
bú kuàilè	5
bù yúkuài	6
bù gāoxìng	4
bú xìngfú	4
Others	12
Total	55

All of the expressions in Table 7.8 start with *bú/bù*,[5] which is an adverb preceding adjectives to indicate negation. *Búxìng* tops the list because it is the closest equivalent to express *unhappy*'s sense of 'unfortunate or unlucky; regrettable'. Consider this example:

(46)　许多在场的人断言，他们在那个不幸 (*búxìng*) 的牧师的胸前看到了 一 个嵌在肉里的红字，与海丝特・白兰所佩戴的 十分 相似

　　　…account of what had been witnessed on the scaffold. Most of the spectators testified to having seen, on the breast of the **unhappy** minister, a SCARLET LETTER – the very semblance of that worn by Hester Prynne – imprinted in the flesh.

In (46), *unhappy* is translated as *búxìng*. According to the OED, the 'not happy' meaning developed from the 'unlucky' meaning. In Chinese, there is a separate word '*búxìng*', literally meaning 'not lucky' or 'unfortunate', to convey this meaning. *Unhappy* and *unlucky* are two distinct concepts both in Chinese and English, but *unhappy* connects 'misfortune' and 'a feeling of displeasure' through a conceptual extension, which is missing in Chinese.

In translating, the sense of 'not happy' is divided by many Chinese phrases with similar meanings. The four most frequent ones are listed in Table 7.8. The last one *bú xìngfú* is based on the evaluation of one's own life. It concerns the satisfaction with different aspects of one's life, depending more on some cognitive appraisal. It has not only to do with 'our personal past experience, but also to our social experience. We are always comparing ourselves to others. And we feel good or bad depending on whom we compare ourselves to' (Myers 1991: 56). 'Our social comparisons concern not only money, but also looks, smarts, and various forms of success' (p. 57). Rich people are not necessarily happier than less wealthy people because the former may compare themselves with those above them or have higher expectations towards life. People from different cultures have different criteria to judge life satisfaction. In Chinese, the closest equivalent to this meaning is *xìngfú*. Its negative form *bú xìngfú* is used to describe life dissatisfaction.

I will discuss the other three expressions meaning 'not happy': *bù yúkuài*, *bú kuàilè* and *bù gāoxìng*. *Bù gāoxìng* is usually a short-term feeling triggered by something specific; *bú kuàilè* is extended in time and more general; *bù yúkuài* is also specific. They can be separated by degree words like *zěnme* (to some degree, used in negatives). Consider this example:

(47) 可凯里·阿什伯恩显得 并不怎么高兴 (*gāoxìng*), 因为他明明很不喜欢
瑞德,他十分愿意站在米德大夫一边可是又不能说假话。
Carey Ashburn looked **unhappy**, for it was obvious that he, too, disliked Rhett intensely. He gladly would have sided with the doctor but he could not lie.

Unhappy in (47) is translated as *bù zěnme gāoxìng*, which means 'not very happy'. In Chinese, it is very common to insert degree words into negative phrases. To explore the finer distinctions of these Chinese phrases, I will analyse them one by one in detail based on the corpus data.

Bù gāoxìng

There are 2,561 hits of *bù gāoxìng* found in the CCL corpus and its significant collocates are shown in Table 7.9.

The first column in Table 7.9 lists the collocates that are semantically associated with outward manifestations: *liǎn/mǎnliǎn/liǎnshàng* (face/full face on the face), *yàngzi* (appearence) and *xiǎnde* (appear). Sometimes, we could

Table 7.9 Significant collocates of *bù gāoxìng* in the CCL corpus

Extroversion	Introversion	Modifier	Others
liǎn 73	*xīnlǐ 117*	*hěn 407*	*rě 40*
mǎnliǎn 48	*xīnzhōng 28*	*hǎo 70*	*dùzi 26*
liǎnshàng 29	*juéde 37*	*lǎodà 45*	*yīnwèi 66*
yàngzi 34	*gǎndào 41*	*fēicháng 33*	*wèishénme 48*
xiǎnde 21		*zhēn 31*	
		tǐng 21	
		xiē/yǒuxiē 32/36	
		diǎn/yǒudiǎn 41/27	

judge whether someone is happy or not based on his or her facial expressions or behaviour. But it is not always so. The collocates in the second column reveal that *bù gāoxìng* is also realized as an inner emotional state: *xīnlǐ/xīnzhōng* (in the heart), *xīn* (heart) and *juéde/gǎndào* (feel). *Unhappy* also tends to co-occur with *feel* and *look*, as discussed earlier, but not with *in the heart*. Different from English, Chinese tends to add *xīnzhōng* or *xīnlǐ* to emphasize that what the person experiences is an *unhappy* feeling, but s/he does not necessarily reveal it on the face. Traditionally, Chinese people have followed the philosophy of 'xǐ nù bù xíng yǔ sè' (do not reveal your joy and anger on your face). In the Chinese culture, it has been taken for granted that people hide their true feelings to others. In such a society, we cannot judge whether a person is happy or unhappy just based on his/her facial expressions. At the same time, in the Chinese discourse, people distinguish clearly an inward feeling from an outward facial expression or bodily manifestation, which might not reflect the true feeling. Consider the following example:

(48) 人家嘴上不说可心里不高兴 (*bù gāoxìng*)
       'He was actually *bù gāoxìng*, though he didn't say so'

Things like this happen quite often. They have to do with the famous Chinese 'face' (*miànzi*) issue, which is said to originate from Confucius' concept of 'míng' (名) (status) (Nongren, available at http://www.my1510.cn/article.php?id= b255454ac 109ed9a). Regarding the Chinese *miànzi*, Shi and Feng (2013: 9) provide the following explanation:

> [T]he Chinese face requires more recognition and respect from social others and is therefore more highly valued and more strongly protected or defended ... In terms of discursive strategies, this may be observed in the fact that Chinese speakers will do much more (than 'politeness strategies', Brown & Levinson, 1987) to keep (up) one's own face and to enhance or protect others' faces than Westerners—sometimes even at heavy costs ... In terms of discursive strategies, Chinese speakers typically create, maintain, show or highlight a positive image of themselves in character, position, worth, etc; given the understanding of the importance of this aspect of the self-concept, they will make efforts to enhance, protect or save others' faces, too (cf. Gu, 1990).

As can be seen from the above quote, Chinese people take their 'faces' very seriously. In speaking or talking, they have to be considerate enough to protect, defend and not to hurt other people's 'faces'. On the other hand, if someone is praised for his/her achievement, the traditional response would be a denial, though s/he is actually very happy. This is due to the well-known modesty of Chinese people.

In the English culture, it is also common to hide the true feelings because it is assumed to be a departure from 'normal behaviour' to show feelings 'over which one has no control' (Wierzbicka 1999: 19). Wierzbicka interprets the word 'emotional' as a certain unconscious 'ideology'—the loss of control of one's feelings would be abnormal. But generally speaking, compared with Chinese, English-speaking people are more direct, frank and transparent. Another reason to account for such a difference might be the Chinese specific way of expressing emotions. Look at the following examples from the Babel Chinese–English Parallel Corpus:[6]

(49) *Xīnzhōng*   *yòu*   *yǒuxiē*   *nánguò*
      In the heart   but   a little bit   unhappy
      'But he felt *nánguò* about it'

(50) *Xiángzi*   *xīnzhōng*   *fēicháng*   *gāoxìng*
      Name   in the heart   very   happy
      'Xiangzi was very *gāoxìng*'

The above examples are not translated word by word. In English, being happy or unhappy by default is an inner state of emotion, so 'xinzhong' can be left out in the translations.

From the third column in Table 7.9, we can see that its modifiers include *hěn/lǎodà/tǐng/hǎo/fēicháng* (very), *zhēn* (really) and *xiē/yǒuxiē/diǎn/yǒudiǎn* (a little). In English, adjectives can also be modified by a little (bit). It seems that both English and Chinese have metaphorized 'small number or amount' as 'to a little degree', which has been referred to as grammaticalization. The last column lists its other meaningful collocates. Among them, *rě* (invite/lead to) is a frequent causative verb to collocate with *bù gāoxìng*. It is usually used in the pattern 'rě mǒurén *bù gāoxìng*' (cause/make someone *unhappy*). *Dùzi* (belly) appears in Table 7.9 because *yī/mǎn dùzi bù gāoxìng* (full of *bù gāoxìng* in one's belly) is a recurrent pattern, meaning 'very unhappy'. The Chinese culture conceptualizes that emotions are located in one's belly. You become *bù gāoxìng* because something bad happened and you do not want this, and the event affects your feeling only temporarily. *Wěiqu* (grievance/feel wronged) and *shēngqì* (annoyance) are often associated with *bù gāoxìng*, as the following examples illustrate:

(51) 老师没听解释就批评了我。我感到很委屈 (*wěiqu*), 好几天不高兴
      (*bù gāoxìng*)。

'The teacher criticized me without listening to my explanation, so I felt
very *wěiqu*. Because of this I felt *bù gāoxìng* for several days.'

(52) 好像今天不高兴, 跟谁生气 (*shēngqì*) 呢?

'You look *bù gāoxìng* today. Who are you *shēngqì* with?'

If someone is wronged, s/he will feel *bù gāoxìng*. If someone is *shēngqì*, s/he must
be *bù gāoxìng*. *Shēngqì* is a weak version of anger. XHCBL glosses it as 'yīn bùhé
xīnyì ér bù yúkuài', which literally means 'not happy due to dissatisfaction'. Bad
events—a rejection, failing in an exam, losing a game—may make you *bù gāoxìng*.
But our moods will return to normal soon, because 'we humans have an enormous
capacity to adapt to changed circumstance' (Myers 1991: 48). In some cases, the
feeling of *bù gāoxìng* may linger longer, but it usually lasts for a short time because
one's current mood is more affected by what is happening. Thus, we can accept
easily the past bad events and adjust our moods to welcome something new.

In the second sense of OALECD, *unhappy* is glossed as 'feeling worried or
annoyed because you do not like what is happening in a particular situation'.
While *unhappy* and *bù gāoxìng* are similar in being annoyed, *bù gāoxìng* has
nothing to do with worry. Like *unhappy*, *bù gāoxìng* is a feeling when something
I do not like happened. It is quite specific. In other words, *bù gāoxìng* has a
definite cause, as indicated in its collocates *yīnwèi* (66/because) and *wèishénme*
(48/why). Further, a simple glance of its concordance reveals that *bù gāoxìng* is
overwhelmingly used predicatively.

Bù yúkuài

Bù yúkuài occurs 1,408 times in the corpus. Table 7.10 presents its significant
collocates.

Table 7.10 Significant collocates of *bù yúkuài* in the CCL corpus

Introversion	Modifier	Verb	Noun	Others
xīnlǐ 40	*hěn 163*	*fāshēng 89*	*shìqíng 133*	*méiyǒu 37*
xīnzhōng 16	*jí 38*	*chǎnshēng 25*	*shì 107*	*zhījiān 22*
xīnqíng 46	*fēicháng 27*	*nào 26*	*shíjiàn 24*	
qíngxù 36	*yīdiǎn 18*	*yǐnqǐ 25*	*jīnglì 21*	
gǎndào 80		*yùdào 23*	*guòqù 22*	
gǎnjué 33		*shǐ 103*	*shēnghuó 31*	
juéde 37		*lìng 99*	*gōngzuò 15*	
		ràng 40		

Table 7.10 shows that, semantically, *bù yúkuài* has a preference for words related to internal states, including sensational verbs, predominantly *gǎndào/gǎnjué/juéde* (feel), prepositions indicating the assumed loci of emotions, typically *xīnlǐ/xīnzhōng* (in the heart), and its superordinates, such as *xīnqíng* (frame of mind), *qíngxù* (mood). Look at the following instance, which clearly shows that *bù yúkuài* is a frame of mind or mood:

(53) 他跳槽到了广东某地的一家外资企业, 工资比康惠高了近一倍,
       但心情并不愉快 (*bù yúkuài*)
       'He changed to another foreign enterprise, with his pay doubled, but
       actually he was *bù yúkuài*'

Hence, it may be argued that *bù yúkuài* is more realized as an internal emotional state, focusing mostly on what is mentally experienced. It can also be seen, from Table 7.10, that *bù yúkuài* colligates frequently with intensifiers, typically *hěn* (very), *jí* (extremely), *fēicháng* (very much) and *yīdiǎn* (slightly). It has a semantic preference for things that might make people *bù yúkuài*, such as *shìqing/shì/shìjiàn* (thing/event), *jīnglì* (experience), *guòqù* (past), and aspects in terms of which *bù yúkuài* might happen, typically *shēnghuó* (life), *gōngzuò* (work), as exemplified in the following example:

(54) 日常生活中处处都可能遇到 不愉快 (*bù yúkuài*) 的事
       'In everyday life, it is likely to encounter *bù yúkuài* things'

It seems that *bù yúkuài* is often used as an attributive, which is different from *bù gāoxìng*, which is more likely to be used as a predicate. Another difference is that 'méiyǒu bù yúkuài' means 'there is nothing unhappy', where *méiyǒu* is the same as 'no' or 'not have', while 'méiyǒu bù gāoxìng' means 'not unhappy', where *méiyǒu* is used to indicate negation. Further, *bù yúkuài* often occurs between two parties, so *zhījiān* (between) is salient in its collocates. Examples are shown below:

(55) 我不想因为这件事情而使我们之间 (*zhījiān*) 发生 (*fāshēng*) 不愉快
       (*bù yúkuài*)
       'I don't want any *bù yúkuài* to happen between us because of this'
(56) 所以我们之间 (*zhījiān*) 并没有 (*méiyǒu*) 什么不愉快 (*bù yúkuài*), 大家
       还是好离好散
       'So there was no *bù yúkuài* between us. We broke up peacefully'

The phrase *bù yúkuài* could be used as a noun, meaning something that makes people *bù yúkuài*, just as shown above. Besides *fāshēng* (occur) and *méiyǒu* (no), it has some other typical verbal collocates:

(57) 人们必须保证不要出现 (*chūxiàn*) 令人震惊的不愉快 (*bù yúkuài*)
      'People must make sure that nothing shockingly *unhappy* occurs'
(58) 洛宾一点也没有察觉三毛因为拍电视而引起 (*yǐnqǐ*) 的不愉快
      (*bù yúkuài*)
      'Robin was not at all aware of Sanmao's sadness caused by TV show
      making'

It should be noted that, in Chinese, *fāshēng/chūxiàn/chǎnshēng* (occur/emerge),
like *yǐnqǐ* (cause), are all transitive verbs. *Nào* is a causative verb, which often
collocates with *bù yúkuài*, meaning 'leading to something unpleasant':

(59) 闹　得　很　不愉快 (*bù yúkuài*)
      'led to something very *bù yúkuài*'

As Table 7.10 shows, *bù yúkuài* frequently co-occurs with *ràng/lìng/shǐ* (make/
cause), suggesting a strong colligation with causative constructions. It is
semantically associated with disappointment, as exemplified below:

(60) 正是事先预料的那样, 是令人失望 (*lìng rén shīwàng*) 和极不愉快
      (*bù yúkuài*) 的
      'As expected, it was disappointing and extremely *bù yúkuài*'

It seems odd to say 'someone is disappointed and very *bù gāoxìng*', because
'disappointed' implies '*bù gāoxìng*', so it's completely redundant to add it. But
disappointment can be juxtaposed with *bù yúkuài* since they each emphasize a
different aspect. *Bù yúkuài* is closer to 'unpleasant' in feeling as both give no
pleasure to the mind. *Bù yúkuài* is more intense than *bù gāoxìng*. I will further
explore the subtle differences between *bù gāoxìng* and *bù yúkuài* by looking at
their causes. Look at these examples:

(61) 然而生活中存在的个别不文明行为却使多数同学感到不愉快
      (*bù yúkuài*)
      'But any uncivilized behaviour in everyday life makes many students feel
      bù yúkuài'
(62) 大部分人闻到这味道就感到不愉快 (*bù yúkuài*)
      'most people feel *bù yúkuài* when smelling this'

It can be seen from the above examples that a bad smell or uncivilized behaviour
can make people *bù yúkuài*. *Bù yúkuài* might mean people feel upset or
uncomfortable. One may feel *bù yúkuài* when one has worries or burdens. The
feeling of *bù yúkuài* can last long or be triggered again even long after the

unpleasant thing. However, one feels *bù gāoxìng* because what happened is not what one wants. *Bù gāoxìng* is quite specific and short. It may disappear soon because the situation changes or something happy happens afterwards.

Bú kuàilè

The CCL corpus only generates 255 instances of *bú kuàilè*, whose significant collocates are shown in Table 7.11.

Table 7.11 Significant collocates of *bú kuàilè* in the CCL corpus

Modifier	Introversion	Others
hěn 19	*xīnlǐ 6*	*yīnwèi 11*
fēicháng 17	*gǎndào 8*	*wèishénme 8*
yīdiǎn 7	*juéde 6*	*yuányīn 7*

Table 7.11 shows that it has a colligation with intensifiers: *hěn* (very), *fēicháng* (very much) and *yīdiǎn* (a little). Its semantic preference for words of introversion, characteristically *gǎndào/juéde* (feel), *xīnlǐ* (in the heart), shows that *bú kuàilè* is more experienced as an inner state. The last column reveals that the reasons why people are *bú kuàilè* are often discussed in the discourse, suggesting that *bú kuàilè* is more specific because it has a definite reason, as indicated in *yīnwèi* (because), *wèishénme* (why) and *yuányīn* (reason). To determine what *bú kuàilè* exactly means, we have to look at some examples:

(63) 结婚是人生最美满快乐的事, 我和我内人都是个中人, 假使结婚不快乐 (*bú kuàilè*), 我们应该苦劝两位别结婚 ...
Marriage is the happiest event of one's life. My wife and I both know what it is. If marriage **weren't happy**, we should be exhorting you not to marry.

(64) 就因为张蕊玲的阴谋, 我们就要永远的不快乐 (*bú kuàilè*) 吗?
'Are we going to be *bú kuàilè* for good, just because of Zhang Ruiling's conspiracy?'

Examples (63) and (64) seem to suggest that *bú kuàilè* lasts long since it is associated with marriage and permanency. More examples:

(65) 有钱的人, 通常并不快乐 (*bú kuàilè*)
'Usually, rich people are actually *bú kuàilè*'

(66) 凡是童年不快乐 (*bú kuàilè*) 的人都特别脆弱

'People with a *bú kuàilè* childhood are especially vulnerable'

(67) '上班族'不快乐 (*bú kuàilè*) 的原因是压力太大,压力主要来自工作、经济因素和家庭.

'The reason why "shangbanzu" are *bú kuàilè* is because they have much pressure from work, financial matters and family'

(68) 但我的心中充满隐忧,我其实是极度地不快乐 (*bú kuàilè*) 的.

'But I have a lot of worries. I'm actually extremely *bú kuàilè*'

(69) 有时候这种反省会把我弄得非常不快乐 (*bú kuàilè*), 惊讶的发现自己的失误竟是那么多.

'Sometimes the reflection made me very *bú kuàilè*, because I found that I had made a surprisingly large number of mistakes'

Rich people are *bú kuàilè* probably because they want more than money can provide. A *bú kuàilè* childhood is often associated with an abnormal life. Usually a child enjoys a carefree life under the care of his/her parents. A *bú kuàilè* childhood often means the child has to live a life with worries. When we say 'a *bú kuàilè* de childhood', we mean that we divide the life into several periods, one of which—childhood—is *bú kuàilè*. It seems that we can limit it to a certain period of time and then judge whether someone is *kuàilè* or *bú kuàilè* in this period. 'Shàngbānzú' in Example (67) are *bú kuàilè* because of their pressure, suggesting that worries lead to *bú kuàilè*. The reflection in Example (69) made me *bú kuàilè* because I found I had made much more mistakes than expected. This might make me think more about what caused these mistakes. *Bú kuàilè*, unlike *bù gāoxìng*, often makes people think more about what happened or what it may further lead to. In other words, one feels *bú kuàilè* because one has something to worry about in life. A carefree person would be *kuàilè* even if s/he is not rich. In this sense, it is related to life dissatisfaction. We say 'shēngrì (birthday) kuàilè' to others because we wish the addressee, at least, a carefree and joyful day. *Bù gāoxìng* is an emotional, and more often also a physical, reaction to a specific thing based on the judgement that what happened is not what s/he wants. People who have worries or cannot forget their worries are unlikely to enjoy life, so they will be *bú kuàilè*.

Comparison

Now let us come to the comparison between *unhappy* and its Chinese translation equivalents. One difference not relevant to meaning analysis is that *bù yúkuài* can also be used as a noun. Another notable difference among *bù gāoxìng*, *bù yúkuài* and *bú kuàilè* would be that *bù yúkuài* can be used to modify a thing, place or situation that makes people unhappy, such as *shì* (event), *chǎnghé* (occasion/ situation), *qìfēn* (atmosphere), *jīnglì* (experience), *jìyì* (memory) and *hūnyīn* (marriage), as shown in Table 7.12.

Table 7.12 Comparison of some collocates of *bù gāoxìng, bù yúkuài* and *bú kuàilè*

	shì	*chǎnghé*	*qìfēn*	*jīnglì*	*jìyì*	*hūnyīn*
bù gāoxìng	18	0	0	0	0	0
bù yúkuài	219	5	5	12	7	7
bú kuàilè	2	0	0	0	0	0

Bù yúkuài seems to be more similar to *unhappy* in terms of its modifying a variety of nouns, as shown in Table 7.12. *Bù gāoxìng* and *bú kuàilè* can only co-occur with thing (event), but not with the others. *Lìng rén/ràng ren* (make/cause) should be added to them to express the making-unhappy meaning. *Shì* (event) seems to be very special in Chinese in that it does not follow the common rules and can collocate with many words. So I will exclude it from the analysis. These expressions also differ in many other aspects. Table 7.13 summarizes their respective features.

It can be seen from Table 7.13 that *unhappy* seems to be a good-for-anything word, which covers the meanings of all four Chinese equivalents. I will focus on the semantic differences caused by cultural specificity. Chinese distinguishes

Table 7.13 Features of *unhappy* expressions

	unhappy	*bù gāoxìng*	*bù yúkuài*	*bú kuàilè*	*bú xìngfú*
Extroverted	√	√			
General	√		√	√	√
Specific	√	√	√		
Length	short or long	usually short	short or long	usually long	long
Making unhappy	√		√		
Annoyed	√	√	√		
Worried	√			√	
Unfortunate	√				
Not suitable	√				

these expressions in terms of the dimensions of extroversion, specificity, generality and length. No Chinese word has all of these features. *Unhappy* and its translational equivalents are seemingly semantically similar, but, if you examine them individually, they will exhibit distinct features. In other words, they have different functional loads. *Unhappy* covers a wider semantic range, also meaning 'making unhappy', 'annoyed', 'worried', 'unfortunate' and 'unsuitable', etc. Interestingly, some Chinese words also have some of these senses, like *bù yúkuài* meaning 'making unhappy' or 'annoyed', *bù gāoxìng* meaning *shēngqì*, and *bú kuàilè* implying 'worried'. However, the meanings of 'unlucky or unfortunate' and 'not suitable' have nothing to do with the Chinese expressions about unhappy feelings.

7.1.3 *Sad** and their Chinese equivalents

*Sad**

Sad is a generic term for unhappy feelings. First, let us look at the senses from the three chosen English dictionaries:

LDCE: 1. [FEELING UNHAPPY] unhappy, especially because something unpleasant has happened 2. [MAKING YOU UNHAPPY] a sad event, situation etc makes you feel unhappy 3. [NOT SATISFACTORY] very bad or unacceptable 4. [LONELY] a *sad* person has a dull, unhappy, or lonely life 5. [BORING] *informal* boring or not deserving any respect

OALECD: 1. showing or causing sorrow; unhappy 悲哀的; 忧愁的; 难过的 2. worthy of blame or criticism; bad 该受责备或批评的; 坏的 3. making one feel pity or regret 令人遗憾或惋惜的 ***sadness*** 1. being sad 悲哀; 忧伤. 2. [C usu *pl*] thing that makes one sad 令人悲哀或忧伤的事物

COBUILD: 1. If you are *sad*, you feel unhappy, usually because something has happened that you do not like. 2. *Sad* stories and *sad* news make you feel sad. 3. A *sad* event or situation is unfortunate or undesirable. 4. If you describe someone as *sad*, you do not have any respect for them and think their behaviour or ideas are ridiculous.

A simple glance at the definitions above will show that these three dictionaries cannot agree about the numbers of the senses *sad* has. A careful analysis of their senses reveals that, basically, they agree about two senses: (a) feeling unhappy and (b) making someone unhappy. OALECD and LDCE share the sense of 'bad'. LDCE and COBUILD agree about the meaning of 'undesirable'. Both OALD and

COBUILD say *sad* is associated with 'unfortunate' in some contexts. All of these meanings can be seen as extensions of its original meaning. The meaning of 'making unhappy' may be associated with numerous things; in other words, *sad* can be used to talk about a large number of things that make someone unhappy. However, in discourse, it has its preferences to describe. The most frequent ones have attained the attention of lexicographers. However, they do not agree about classifying criteria, so they produce a different number of senses and define them in different ways.

Now let us look at the data for *sad* (18,212 hits) and *sadness* (4,161 hits) from the BOE. From their top 50 collocates, we can roughly set out the components of *sad* and *sadness* as follows:

Core: *sad*

Colligations:

(a) article-determiners: *a (2,689), the (2,073)*

(b) link verbs: *be (3,009), feel (428), look (194)*[7]

(c) prepositions: *about (270), for (426), to (1,158)*

(d) modifiers: *very (1,612), really (318), little (230), rather (128), terribly (90), extremely (69)*

Semantic preferences:

(a) nouns modified by *sad* (making unhappy): *day (592), thing (418), story (243), fact (225), news (175), truth (155), part (128), state (123), time (116), case (105), song (89), tale (85), reality (76), loss (75), end (87), commentary (65)*

(b) facial parts or expressions (showing sadness): *eye (89), face (80), smile (68)*

Core: *sadness*

Colligations:

(a) article-determiner: *the (490)*

(b) possessive adjectives: *her (79), his (68), their (42), my (35), your (20), our (18)*

(c) prepositions: *of (795), with (245), in (237), at (142), for (133), about (61), over (37)*

(d) modifiers: *great (213), deep (80), profound (39), real (31), terrible (28), overwhelming (20), huge (12), intense (11), immense (10), extreme (10), some (50), much (34), little (20)*

Semantic preference:

verbs of feeling or expressing: *express (46), feel (25)*

The frequent co-occurrence of *sad* with both *feel* and *look*, as well as the semantic preference of sadness for *express* and *feel*, seems to suggest that *sad* is both extroverted and introverted. The corpus data presented above show that, different from *unhappy*, which is often intensified by amplifiers but not downtoners, *sad* frequently collocates with *(a) little (230)*. This is consistent with Wierzbicka's claim that *unhappy* is conceived as a more 'intense' feeling and a 'stronger' negative evaluation than *sad* (Wierzbicka, 1999: 63). Speaking of their difference, Wierzbicka makes the following comments (1999: 63):

> . . . *unhappy* – in contrast to sad – does not suggest a resigned state of mind. If in the case of *sadness* the experiencer focuses on the thought 'I can't do anything about it', in the case of *unhappiness* he/she focuses on some thwarted desires ('I wanted things like this not to happen to me'), and hence it is more closely associated semantically with *unhappy*. The attitude is not exactly 'active' because one doesn't necessarily want anything to happen, but it is not 'passive' either, for one doesn't take the perspective 'I can't do anything about it'.

According to Wierzbicka, the experiencer of *sadness* is quite passive due to helplessness, while the experiencer of *unhappiness* is much less so because its focus is on 'some thwarted desires'. Let us look at their significant collocates in the 'and/or' pattern to see whether *unhappy* and *sad* differ in resignation:

Sad: lonely (109), disappointed (25), regrettable (17), pathetic (26)
Sadness: regret (32), disappointment (24), loneliness (15), hopelessness (11),
    pity (11), vulnerability (8), self-pity (5)
Unhappy: lonely (32), confused (23), depressed (18), insecure (17), anxious (16),
    angry (16), tense (14), uncomfortable (13)
Unhappiness: frustration (13), stress (10), depression (8), pain (8), misery (6),
    anxiety (6), loneliness (6)

The data presented above indicate that *sadness* is closely associated with *regret, disappointment, loneliness, hopelessness, pity, self-pity* and *vulnerability*. It can be inferred that the core of *sadness* is that 'I am disappointed and hopeless about what happened and I wish things could happen differently'. This is in line with Wierzbicka's claim that *sadness* implies being more passive. It is also true that the above collocates for *unhappy* and *unhappiness* do not show any apparent resignation. Nonetheless, as mentioned in Section 7.1.2, *unhappy* has a marked tendency to occur with *result, situation, decision, life, outcome, performance, plan, idea*, etc., implying a semantic core of dissatisfaction. This shows that the typical cognitive scenario of 'unhappy' would be that 'this is not what I want and I am not satisfied with this'. In other words, the main differences between these two concepts lie in the contrast between helplessness and dissatisfaction. Further, as presented earlier, the nouns modified by *sad* are usually short or specific, such as *day, thing, story, fact, news, truth, case, song, tale*, or facial parts or expressions, like *eye, face, smile*. However, *unhappy* tends to modify *marriage, childhood, family, life, relationship*. We may speak of *unhappiness* of a moment or of something rather specific, but we often reserve the term for longer periods or something more general, which often needs to be measured or judged from a certain perspective.

Now let us move on to examine *sadly*. Below are its dictionary entries:

LDCE: 1. in a way that shows that you are *sad* = unhappily 2. [sentence adverb] unfortunately 3. very much – used when talking about bad situations or states: *The garden's been sadly neglected.*

OALECD: 1. in a *sad* manner 悲哀地; 忧愁地 2. regrettably 令人遗憾地; 惋惜地: *a sadly neglected garden*. 3. unfortunately 不幸地

It can be seen that LDCE lacks the sense of 'regrettably', but it includes the sense of 'very much'. Their examples show that the two dictionaries interpret 'a sadly neglected garden' in different ways. This is quite common in lexicography. They are only interpretations of lexicographers, rather than the absolute truth. Now we come to its corpus data. These are 8,178 hits of *sadly* in the corpus. An examination of its top 50 collocates shows that it has a strong colligation with verbs. On the one hand, *sadly* has a semantic preference for verbs to do with physical manifestations, such as *(shake one's) head (197), smile (140), nod (26), stare (22), seem (19)*, suggesting that *sad* is very much outwardly shown via facial expressions or bodily events. On the other hand, it is semantically associated with a group of words that are related to bad situations or states, like *miss/235* (sadly missed), *lack/97* (sadly lacking), *mistake/48* (sadly mistaken), *overlook/29* (sadly overlooked), *neglect/28* (sadly neglected), *disappoint/19* (sadly disappointed), etc., where *sadly* can be interpreted either as 'regrettably' or 'very much'. For its sense of 'unfortunately', *die sadly* is a frequent collocation. In addition, its modifiers include *rather (31), very (37), (a) little (27)*.

Sadden is glossed as '(cause sb to) become sad (使某人) 悲哀, 忧愁' [to make someone *bēiāi* or *yōuchóu*] in OALECD. Actually, I do not think *yōuchóu* is the main component of *sadden*, but this is not the focus of my research. Its top collocates, based on 1,785 hits of *sadden*, show that it colligates strongly with *be (550)*, the preposition *by (521)*, and modifiers, typically *deeply (189)*, *very (54)*, *greatly (21)*, *really (20)*, *profoundly (11)*, *extremely (9)*, *particularly (7)*, *genuinely (5)*, *terribly (5)*, *little (5)*. Its concordance reveals that the causes for being *saddened* include *passing, death, loss, departure, news, verdict, accident, decision, tragic events/tragedy*, etc. Its 'and/or' word sketch tells us that being *saddened* tends to occur after being *shocked (112)* and/or *disappointed (24)* and/or being *sickened (11)*. Most of us could manage to regain our equilibrium soon and move on.

Chinese equivalents of sad*

One hundred and thirty-three instances of *sad** occur in the BPC and their most frequent Chinese equivalents are shown in Table 7.14. In English, *sad* can be used to describe not only people, expressions, feelings, but also things and situations causing sadness. However, as mentioned earlier, Chinese emotion words have to be preceded by 'lìng rén/jiào rén/ràng rén/shǐ rén' (make/cause) to express causative meanings, as shown in Table 7.14. There are specific Chinese words that are used to describe different things and situations. For example, *bēicǎn* is used to talk about a miserable situation or bitter experience, as illustrated in the following example:

(70)   You think that her father, even in this **sad** state, will submit himself to her; do you not?
       你相信她的父亲即使在目前这种 悲惨 (*bēicǎn*) 的状况下也会服从她 么?

Table 7.14 The most frequent Chinese equivalents of *sad** in the BPC

Chinese translational equivalent	Frequency
(*lìng rén /ràng rén/ jiào rén) shāngxīn*	39
(*lìng rén) bēishāng*	37
bēicǎn	11
yōushāng	10
bēiāi	10
(*ràng rén) nánguò*	8
Others	18
Total:	133

Consider more examples from the parallel corpus:

(71) Then she had been pale and *sad* but there had been buoyancy about
her.
那时她尽管面黄瘦 (*miàn huáng shòu*)，但还显得比较轻松活泼。

(72) 'Oh, 'it's only – about my own self,' she said, with a frail **laugh of *sadness***,
fitfully beginning to peel 'a lady' meanwhile.
'哦，这只是——关于我自己的事；她说完，苦笑 (*kǔxiào*) 了一下，同时
又断断续续地动手把 '夫人' 的花蕾剥开。

(73) It was a *sad* sight, but it showed us that the anchorage was calm.
这是幅凄凉 (*qīliáng*) 的景象，但这也告诉我们这锚地非常平静。

(74) In the *sad* moonlight, she clasped him by the neck, and laid her face
upon his breast.
她在凄清 (*qīqīng*) 的月光下搂住了爸爸的脖子，把脸靠在他的胸
脯上。

(75) But she can be so cruel and it comes so suddenly and such birds that fly,
dipping and hunting, with their small *sad* voices are made too delicately
for the sea.
然而她能变得这样残暴，又是来得这样突然，而这些飞翔的鸟儿，从空
中落下觅食，发出细微的哀鸣 (*aīmíng*)，却生来就柔弱得不适宜在海上
生活。

(76) Her face was puckered in the *sad* bewilderment of an old ape but there
was determination in her jaw.
她那张皱脸孔，像只惶惑不安的老猴似的，不过那下颚却说明她心中早
已打定了主意。

(77) But he made a *sad* business of it with his unsteady hand, and a smothered
titter rippled over the house.
可他的手不听使唤，结果把图画得不象样，引得大家暗地里忍俊不禁。

(78) The piano was *sadly* out of tune but some of the chords were musical…
钢琴是严重 (*yánzhòng*) 走调了，但有的和弦听起来仍然很美 …

(79) In their *sad* doubts as to whether their son had himself any right
whatever to the title he claimed for the unknown young woman, Mr and
Mrs Clare began to feel it as an advantage not to be overlooked that she at
least was sound in her views.
克莱尔先生和克莱尔太太很有些 (*hěn yǒuxiē*) 怀疑他们的儿子声明那
个他们不认识的年轻姑娘拥有的资格，他们的儿子是不是就有权利得
到他说的那种资格，他们开始觉得有一个不能忽视的优点，那就是他的
见解至少是正确的。

(80)   Behind those doors lay the beauty of the old days, and a *sad* hunger for
       them welled up within her.
       那些门背后藏着往日的美好,而现在她心里正苦苦 (*kǔkǔ*) 渴望着重新
       见到它。

If *sad* is associated with a countenance, the Chinese translation would often be
huángshòu (yellow and thin), as shown in (71). If it is used to modify a smile or
laugh, the Chinese translation will be *kǔxiào* (lit. bitter laugh/smile), as
exemplified in (72). In (73), (74) and (75), *sad* was translated as *qīliáng* in *a sad
sight*, *qīqīng* in *sad moonlight*, and *āimíng* in *sad voices*. Chinese has specific
words to describe these things. *Sad* can collocate with numerous words from a
wide range of domains, concrete or abstract, such as *bewilderment* and *business*
shown in (76) and (77). It seems that *sadly* can also be used to indicate a degree,
as exemplified in (78). Examples (79) and (80) suggest that *sad* also has such a
function, which is missing in dictionary descriptions.

   I have discussed *bēishāng* and *bēiāi* in Section 7.1.1, so here I will only look
at the other three Chinese equivalents of *sad*: *shāngxīn*, *nánguò* and *yōushāng*.
Shāngxīn occurs 39 times in the parallel corpus and it is significantly higher
than the frequency of any other equivalent shown in Table 7.14. It seems
that *shāngxīn* is the commonest Chinese word to describe a sad feeling. It
literally means the heart is hurt and has taken on a metaphorical meaning of
denoting a sad feeling. This is reminiscent of the English *heart-broken*. But they
actually have different meanings, to which I will return in Section 7.1.4.
In Chinese, XHCBL provides the definition for *shāngxīn*: 由于遭受不如意的
事情而心里痛苦 (*yōuyù zāoshòu bú rúyì de shìqíng ér xīnlǐ tòngkǔ*/suffer
mentally because of an unpleasant event), where 痛苦 (*tòngkǔ*) is found. Then
what does *tòngkǔ* mean? It is defined by XHCBL as '身体或精神感到非常难受
(*shēntǐ huò jīngshén gǎndào fēicháng nánshòu* [feeling very uncomfortable,
physically or mentally])'. The above definition introduces another new feeling
nánshòu, which is '伤心; 不痛快 (*shāngxīn; bú tòngkuài*/not happy)', according
to XHCBL. *Shāngxīn*'s occurrence again suggests that if we restrict ourselves
to dictionaries we will never get out of the circle of cross-explanation; therefore,
a corpus exploration is necessary to achieve our purpose to tease out their
meanings.

Shāngxīn

Table 7.15 presents the significant collocates of *shāngxīn* (4,219 hits) from the
CCL corpus.

Table 7.15 Significant collocates of *shāngxīn* in the CCL corpus

Introversion/ extroversion	Cause + causative verb	Modifier	Feeling	Others
gǎndào 143	*yīnwèi 90*	*hěn 338*	*tòngkǔ 55*	*xiǎngqǐ 24*
gǎnjué 13	*yīn 29*	*fēicháng 78*	*hàipà 18*	*shì 232*
juéde 60	*sǐ/sǐqù 95/15*	*shífēn 65*	*shīwàng 39*	*guòqù 27*
xīnlǐ/xīnzhōng 17/12	*líkāi 28*	*tèbié 20*	*fènnù 29*	*wǎngshì 24*
yàngzi 30	*shīqù 18*	*shízài 26*	*shēngqì 30*	*gùshì 18*
kàn/kàndào 87/27	*búxìng 15*	*jíle 45*	*qì 37*	*ānwèi 20*
liǎnshàng/liǎn 16/13	*shǐ 223*	*jí 33*	*nánguò 23*	*quàn 18*
kū/kūqì 436/33	*jiào 127*	*guòdù 17*	*juéwàng 22*	*chù 53*
lèi/yǎnlèi 75/72	*lìng 113*	*bùyǐ 18*	*wěiqu 21*	*cì 42*
lèishuǐ 18	*lìngrén 33*	*yīdiǎn 19*		*yīzhèn 19*
luòlèi/liúlèi 74/27	*rě 29*	*yīxiē 15*		*zìjǐ 139*
tòngkǔ 35				

From the first column in Table 7.15, it can be clearly seen that *shāngxīn* is something one feels (*gǎndào/gǎnjué/juéde*) in the heart (*xīnlǐ/xīnzhōng*). *Shāngxīn* is also an emotion involving external manifestations, as implied in its collocates: *liǎnshàng/liǎn* (on the face/face), *yàngzi* (appearance), *kàn/kàndào* (see), *kū* (cry), *kūqì* (weep), *lèi/yǎnlèi/lèishuǐ* (tears), *luòlèi/liúlèi* (shed tears) and *tòngkǔ* (cry bitterly). The second column shows that *shāngxīn* co-occurs frequently with *yīnwèi/yīn* (because), suggesting that it is an emotion with a clear reason, such as death (*sǐ/sǐqù*), departure (*líkāi*), loss (*shīqù*) and misfortune (*búxìng*). Its frequent collocation with causative verbs, like *shǐ/jiào/lìng* (*rén*) (cause/make), *rě* (invite/lead to), suggests that it has a strong colligation with causative construction. The third column gives its modifiers, typically *hěn/fēicháng/shífēn* (very), *tèbié* (particularly), *shízài* (really), *guòdù* (exceedingly), *jí/jíle* (extremely), *bùyǐ* (endlessly), *yīxiē/yīdiǎn* (a little).

From the fourth column, it can be seen that, like *sadness*, *shāngxīn* has various negative feelings in its company, such as *tòngkǔ* (anguish), *hàipà* (fear), *shīwàng* (disappointment), *fènnù* (indignation), *qì/shēngqì* (annoyance), *nánguò* (sadness), *juéwàng* (despair) and grievance (*wěiqu*). The last column lists its other collocates, which can contribute to disclosing its meaning. *Xiǎngqǐ* (think of) might suggest that *shāngxīn* is a feeling stirred up by thinking of something *sad*. Usually *shāngxīn* is not used to describe things or situations that make people *shāngxīn*. It can be preceded by causative verbs to fulfil such a function.

However, it has some exceptions. Some specific things can be modified by *shāngxīn*, such as *shì* (thing), *wǎngshì* (past events), *guòqù* (past) and *gùshì* (story). One's *shāngxīn* could be mitigated or overcome after being consoled (*ānwèi*) or persuaded (*quàn*). *Shāngxīn chù* (place) means what exactly makes someone *shāngxīn*. This is Chinese-specific. Chinese tends to use *chù* or *diǎn* (point) to highlight what really matters. Another Chinese-specific feature is that it tends to use *cì* (number of times) to indicate the frequency of *shāngxīn*. In other words, *shāngxīn* in Chinese is conceptualized as repeated happenings. *Shāngxīn* could last for a short period (*yīzhèn*). In addition, one often feels *shāngxīn* on one's own (*zìjǐ*), not wanting others to know one's true feelings. From *shāngxīn*'s external manifestations, such as *kū*, we may infer that *shāngxīn* is prototypically a transient emotion.

The CCL corpus tells us that you may feel *shāngxīn* if your pet has just died, if you have broken up with your girl/boyfriend, if you encounter failure, if the person you love does not love you or not any more, if one of your close relatives or someone you have respected has died recently, if you have been cheated by your best friend, if you have learned that your former classmate in college is much more successful than you in both career and family life, if your kid cannot come up to your expectations or does not follow your advice, if you have been misunderstood, or if you have just learned that you were deserted by your mother when you were very young, etc.

Nánguò

Another similar term to describe sadness is *nánguò*. The internal structure of this disyllabic lexeme is 'the adjective prefix *nán* + *guo*' difficult + live. *Nánguò* is simple and less formal. Below is the definition for *nánguò* found in XHCBL:

1. *bù róngyì guòhuó* (be hard off; have a hard time)
2. *the same as nánshòu* (*shāngxīn*; *bú tòngkuài*)

Nánshòu is an even less formal version of *nánguò*. Let us look at the corpus data. The significant collocates of *nánguò* (4,152 hits) are shown in Table 7.16.

The explanation of Table 7.16 will start with the second column showing its modifiers: *hěn/fēicháng* (very), *tèbié* (particularly), *wànfēn/jí/jíle* (extremely), *yǒuxiē/yīxiē/yīdiǎn/yǒudiǎn* (a little). *Nánguò* also co-occurs with various negative feelings, such as *shāngxīn* (sadness), *tòngkǔ* (anguish), *shēngqì* (annoyance), *bēishāng* (sorrow), *wěiqu* (grievance), *zhènjīng* (shock), *shīwàng* (disappointment), *hàipà* (fear), *hòuhuǐ* (regret), *xiūkuì* (shame), etc. A glance at the concordance of *shāngxīn* reveals that *hòuhuǐ* and *xiūkuì* seldom co-occur

Table 7.16 Significant collocates of *nánguò* in the CCL corpus

Introversion/ extroversion	Modifier	Feeling	Others
xīnlǐ 622	*hěn 642*	*shāngxīn 45*	*xiǎngdào 19*
xīnzhōng 152	*fēicháng 208*	*tòngkǔ 22*	*xiǎngqǐ 17*
xīnqíng 36	*wànfēn 12*	*shēngqì 16*	*shǐ 185*
gǎndào 355	*tèbié 34*	*bēishāng 14*	*ràng 120*
juéde 146	*jí/jíle 22/82*	*wěiqu 14*	*jiào 87*
gǎnjué 17	*yǒuxiē 21*	*zhènjīng 13*	*lìng 55*
yàngzi 55	*yīxiē 18*	*shīwàng 13*	*cì 12*
liǎn 15	*yīdiǎn 27*	*hàipà 13*	*yīzhèn 53*
kàndào 108	*yǒudiǎn 21*	*hòuhuǐ 12*	*ānwèi 25*
kànjiàn 22		*xiūkuì 12*	*quàn 21*
kū 69			*rìzi 157*
lèi 18			*shīqù 15*
luòlèi 12			*bìng 15*
			qùshì 13
			zìjǐ 176

with *shāngxīn*, which might suggest that *nánguò* is the result of the general evaluation of what happened, whether it is caused by oneself or someone else, while *shāngxīn* is more likely to emphasize the pain on 'ME' caused by other people or some external forces.

The last column gives its other collocates, which help understand the meaning of *nánguò*. We find *shāngxīn, xiǎngqǐ/xiǎngdào* (think of), *shǐ/ràng/jiào/lìng* (cause/make), *cì* (number of times) and *yīzhèn* (a short period of time) here. Like *shāngxīn*, the feeling of *nánguò* can be mitigated or overcome after being consoled (*ānwèi*) or persuaded (*quàn*). *Rìzi* (life) is a collocate for its literary meaning—'difficult to live' (have a hard time). It is clear from its collocates that *nánguò* is overwhelmingly used in its metaphorical sense in the modern discourse.

Let us come back to the first column of Table 7.16, from which it can be seen that, like *shāngxīn, nánguò* is also something one feels (*gǎndào/gǎnjué/juéde*) in the heart (*xīnlǐ/xīnzhōng*). *Nánguò* is more experienced as a *xīnqíng* (frame of mind). *Nánguò*, like *shāngxīn*, is also an emotion involving physical manifestations, as suggested by its collocates: *liǎnshàng/liǎn* (on the face/face), *kàndào/kànjiàn* (see), *yàngzi* (appearance), *kū* (cry), *lèi* (tears), *luòlèi* (shed tears), etc. The corpus tells us that you may feel *nánguò* if you have been scolded by your boss, if you, as an athlete, have not entered the final rounds, if you are going to leave your colleagues with whom you have worked for many years, if you learn that the children in some rural areas cannot afford their textbooks and tuition fees, if one of the people you have respected has been diagnosed with a cancer, if you cannot reunite with your family at the Spring Festival, or if you have failed in an entrance exam, etc.

Shāngxīn and *nánguò* occur in the CCL corpus with almost the same frequency (*shāngxīn* 4,219 hits/*nánguò* 4,152 hits). Table 7.17 summarizes their collocates indicating features of extroversion and introversion. From the numbers and percentages of the extroversion and introversion collocates for *shāngxīn* and *nánguò* shown in Table 7.17, it can be clearly seen that *shāngxīn* tends to be shown more outwardly than *nánguò* (224 > 72; 943 > 299). *Nánguò* is more likely to be used to describe what is happening internally than *shāngxīn* (320 > 58; 1,328 > 245). Table 7.17 also show that *shāngxīn* is a more intense

Table 7.17 Comparison of the collocates for *shāngxīn* & *nánguò*

	shāngxīn 4,219 hits	*nánguò* 4,152 hits
Introversion	*gǎndào 143*	*xīnlǐ 622*
	gǎnjué 13	*xīnzhōng 152*
	juéde 60	*xīnqíng 36*
	xīnlǐ/xīnzhōng 17/12	*gǎndào 355*
		juéde 146
		gǎnjué 17
	Total 245	Total 1,328
	Percentage 58‰	Percentage 320‰
Extroversion	*yàngzi 30*	*yàngzi 55*
	kàn/kàndào 87/27	*liǎn 15*
	liǎnshàng/liǎn 16/13	*kàndào 108*
	kū/kūqì 436/33	*kànjiàn 22*
	lèi/yǎnlèi 75/72	*kū 69*
	lèishuǐ 18	*lèi 18*
	luòlèi/kiulie 74/27	*luòlèi 12*
	tòngkǔ 35	
	Total 943	Total 299
	Percentage 224‰	Percentage 72‰

feeling than *nánguò* because the percentage of collocates associated with *kū/lèi* for the former is much bigger (735 > 99; 17.4% > 2.4%) than that for the latter. As mentioned earlier, in Chinese, it is believed that the behaviour of the heart has a lot to do with a person's emotional state. If you feel *nánguò*, your heart will feel uncomfortable. *Shāngxīn* is a metaphorized word, which has been frequently used independently, while *nánguò* is used to describe what is taking place in the heart in a metaphorical way. It is undergoing the change. This is why *nánguò* co-occurs more frequently with *xīnlǐ* or *xīnzhōng* and is less often used as an attributive.

Yōushāng

The last word I will examine in this section is *yōushāng*. It is a combination of *yōu* (worried) and *shāng* (sorrowful), meaning 'yōuchóu (worried) bēishāng (sorrowful)' (XHCBL), so it is also associated with the fatalistic view. There are 1,175 hits of *yōushāng* in the CCL corpus and its significant collocates are presented in Table 7.18.

Table 7.18 Significant collocates of *yōushāng* in the CCL corpus

Introversion	Extroversion	Verb & modifier	Feeling	Others
gǎndào 44	yǎnjing 27	chōngmǎn 44	tòngkǔ 33	sǐ 15
juéde 11	liǎnshàng 23	mǎnhuái 9	fánnǎo 12	zhǒng 43
nèixīn 12	biǎoqíng 16	liúlù 10	bēitòng 10	zhèzhǒng 18
xīnzhōng 14	yǎnshén 14	lòuchū 8	gūdú 9	nàzhǒng 15
xīnlǐ 19	shénqíng 13	shēnshēn 12	juéwàng 9	fèn 7
xīnlǐng 11		dàndàn de 18	fènnù 9	měilì 25
xīnqíng 10		sǐ 9	kǒngjù 9	
qíngxù 11		jǐfēn 6	bēiāi 9	

Table 7.18 shows that *yōushāng* is semantically associated with introversion-words, such as *gǎndào/juéde* (feel), *xīn/xīnlǐ/xīnzhōng* (in the heart), *xīnlǐng* (mind), *xīnqíng* (frame of mind), *qíngxù* (mood), and extroversion-words, like *yǎnjing* (eye), *liǎnshàng* (on one's face), *biǎoqíng/shénqíng* (facial expression), *yǎnshén* (expression in one's eyes). It semantically prefers verbs of 'being brimming with', typically *chōngmǎn* (be filled with) and *mǎnhuái* (be filled in one's bosom), and verbs of 'revealing', such as *liúlù, lòuchū*. Its typical modifiers include *shēnshēn* (deep), *dàndàn de* (faint), *sǐ* (a minute quantity) and *jǐfēn* (small amount). *Sǐ* (lit. silk) and *jǐfēn* (lit. a few + a unit of length) are Chinese-specific literary modifiers to describe a slight degree of intensity for emotions.

Like *shāngxīn* and *nánguò*, *yōushāng* also tends to co-occur with other negative feelings, such as *tòngkǔ* (anguish), *fánnǎo* (vexation), *bēitòng* (grief), *gūdú* (loneliness), *juéwàng* (despair), *bēifèn* (grief and indignation), *fènnù* (indignation), *kǒngjù* (fear), *bēiāi* (sorrow). The last column gives *yōushāng*'s other collocates, which are helpful for revealing its meaning. As a word to denote sadness, unavoidably, *yōushāng* is sometimes associated with *sǐ* (death). One unique feature for *yōushāng* is that it is more likely to co-occur with classifiers, like *zhǒng* (*zhèzhǒng*/this kind, *nàzhǒng*/that kind) and *fèn* (portion), when it is used as a noun. Consider the following examples from the CCL:

(81) 这个"神秘"的音乐组合以他们优美 (*yōuměi*) exquisite, 宁静 (*níngjìng*) 而带着忧伤 (*yōushāng*) 的音乐吸引了众多的媒体和乐迷

(82) 似一幅温和 (*wēnhé*), 优雅 (*yōuyā*) 而又让人品出一缕淡淡忧伤 (*yōushāng*) 的风景画

(83) 擦亮前额使我的忧伤 (*yōushāng*) 也楚楚动人 (*chǔchǔdòngrén*)

(84) 她显得很文静 (*wénjìng*), 微笑 (*wēixiào*) 的脸上带着几丝淡淡的忧伤 (*yōushāng*)

(85) 她的笑里有一种宁静 (*níngjìng*), 微笑 (*chúnzhēn*) 与忧伤 (*yōushāng*) 糅合在一起的东西, 使天成感动

All the Chinese words in bold in (81)–(85) are absolutely positive: *yōuměi* (exquisite), *níngjìng* (calmness), *wēnhé* (gentle), *yōuyā* (elegant), *chǔchǔdòngrén*[8] (moving), *wénjìng* (gentle and quiet), *wēixiào* (smiling) and *chúnzhēn* (innocence). As *yōushāng* is often associated with concepts with very good connotations, we may argue that it has a less negative semantic prosody and is not perceived as a fully negative emotion. This might be due to its constituent character *yōu*, which was a quite positive concept in Old Chinese. We will come back to this issue when we deal with *yōuyù*.

Comparison

The concept of *sadness* has been well researched in the literature. The claim that *sadness* is one of the universal human emotions has also been challenged by many scholars (see Levy 1973; Stearns 1993; Wierzbicka 1999). Their studies show that some languages do not have corresponding words to *sadness*, and others only have some words that are roughly equivalent to it. Wierzbicka claims that people 'may not be conscious of the reason for the *sadness*' (Wierzbicka 1999: 62). Ekman and Friesen (1975: 117) argue that '*sadness* is a passive, not an active feeling', suggesting one is resigned to what happened.

After examining so many sad-feeling words in Chinese, I would argue that none of them is equivalent to *sad*. *Sad* seems to be a generic term covering many sad-related concepts, such as *sorrow, grief, heartbreak, mourn, doleful, woeful*, etc. Each of them differs in many dimensions from others, but the basic semantic component seems to be the same, i.e. *sadness*. In Chinese, however, there is no such word that can cover all those sadness-denoting words. Besides, *sad* means 'feeling unhappy', 'showing unhappiness' and 'making you unhappy'. It can be used to describe unhappy feelings, unhappy expressions or things and situations that make people unhappy. Chinese sadness words can only describe people's feelings, expressions and some facial parts or physical events. For example, Chinese sadness words are seldom used to modify a face, such as **nánguò de liǎn*. In the sense of feeling unhappy, *shāngxīn* seems to be the closest one since it is often used to explain other sadness words in the dictionary definitions. But *shāngxīn* is more intense and extroverted than *sad*. *Nánguò* is similar in intensity to *sad*, but more specific because it focuses on the emotional discomfort brought by what happened. In addition, *nánguò* is less formal. *Yōushāng* is a Chinese-specific concept that is a mixture of worry and sorrow. Like *sad*, someone who feels *yōushāng* may not be conscious of the reason for *yōushāng*. *Yōushāng* is also a passive feeling, i.e. the experiencer of *yōushāng* may be resigned to what happened. *Yōushāng* is often associated with *píngjìng* (calmness) and *měilì* (beauty), and sometimes it is viewed as something people may enjoy. *Yōushāng* and *sadness* are similar in being non-specific and passive. But *yōushāng* is more intense, more formal, more literary, more introverted than *sadness*.

7.1.4 *Heartbreak** and their Chinese equivalents

*Heartbreak**

Heartbreak is a concept metaphorically conceptualized in terms of a bodily image, namely 'heart is broken'. Let us look at the relevant entries in the dictionaries:

LDCE:
heartbreak: great sadness or disappointment
heartbroken: extremely sad because of something that has happened
broken-hearted: extremely sad, especially because someone you love has died or left you
heartbreaking: making you feel extremely sad or disappointed

OALECD:

break sb's/one's heart: make sb/one feel very sad 使某人自己很伤心`

heart-break: (cause of) very great unhappiness 很大的不幸; 造成很大不幸的原因

heart-breaking adj.

heart-broken (of a person) feeling great sadness (指人) 极其伤心的

COBUILD:

Heartbreak is very great sadness and emotional suffering, especially after the end of a love affair or close relationship.

Someone who is *heartbroken* is very sad and emotionally upset.

Someone who is *broken-hearted* is very sad and upset because they have had a serious disappointment.

Something that is *heartbreaking* makes you feel extremely sad and upset.

A summary of the above definitions shows that *heartbreak* is great sadness mainly caused by disappointment, the end of a close relationship or someone's death. In OALECD, ironically, it is translated as *búxìng*, which means 'misfortune'. In the example, fortunately, its translation *shāngxīnshì* does not deviate too much from its real meaning. According to this dictionary, the Chinese equivalent of *heart-broken* is *jíqí* (extremely) *shāngxīn*.

Now let us turn to the corpus search (*heart-break 6, heartbreak 1,157*). A close examination of its concordance and its top 50 collocates reveals that *heartbreak* colligates strongly with the definite article *the (226)*, possessive adjectives, typically *his (28)*, *her (24)*, *their (10)*, prepositions, predominantly *of (221)*, *for (80)*, *at (29)*, *over (14)*. Its word sketch shows that the verbs it often co-occurs with include *suffer (49)*, *face (13)*, *experience (3)*, *cause (7)*, *bring (7)*, etc. *Cause* and *bring* appear to show that there is an explicit reason for *heartbreak*. Consider the following examples:

(86)　To many people, such a recognition requires considerable courage, for casting away anything may seem an intolerable action, just as failing at anything is a great **heartbreak**.

(87)　Mr Justice Waite described his ruling as a happy ending, but warned that people who failed to go through government-approved adoption agencies faced a grave risk of disappointment and even **heartbreak**.

(88)　Partnership—a deep relationship with another person is essential to the Libran's very being, and all too often they rush into total commitment before they are really ready for it; such partnerships can often end in **heartbreak** and disaster.

(89) Jealousy flamed in her that she had never known that part of his life, that it belonged to his wife, Elizabeth. The blood was pounding in her cheeks. She put up her hands to cover them. 'I'm just someone . . . to pass the time with. I blame myself entirely. Anna thinks I'm stupid, that it's pointless, that there's nothing in it for me but **heartbreak**.' The pain was unendurable.

Examples (86), (87) and (89) seem to suggest that the principal determinant of *heartbreak* is disappointment, either about oneself or someone else. Example (88) seems to show that the end of a close or deep relationship, whether partnership or love, usually leads to *heartbreak*. One might wish the relationship to continue and it is the disappointment about the person with whom one used to have the relationship that leads to the feeling of *heartbreak*. However, for the *heartbreak* caused by someone's death, the loss, instead of the disappointment, is the main factor.

Now let us look at *heartbroken*. There are 1,420 hits of *heartbroken** (*heartbroken, 1,197; heart-broken, 43; brokenhearted, 56; broken-hearted 124*) in the BOE. A close inspection of its concordance and its top 50 collocates reveals that *be (434)* dominates the picture. It also has a colligation with prepositions, typically *over (31), at (38)*. It is interesting to find *parent (34), family (30), mum (25), mother (21), father (16), dad (14), wife (10), relative (6), husband (6), brother (5)* in the top collocates. It suggests that *heartbroken** has a semantic preference for family connections because the 'heartbroken' feeling is closely associated with family members. Both *feel (7)* and *look (7)* are found to occur with *heartbroken**, suggesting that *heartbroken* is both extroverted and introverted. 'Be left heartbroken' is a recurrent pattern that occurs 40 times in the BOE. It shows that getting *heartbroken* is the immediate result of something bad. Its word sketch shows that *heartbroken* is often modified by maximizers, such as *absolutely (21), utterly (3), truly (3)* and *totally (3)*, showing that *heartbroken* can only be reinforced but not weakened. We will come back to this issue when we talk about its Chinese equivalents.

For *heartbreaking*, 1,446 occurrences (*heartbreaking 1,214 + heart-breaking 232*) are found in the BOE. An inspection of its concordance listing and its top 50 collocates shows that it has colligations with *be (369)*, the article-determiners *a (239), the (158)*, possessive adjectives, typically *his (20), their (17)*, and the preposition *for (66)*. Its word sketch shows that it is often modified by *absolutely (5), truly (3), especially (4), pretty (4), particularly (3)*. It should be noted that, different from *heartbroken, heartbreaking* can be modified by the compromiser *pretty*, suggesting that *heartbreaking* is a less strong word than *heartbroken*.

According to its word sketch, *heartbreaking* is semantically associated with negative words that can make one extremely sad or upset, such as *loss (51)*, *defeat (28)*, or words that have such a quality, like *story (21)*, *decision (19)*, *letter (17)*, *news (13)*, *moment (12)*, *performance (10)*, *plea (9)*, etc.

Only 81 instances of *heartbreakingly* are found in the corpus. Although it does co-occur with adjectives with negative connotations, such as *naff (1)*, *ineffective (1)*, *fragile (1)*, *inadequate (1)*, *awful (1)*, *stupid (1)*, *sad (1)*, *thin (1)*, it co-occurs more frequently with positive words, like *beautiful (16)*, *lovely (3)*, *handsome (2)*, *delicious (1)*, *unspoilt (1)*, *touching (1)*, *hopeful (1)*, *brave (1)*, *pleasant (1)*, *poetic (1)*. So it may be argued that *heartbreakingly* has evolved into a pure intensifier with a more positive semantic prosody.

Xīnsuì

Thirty hits of *heartbreak** (incl. *heartbreaking*, *broken(-)hearted*, *heartbroken*) are found in the BPC. Table 7.19 presents the result of my search.

Table 7.19 Chinese equivalents of *heartbreak** in the BPC

Chinese equivalents	Frequency
shāngxīn	20 *(shāng tòu le xīn* 1 + *shāngxīn tòu le* 1)
xīnsuì	3
bēitòng	3
others	4
Total	30

It is understandable that the great majority (20 out of 30) of the instances of *heartbreak** are translated as *shāngxīn*, as shown in Table 7.19, because it is almost a cover term to indicate a sad emotional state. If the translator cannot find an appropriate word to describe a sad state, s/he would resort to this word and put an intensifier before it. For example:

(90) '一想起你这么快便忘记了自己的教养, 我就**伤心透了** (*shāngxīn tòu le*)'。

'I am **heartbroken** to think that you could so soon forget your rearing.'

(91) 并且波琳上星期还写了信来, 说他名声很坏, 在查尔斯顿, 连他自己家里也没有接待他, 只是他那位**伤透了心** (*shāng tòu le xīn*) 的母亲例外。

... and Pauline wrote me only last week that he is a man of bad repute and not even received by his own family in Charleston, except of course by his **heartbroken** mother.

In the above examples, *(shāngxīn) tòu le* / *(shāng) tòu le (xīn)* are used to indicate the degree of *shāngxīn*. *Tòu* literally means 'pass through'. The whole construction means the heart is penetrated through, i.e. the heart is badly hurt. In some contexts, if someone you love has died, you will be in *heartbreak*. In the following examples, *heartbreak** is translated as *bēitòng (3)*, which is a word usually denoting grief due to the death of a beloved person:

(92) 她虽然处于**悲痛** (*bēitòng*) 之中, 然而一想到和他见面, 而她怀的又是另外一个男人的孩子, 就感到不寒而栗.

Even in her ***heartbreak***, she shrank from the thought of facing him when she was carrying another man's child.

(93) 她 本来会奉献给教堂的那 分悲痛 (*bēitòng*) 和无私, 如今都全部用来服务于自己的儿女和家庭以及那位带她离开萨凡纳的男人了…

The ***heartbreak*** and selflessness that she would have dedicated to the Church were devoted instead to the service of her child, her household and the man who had taken her out of Savannah …

(94) 如今他那双光亮的马靴 踏上了苦难的道路, 那儿充满了饥饿、疲惫、行军、苦战、创伤、**悲痛** (*bēitòng*) 等等, 像无数狂叫的恶狼在等着他, 最后的结局 就是死亡呢。

Now he had set his varnished boots upon a bitter road where hunger tramped with tireless stride and wounds and weariness and ***heartbreak*** ran like yelping wolves. And the end of the road was death. He need not have gone.

Another Chinese near-equivalent of *heartbreak** is *xīnsuì (3)*, which literally means 'heart is broken into pieces'. Look at the examples from the BPC:

(95) 她呼唤着孩子的名字, 有时头抬起来整整有一 分钟时间那么长听着, 然后无力地呻吟着一头倒在床上。见此情形, 大家都说真叫人**心碎** (*xīnsuì*)。

People said it was ***heartbreaking*** to hear her call her child, and raise her head and listen a whole minute at a time, then lay it wearily down again with a moan.

(96) 人们从媚兰那年轻的脸上可以看出, 她对过去的一切是忠贞不渝的。这使人们会暂时忘记自己一伙人中那些使人愤怒、害怕、**心碎** (*xīnsuì*) 的败类。

When they looked into her young face and saw there the inflexible loyalty to the old days, they could forget, for a moment, the traitors within their own class who were causing fury, fear and **heartbreak**. And there were many such.

(97) 我知道, 她在爱你时, 看到了跟她同龄的母亲, 也在爱着她, 看到了跟我同龄时的你, 也在爱着我。她爱她**心碎** (xīnsuì) 的母亲, 她爱那经历了可怕的考验和成功的恢复过程的你。

I know that in loving you she sees and loves her mother at her own age, sees and loves you at my age, loves her mother **broken-hearted**, loves you through your dreadful trial and in your blessed restoration.

Xīnsuì is not included in the XHCBL, probably because it is not a frequent word. Only 430 hits of *xīnsuì* are found in the CCL corpus and its significant collocates are shown in Table 7.20.

Table 7.20 Significant collocates of *xīnsuì* in the CCL corpus

Collocate	Frequency
lìng 163/ràng 36/shǐ 50/jiào 20 (rén)	269
sǐ	14
kū/kūqì	21
gùshì	6
xiāoxī	7
mǔqīn	9
qīliáng	5
cháng	14
liè	6

It is interesting to find the most significant collocates for *xīnsuì* in Table 7.20 are *lìng/ràng/shǐ/jiào* (cause/make). It can be seen that, in more than half of the occurrences (269/430, 63%), *xīnsuì* is used in a causative construction, whose function in English can be fulfilled by a single adjective, such as *sad, sorrowful, heartbreaking*. Of course, some other expressions can also be translated as *xīnsuì*. For example:

(98) '我的天哪!**心碎** (xīnsuì) 的人多了, 也没见谁去当修女。就拿我来说吧, 我送掉了一个丈夫'。

'Lots of people's **hearts** have been **broken** and they didn't run off to convents. Look at me. I lost a husband.'

(99) '你认为我可以丢下媚兰和孩子自己跑掉, 就算我恨他们两个人, 难道我能让媚兰**心碎** (*xīnsuì*)?...'

'Do you think I could go off and leave Melanie and the baby, even if I hated them both? **Break** Melanie's **heart**? ...'

(100) 在路上看见她路过, 把消息带回家里, 我爸爸便**心碎** (*xīnsuì*) 而死。他满腹冤屈, 却一个字也没说。

I saw her pass me on the road. When I took the tidings home, our father's **heart burst**. He never spoke one of the words that filled it.

It seems that in the English source texts, if expressions like 'hearts have been broken or break someone's heart' are used to describe the great sadness, then probably, their Chinese translation would be *xīnsuì*. If *heart burst* is used instead of *heart break*, then *xīnsuì* is also highly likely to be used as its translation equivalent. The reason for this would be that cleft expressions are more intense than single words.

In Chinese, *xīnsuì* is also closely related to *sǐ* (death) and *kū*/*kūqì* (cry/weep). *Xīnsuì* is often used in a causative construction to describe things that make people extremely sad, such as *lìngrén xīnsuì de gùshì* (sad story) or *lìngrén xīnsuì de xiāoxī* (sad news). *Mǔqīn* (mother) often co-occurs with *xīnsuì* probably because a mother is often sentimental and tends to be the experiencer of *xīnsuì*. A *qīliáng* (desolate) place may make one *xīnsuì* because it is unbearable to see that exceedingly sad scene and one's feeling in such a situation is also conceptualized as *xīnsuì*. *Cháng* (intestine) and *liè* (crack) appear in Table 7.20 because, in the Chinese culture, *xīnsuì*, *chángduàn* (intestine-broken) and *dǎnliè* (gall bladder-crack) are common metaphorical images to understand great sadness. One thing that needs to be noted is that *xīnsuì* is not always used to denote a sad feeling, sometimes it is positive. Consider the following examples:

(101) 一片令人**心碎** (*xīnsuì*) 的温柔

'lìng rén xīnsuì de gentleness'

(102) 那声声妈妈, 叫得好甜哟, 叫得让人**心碎** (*xīnsuì*) 哟 ...

'the calling of "mama" was so sweet and *lìngrén xīnsuì*'

(103) 美得令人**心碎** (*xīnsuì*)

'so beautiful that it made someone *xīnsuì*'

The above examples show that *xīnsuì* is not necessarily bad or sad. It is used to describe an immensely strong feeling, regardless of whether it is positive or negative.

Comparison

Heartbreak is associated with great sadness, caused by breaking up, the ending of a close relationship, the death of a beloved person, or something very bad that happened. *Heartbreak* is absolutely personal, i.e. it is characterized by 'something bad happened TO ME'. It is more an internal state, a mental suffering or pain. It is more related to family or a close relationship. Its Chinese counterparts could be *shāngxīn*, *bēitòng* or *xīnsuì*. Among them, *shāngxīn*, often with its premodifier, is the most common translation equivalent in Chinese. *Shāngxīn* alone is not intense enough to express *heartbreak*. *Bēitòng* is only used when it is associated with someone's death. *Xīnsuì* is an intense feeling mainly used in causative constructions like 'lìngrén *xīnsuì* de'. In addition, *xīnsuì* is not necessarily sad or bad. Therefore, in Chinese, there is no word that corresponds to *heartbreak* or any of its cognates. English and Chinese conceptualize sadness by associating the heart with different metaphorical images. *Suì* means '完整的东西破成零片零块 break to pieces; smash' (XHCBL). LDCE contains the definition of *break*:

> If you break something, you make it separate into two or more pieces, for example by hitting it, dropping it, or bending it.

It is clear that 'two or more pieces' is used to describe the extent to which something is broken. So, in terms of intensity, *heartbreak* is halfway between *shāngxīn* (heart-hurt) and *xīnsuì* (heart-fragmented). Usually, the translator increases the intensity of *shāngxīn* by adding an amplifier to it to match *heartbreak*. Sometimes, *xīnsuì* is used instead, but *xīnsuì* is far less frequent than *shāngxīn*, and it has a literary flavour. To sum up, Chinese and English encode different meanings in their sadness words, which do not correspond neatly to each other. We have to rely on the corpus data to find out their subtle nuances of meaning.

7.1.5 *Doleful* & woe** and their Chinese equivalents

*Doleful**

The dictionary entries for the *doleful* family are shown below:

> LDCE: *formal* very sad [Origin: dole 'sadness' (13–19 centuries), from *Latin* dolere 'to be sad'] *a doleful song about lost love*

> OALECD: sad; mournful 悲伤的; 令人沮丧的: *a doleful face, manner, expression, etc* 愁眉苦脸/垂头丧气的样子/忧郁的表情

COBUILD: A *doleful* expression, manner, or voice is depressing and miserable. = mournful

LDCE says that *doleful* derives from *dole*, which comes from a Latin word *dolere*, meaning 'to be sad'. According to the other two dictionaries, *doleful* is very close to *mournful*. There are 157 hits of *doleful* found in the BOE. According to its top collocates,[9] its colligational properties include the article-determiners *a (34), the (23)*, possessive adjectives, typically *his (7), their (5), our (5)*, and nouns. *Doleful* semantically prefers words relating to external, especially visible, manifestations, such as *expression (8), eye (6), face (4)* and *look (4)*. It implies that *doleful* describes outward expressions. *Be* or any of its variant forms, like *is, are, am*, does not occur before *doleful*, suggesting that *doleful* is usually used as an adjectival modifier. Unlike *sad*, it is seldom used for predicating.

Now let us turn to its adverbial form. *Dolefully* only occurs 88 times in the BOE. Its top 50 collocates show that *dolefully* is semantically associated with physical action verbs, like *say (11), nod (3), stare (3)*, etc. An edited concordance listing is shown in Figure 7.2.

1)	to the bar. Jewel shook her head	*dolefully.*	<p> 'Me neither. She better
2)	Sympathizing, Mabel shook her head	*dolefully.*	'Just sittin' there, huh?'
3)	e Earthmen.' Sefan shook his head	*dolefully.*	'This is a bad business.'
4)	them under fifty, shook their heads	*dolefully*	in perfect agreement with their
5)	race ended. Keeler **glanced** back	*dolefully*	and shook his head. Suckers.
6)	see you, others laze in the sun and	*dolefully*	**watch** you wander by. These are
7)	you like it, but. .' She **looks** around	*dolefully,*	a smile for the cat, '. . .why'

Figure 7.2 Concordance listing of *dolefully*

A simple glimpse of the concordance lines in Figure 7.2 reveals that 'shook one's head dolefully' is a frequent pattern. 'Keeler glanced back dolefully' in line 5, 'others laze in the sun and dolefully watch you wander by' in line 6 and 'looks around *dolefully*' seem to suggest that *dolefully* can collocate with any looking verb, such as *look, watch, glance*.

To determine the Chinese equivelants of *doleful* and *dolefully*, we still need to look at the BPC, in which only 6 instances are found:

(104) 贾维斯罗瑞因为心绪不宁, 也因为他年轻的同伴越来越激动, 也曾两次停下步来休息, 每次都在一道**凄凉** (qīliáng) 的栅栏旁边。还没有完全 败坏, 却已失去动力的新鲜空气似乎在从那栅栏逃逸, 而一切败坏了的带病 的潮气则似乎从那里扑了进来。

Yielding to his own disturbance of mind, and to his young companion's agitation, which became greater every instant, Mr. Jarvis Lorry twice stopped to rest. Each of these stoppages was made at a ***doleful*** grating, by which any languishing good airs that were left uncorrupted seemed to escape, and all spoilt and sickly vapours seemed to crawl in.

(105) '我, 不幸的医生 亚历山大·曼内特, 波维市人, 后居巴黎, 于 一七六七年 最后 一个月在 巴士底狱**凄凉** (qīliáng) 的牢房里写下这份 悲惨的记录。'

'I, Alexandre Manette, unfortunate physician, native of Beauvais, and afterwards resident in Paris, write this melancholy paper in my ***doleful*** cell in the Bastille, during the last month of the year, 1767.'

(106) 他为她们又是着急又是**痛苦** (tòngkǔ), 日子过得极其缓慢沉重。

A disturbed and ***doleful*** mind he brought to bear upon them, and slowly and heavily the day lagged on with him.

(107) '我的小女儿。' 派逊斯答道, 神情有些 **悲哀** (bēiāi), 但又自豪。

'It was my little daughter,' said Parsons with a sort of ***doleful*** pride.

(108) 一 棵肃穆的老树对另一棵树**悲声** (bēishēng) 低吟, 仿佛在倾诉树下坐着的这一对人儿的伤心的故事, 或是在不得不预告那行将到来**的**邪恶。

. . . while one solemn old tree groaned ***dolefully*** to another, as if telling the sad story of the pair that sat beneath, or constrained to forebode evil to come.

(109) 我觉得, 对于早晨伤亡惨重的这帮家伙来说, 这支歌是**再** (zài) 合适不过 (búguò) 了。

And I thought it was a ditty rather too ***dolefully*** appropriate for a company that had met such cruel losses in the morning.

In (109), *dolefully* is used as a degree adverb to modify the adjective *appropriate*. So we will focus on the others. *Dolefully* can be translated as *shāngxīn (de)* or *bēishāng (de)*, but usually, in fiction, it is translated as something more literary, like *bēishēng díyín* in Example (108). In Examples (104)–(107), *doleful* is used as an attributive to modify things: *grating, cell, mind* and *pride* respectively. Among them, the first two are translated as *qīliáng*, which in Chinese is only used to describe surroundings or things, meaning 'being lonely and can arouse sad feelings'. *Doleful* in *doleful mind* is translated as *tòngkǔ* and in *doleful pride* as *bēiāi*.

Unlike *sad*, *doleful* is hardly used to modify someone who feels sad and only used to modify things that show *sadness* or make people *sad*, such as *look, eyes, face, facial expressions, song* as revealed in the BOE, and *grating, cell, mind, pride* as shown in the above examples. OALECD, as presented earlier, gives five different equivalents: *bēishāng de* (悲伤的), *lìngrén jǔsàng de* (令人沮丧的) in the definition, and *chóuméikǔliǎn* (愁眉苦脸), *chuítóusàngqì* (垂头丧气) and *yōuyù* (忧郁) in the translations of its examples—'a *doleful face, manner, expression*'. We can see that, for a *doleful* face, we find '*chóuméikǔliǎn*'; for a *doleful* manner/expression, *chuítóusàngqì* and *yōuyù* are used respectively. These words are chosen to translate these phrases just because they are frequent collocations of the modified words in Chinese. In effect, they all denote quite specific feelings and none of them is equivalent to *doleful*. *Lìng rén jǔsàng de* is used to match *doleful* because both are extroverted. *Bēishāng* is used because they are similar in intensity, but the difference between them is that *bēishāng* is more introverted and *doleful* is more extroverted. *Doleful* has a much broader range of collocations, such as *cell, pride* and the like, but any above-mentioned Chinese word tends to modify a rather limited range of things. So no Chinese word corresponds well to *doleful*. Chinese emotion words are relatively limited in their collocating behaviour, while their English counterparts tend to be more flexible in collocations.

*Woe**

This section will look at *woeful, woefully* and *woebegone*. Before examining them, I will first look at *woe*. Below are the entries of *woe* from the three dictionaries:

LDCE: 1. **woes** [pl] *formal* the problems and troubles affecting someone 2. [U] *literary* great sadness

OALECD: *n* (*dated or fml or joc*) 1. [U] great sorrow or distress 悲哀; 悲痛; 苦恼 2. **woes** [pl] things that cause sorrow or distress; troubles or misfortunes 引起悲哀或苦恼的事物; 麻烦事; 不幸的事

COBUILD: 1. ≠ joy *Woe* is very great sadness. (LITERARY) 2. usu with poss You can refer to someone's problems as their *woes*. (WRITTEN)

These dictionaries provide the same senses about *woe*: 'great sadness' (U) and 'problems' (pl). Now let us look at what it is like in the corpus. Since only its singular form denotes sadness, I will focus on this form. I got 1,092 hits of *woe* (U) from the BOE. A glance at its top 50 collocates reveals that *woe* colligates strongly with possessive markers, such as *of (260), 's (32)* (indicating possessive case). Its concordance shows that, in modern discourse, *woe* is usually used in (half-)fixed expressions like *woe betide somebody, woe of tale(s), woe is me, full of woe, in weal and/or woe*, and *add woe*, etc.

Now let us turn to *woeful* and *woefully*. About *woeful*, the dictionaries say:

LDCE: 1. very bad or serious = *deplorable* 2. *literary* very sad = *pathetic*

OALECD: (*fml* 文) 1. full of woe; sad 悲哀的; 伤心的 2. [usu attrib] undesirable or regrettable; very bad 不合意的; 令人惋惜的; 糟糕的

COBUILD: 1. If someone or something is *woeful*, they are very sad. 2. You can use *woeful* to emphasise that something is very bad or undesirable.

From the definitions above, it is quite obvious that *woeful* is basically defined as 'sad' or 'bad/undesirable', and that *woefully* can be used to modify a verb to indicate a sad manner, or used as a degree modifier. *Woeful* occurs 912 times in the BOE. By inspection of its top 50 collocates, it is clear that *woeful* has colligations with *be* (126), the article-determiners *a (171)*, *the (140)*, possessive adjectives, typically *their (37)*, *his (21)*, and determiners, predominantly *this (11)*. According to its word sketch, its intensifiers are *truly (7)*, *utterly (2)* and *pretty (4)*. The words modified by *woeful* include *display (27)*, *record (27)*, *performance (23)*, *start (13)*, *lack (13)*, *defeat (6)*, *showing (4)*, *miscalculation (4)*, *inadequacy (3)*, *ignorance (3)*, *calamity (2)*, *inconsistency (2)*, etc. It can be seen that almost all of these words are associated with its sense of 'bad/undesirable'. I can hardly recognize any word that is surely related to 'sad'. Many of them talk about football or other sports. This might be due to the composition of the BOE, which contains a lot of newspaper articles. It shows that, in modern discourse, *woeful* is much more used in the sense of 'bad' than 'sad'.

Now let us move on to the discussion of its adverbial form. There are 698 hits of *woefully* in the corpus. In its top 50 collocates, I find *look (8)* and *head (6)* (in *shake/nod one's head*), which show that *woefully* is used to modify an action verb to indicate an emotional manner. However, its word sketch reveals that, in most of the cases, *woefully* is used to modify an adjective to indicate a degree. The modified adjectives include *inadequate (162)*, *short (74)*, *underprepared (22)*, *ignorant (14)*, *ill-prepared (7)*, *deficient (7)*, *underpaid (6)*, *insufficient (4)*, *understaffed (4)*, *ill-informed (3)*, *undermanned (3)*, *inept (3)*, *outdated (3)*, *misguided (3)*, *inexperienced (3)*, etc. It is clear from the above list that *woefully* has evolved into a complete intensifier with a negative semantic prosody.

Now let us turn to look at their Chinese equivalents. *Woe** occurs only 23 times in the BPC. Table 7.21 shows the searching result.

As mentioned in Chapter 6, the parallel corpus used for this research is composed of fiction alone. In fictional writing, it is one of the main features to

Table 7.21 Chinese equivalents of *woe** in the BPC

Sense	Chinese equivalents
Sad	*tòngkǔ 6, āiyuàn 1, shāngxīnshì 1, zhuīxīnqīxuè 1, āishāng 1, bēishāng 1, nánshòu 1, bēitòng 1*
Bad/undesirable	*dǎoméi 2, kělián 1, zāinàn 1, mùbùrěndǔ 1 (in woefully visible)*
Chóu	*bēikǔ 1, kǔnǎo 1, chóuméikǔliǎn 1, chóukǔbùkān 1, chóuróngmǎnmiàn 1*

describe people's feelings or emotional states. So, unlike the BOE, no instance of *woefully* from this corpus is related to the degree adverb sense. Table 7.21 shows that *woe** is often translated as *tòngkǔ* in Chinese. The translators use many Chinese words to express the concept of *woe*, but, basically, these words can be categorized into three classes: one is to do with the feeling of sadness, like *tòngkǔ*, *āiyuàn*, *āishāng*, *bēitòng*; the second one is related to something that is bad or undesirable, like *dǎoméi*, *kělián*, *zāinàn*; and the third one is associated with *chóu*, which is close to *woes*. Since the focus of this research is to examine the concept of sadness, I will only look at the first group.

Woe is a literary word, so Chinese translators use formal or literary words, like *āiyuàn*, *āishāng*, *zhuīxīnqīxuè*, *bēishāng*, *bēitòng*, to express this concept. *Tòngkǔ* focuses on the unacceptability of the bad events and the sufferer's incompetence to solve the problem. The pain comes mainly from the helplessness of the experiencer. We will discuss this concept in detail in Section 7.1.11. Translators use *tòngkǔ* to express *woe* probably because they view *woe* as a concept between *tòngkǔ* and *bēishāng*. Look at the following example from the BPC:

(110) Cried he, with a voice that rose over them, high, solemn, and majestic, yet had always a tremor through it, and sometimes a shriek, struggling up out of a fathomless depth of remorse and ***woe*** — 'ye, that have loved me!'
他的声音高昂、庄严而雄浑, 一直越过他们的 头顶, 但那声音是从**痛苦** (*tòngkǔ*) 与悔恨的无底深渊中挣扎出来的, '你们这些热爱我的人!'

In Chinese, *bēishāng* is something you suffer from but you do not fight against actively. You just let it turn weaker gradually. But it is quite common to say you should fight against *tòngkǔ* and try to get out of it as soon as possible. In Example 110, the original 'out of' might be the reason why the translator uses *tòngkǔ* instead of *bēishāng*. Consider another example:

(111) With a hand's breadth flight, it would have fallen into the water, and have
given the little brook another **woe** to carry onward, besides the
unintelligible tale, which it is still murmuring about.
只消再飞这几指宽的距离, 红字就会落进水里, 那样的话, 小溪除去喃
喃不断 诉说着的莫测的故事之外, 又要载着另一 段**哀怨** (*āiyuàn*)
流淌了。

In the above citation, *āiyuàn* is used presumably because *āiyuàn*, meaning
'aggrieved or resentful', is more literary than either *tòngkǔ* or *bēishāng*.

Let us move on to look at *woebegone*, a compound made up of *woe* and *begone*.
Its dictionary entries are shown below:

LDCE: *literary* looking very sad: *her woebegone expression*

OALECD: (*fml*) looking unhappy 显出悲伤的; 忧愁的; 愁眉苦脸的:
a woebegone child, expression, face

COBUILD: Someone who is *woebegone* is very sad. (WRITTEN)
She sniffed and looked woebegone.

Both LDCE and OALECD agree that *woebegone* is an emotion characterized by
extroversion. COBUILD does not say so explicitly, but its example betrays this
feature. Its dictionary definitions all point to its feature of extroversion. The OED
lists its first sense as follows:

'Beset with woe'; oppressed with misfortune, distress, sorrow, or grief. *Obs.* or
arch.

According to the OED, it appears that the above sense is its original meaning, but
this sense has become inactive in modern usage. Its corpus data provide further
evidence for this change. Seventy-one hits of *woebegone* are found in the BOE.
Expression (5) and *look (5)*, but not *be*, are found most in its top collocates,
suggesting that *woebegone* has become an emotion word that is specifically used
to describe the exhibition of sadness.

Six hits of *woebegone* are found in the BPC: *chóuméikǔliǎn, chóuróngmǎnmiàn,
mǎnliǎnbēishāng, chóukǔbùkān, kǔnǎo, kělián de. Chóuméikǔliǎn*
(sadness + eyebrow + bitter + face) is the Chinese equivalent used in the
OALECD and is also the closest in meaning. *Chóuróngmǎnmiàn* (face covered
with sadness) is much less frequent and only used in certain contexts.
Mǎnliǎnbēishāng (full face + sadness) is hardly a word. Both *chóukǔbùkān*
(sadness + bitterness + unbearable) and *kǔnǎo* (vexation) more describe the

inner emotional state. *Kělián de* (poor) can not be taken as its equivalent. So the following discussion will focus on *chóuméikǔliǎn*, which occurs 362 times in the CCL corpus. An inspection of its collocates reveals that it co-occurs predominantly with *shuō* (say/46), *kàn/kàndào/kànjiàn/jiàn* (see/23/13/6/5), *yàngzi* (appearance/21), *biǎoqíng* (expression/5), all of which indicate that it is closely associated with external manifestations of sadness. It also collocates with *zhěngtiān/zhěngrì* (all the day: 19 + 5) and *zǒngshì/yīzhí* (always: 7 + 5), both showing that it is a long-lasting emotional state. It co-occurs with *āishēngtànqì* (have deep signs) nine times in the corpus, describing vividly what a sad person looks like and suggesting that it is an emotion of resignation. *Chóuméikǔliǎn* usually has a cause (*yīnwèi*/because, 8) and a mother (*mǔqīn*, 7) tends more to be in such an emotional state.

Comparison

As stated earlier, there is no Chinese word that corresponds to *doleful*. It is also true of *woeful*. In English, *sad* can be used to modify a person who is sad, an expression, facial part or anything showing sadness, or a thing causing a sad feeling, but *doleful* is mainly used to modify a thing that shows sadness, like *doleful song, doleful eyes*. Sometimes it is also used to modify a thing that makes people sad, like *doleful cell*, but it is hardly used to describe a person who feels sad, such as *a doleful boy*. *Woeful* may be used to talk about a person, but not often. Both *dolefully* and *woefully* can be used to describe an action to indicate a manner, such as *say, groan, talk, nod, shake one's head*, etc. Both *doleful* and *woeful* are very formal and literary words. *Doleful* is used to modify things causing or showing sadness and Chinese has many words to describe such things, so its Chinese equivalents are not restricted to a few words, but none of them corresponds exactly with it. In the case of *woe*, it is even more complex. From the previous discussion, it seems that *woe* is a concept that combines *tòngkǔ* and *bēishāng*, so it makes the matching job more challenging. *Woebegone* is a literary word that is specifically used to describe the external manifestation of a sad person. Chinese tends to combine emotion words and facial organs to give an account of what a person looks like when s/he is very sad, such as *mǎnliǎnbēishāng*, *chóuróngmǎnmiàn* and *chóuméikǔliǎn*, of which *chóuméikǔliǎn* has developed into a word due to its high frequency.

It should be noted that the parallel corpus I used for this research is not big, so it yields only a small number of instances of *woe** and *doleful**. The claims based on this corpus still await a further test from bigger parallel corpora. What we can surely see is that English and Chinese encode quite different meanings in these words, which makes it impossible to match the two languages on a word-to-word basis. If a word is looked at in isolation, it shows a complicated picture. However, if it is put in a concrete context, its ambiguity will disappear. In translating, the translator can only decide which aspect is emphasized by relying on the context and select the closest word to it.

7.1.6 *Mourn** and their Chinese equivalents

*Mourn**

In this section, we will discuss the *mourn* family. Before we examine *mourn* in the corpus, let us look at what the dictionaries say about it:

> LDCE: 1. to feel very sad and to miss someone after they have died 2. to feel very sad because something no longer exists or is no longer as good as it used to be

> OALECD: feel or show sorrow or regret for the loss of sb/sth 因丧失某人[某事物]而悲痛或表示哀悼

> COBUILD: 1. If you *mourn* someone who has died or *mourn for* them, you are very sad that they have died and show your sorrow in the way that you behave. 2. If you *mourn* something or *mourn for* it, you regret that you no longer have it and show your regret in the way that you behave.

From LDCE's definitions, i.e. 'to feel very sad and to miss someone after they have died' and 'to feel very sad because something no longer exists or is no longer as good as it used to be', it can be seen that the determinant of '*mourn*' is loss. The loss may be material or mental. It may refer to the loss of something or somebody. It seems that the person who mourns feels sad because s/he is always thinking about the past when what is mourned was still there and comparing the difference. OALECD includes the meaning of 'show one's sorrow or regret', which is consistent with COBUILD's explanation: 'If you mourn someone who has died or mourn for them, you are very sad that they have died and show your sorrow in the way that you behave'. So, it can be said that *mourn* means two layers of meaning: one is that you are sad and the other is that you show your sadness. Now let us turn to the BOE. A search for *mourn* generates many instances of *mourning*, which are tagged as VVG but are actually nouns, as exemplified in Figure 7.3.

1	'In France, Napoleon Bonaparte ordered ten days *of mourning*.
2	'She touched Sheilah's arm across the table, her long slender arm in its black stretch lycra, the colour *of mourning*, clinging to life.
3	No sense *of mourning*.
4	The Archbishop of Canterbury, the Catholic Bishop of Westminster and the Chief Rabbi issued a joint statement calling for a national day *of mourning* and prayer; flags on all public buildings were flown at half-mast; and a Book of Remembrance opened at the American embassy in Grosvenor; by the end of the day it had been signed by three thousand people.
5	'That period *of mourning* was a short one, mate.
6	A separation was a bereavement and called for a period *of mourning*, she explained to one of her girlfriends who accused her of being 'unsociable' when she declined an invitation to a billionaire's private Caribbean island for a week's vacation.

Figure 7.3 List of instances of *mourning*

The discussion of the inaccuracy of its POS tagging is out of the scope of the research. Since it is inaccurate to examine *mourn* as a lemma, I searched for *mourn|mourns|mourned* (2,561 hits) in the corpus. An examination of their top 50 collocates shows that *mourn* has colligations with the prepositions *for (159)* and *over (16)*, possessive adjectives, typically *his (91), her (85), their (71)*, and pronouns, predominantly *her (85), she (50), him (48), he (42)*. The nouns associated with *mourn* include *nation (52), family (42), death (36), world (36), loss (30), crowd (19)* and *victim (30)*. As expected, the most significant component of *mourn* is *loss*. It is often related to someone's death. *Mourning* could be personal. You *mourn* them because they are very close to you. After losing them, you miss them and feel sad. However, we can also find *victim, nation, world*, etc., which show that *mourning* could also be social, communal or culturally mediated. In other words, people *mourn* not only for those they love deeply, but also for those about whom they think they should show their sorrow.

Its word sketch shows that *mourn* often co-occurs with *privately (11), openly (5), publicly (5), together (11), alone (5), deeply (7)*. So *mourning* can happen in a private or public way; people *mourn* together or alone. The only intensifier is *deeply*.

Now we come to the discussion of *mourning*:

LDCE: 1. great sadness because someone has died: in *mourning* (= feeling great sadness) 2. black clothes worn to show that you are very sad that someone has died

OALECD: black or dark clothes worn as a (conventional) sign of grief at sb's death (丧服(黑色或深色的))

COBUILD: 1. *Mourning* is behaviour in which you show sadness about a person's death. 2. If you are *in mourning*, you are dressed or behaving in a particular way because someone you love or respect has died.

LDCE says *mourning* means both 'great sadness because someone has died' and 'black clothes worn to show that you are very sad that someone has died'. OALECD only gives its meaning as clothes. COBUILD says '*mourning* is behaviour in which you show sadness about a person's death'. These three dictionaries differ in the explanation of 'mourning' and the phrase 'in mourning'. Its corpus data show that 4,038 hits of *mourning*, either tagged as VVG or NOUN, are found in the BOE. A careful inspection of its top 50 collocates reveals that *mourning* has colligations with prepositions, typically *of (854), in (546), for (418), over (35)*, the definite article *the (520)*, and possessive adjectives, predominantly *her (70), his (40), their (37)*. The adjectives associated with *mourning* include *private (13), public (33), official (54), national (118)* and *deep (29)*. Its nominal collocates contain *family (17), period (102), process (24), clothes (21), ritual (24), ring (11)*. It seems that *mourning* in the BOE is more talked about as a public *mourning* and this is due to its composition. Overall, it has a semantic preference for words related to the *mourning* event.

Next let us turn to look at *mournful* and *mournfully*. The dictionaries give the following about *mournful*:

LDCE: very sad

OALECD: (often derog) sad; sorrowful 悲哀的; 令人悲痛的:

COBUILD: 1. If you are *mournful*, you are very sad. 2. A *mournful* sound seems very sad.

There are 594 hits of *mournful* in the BOE. Its top 50 collocates show that *mournful* colligates with the article-determiners *a (122), the (109)*, and nouns, typically *sound (22), tune (14), cry (13), look (11), wail (10), expressions (10), face (9), tone (9), song (9), eye (8), voice (7), dirge (6), ballad (6), melody (5), music (5), howl (5), note (5), moan (5)*, etc. From its collocates, we can see that it has a semantic preference for words that are related to facial expressions, like *face, eyes, look, expression*, or sound, such as *sound, tune, cry, wail, tone, song, voice, dirge, ballad, melody, music, howl, note, moan*. Its word sketch shows that the verbs collocating with *mournful* are mainly *look (11)* and *sound (2)*, and the only degree modifier is the compromiser *rather (8)*. So it may be argued that *mournful* is mainly external because it has visible or audible features to show the sadness, instead of only suffering it mentally; in other words, it is an externalized emotion, which is mainly expressed by facial expressions, sound or music. *Mournful* focuses on making other people think you are sad. *Mournful* music makes listeners sad. So *mournful* does not talk much about someone's own sadness, but more about making other people think you are sad.

Now we come to examine the top 50 collocates of *mournfully* (236 hits). As expected, *mournfully* has a semantic preference for physical action verbs, like *say/add/recite (23/23/5), gaze (8), look/stare (7/5), sign (6), sit (4)*, etc. So the data support the claim I made earlier that *mournful(ly)* is more extroverted than introverted. Like *mournful, mournfully* is only modified by the downtoner *rather*.

Āidào

The BPC yields 90 hits of *mourn**. The search findings are presented in Table 7.22.

Table 7.22 Chinese equivalents of *mourn** in the BPC

sāng	*31 [sāngfú 17* (including *mourning brooch, mourning bonnet, mourning clothes, mourning dress), fúsāng 10, bàosāng 1, shǒuxiào 2, huāquān 1]*
zàng	*5 [sòngzàngchē]*
bēiāi	*7*
āidào	*6*
shāngxīn	*6*
bēishāng	*5*
bēitòng	*4*
Others	*qīliáng 2, qīkǔ 1, cǎndàn 1,* etc.

Table 7.22 shows that in 31 of 90 occurrences of *mourn** the translation is related to the Chinese concept of *sāng* (a broad concept related to dead people, including mourning, funeral, etc.), such as *sāngfú* (mourning clothes), *fúsāng* (go into mourning), *bàosāng* (announce the death), *shǒuxiào* (in mourning), *huāquān* (mourning wreath). Five of them are translated as *sòngzàngchē* (mourning coach), where *zàng* is a Chinese concept meaning the burial ceremony. Most of the above-discussed instances contain *mourning*. For the remaining occurrences, 6 of them are translated as *āidào*, 7 as *bēiāi*, 6 as *shāngxīn*, 5 as *bēishāng* and 4 as *bēitòng*. Other translations include *qīliáng, qīkǔ, cǎndàn*, which are used to describe things or situations causing sad feelings. *Shāngxīn,*

bēishāng and *bēitòng* are used to translate its sense 'to feel sad especially about someone's death', as revealed in the following examples:

(112) 现在他的躯体去和他的心会合了，我们就没有理由为他感到悲痛了。如果还感到**悲痛** (*bēitòng*) 就太自私了。我爱他就像爱自己的父亲，所以才这样说。

Now that his body's gone to join his heart, I don't see that we got reason to **mourn**, unless we're pretty damned selfish, and I'm sayin' it who loved him like he was my own pa.

(113) 思嘉也曾想把皮蒂姑妈找来，缓和一下她良心上的不安，但是她又犹豫了，姑妈要是来了也许会更糟，因为她对弗兰克的死由衷地感到**悲痛** (*bēitòng*)。

For a moment Scarlett thought of summoning Pittypat to stand between her and her conscience but she hesitated. Pitty would probably make matters worse, for she honestly **mourned** Frank.

The sense of showing sadness about someone's death is reflected in the Chinese translation equivalents related to funeral or other relevant communal or social practices, such as *sang-words*, *āidào* and *bēiāi*.

Bēiāi, *shāngxīn*, *bēishāng* and *bēitòng* have been discussed in earlier sections, so this section will only focus on *āidào*. Table 7.23 presents the search result for *āidào* (1,402 hits) from the CCL corpus.

From Table 7.23, it can be seen that *āidào* is 'to show one's regret or sadness about someone's death', which is clearly reflected in its verbal collocates in the first column: *biǎoshì/biǎodá* (express), *zhuǎndá* (convey). It is a social practice to

Table 7.23 Significant collocates of *āidào* in the CCL corpus

Showing	Modifier	Cause	Object	Subject	Others
biǎoshì 832	shēnqiè 205	yùnàn 195	sǐzhě 46	quánguó 56	jiāshǔ 126
zhuǎndá 11	chéntòng 124	shìshì 189	sǐnànzhě 63	rénmín 46	qīnshǔ 63
biǎodá 10	chéngzhì 17	búxìng 59	línànzhě 15	tóngbāo 25	wèiwèn 115
xià bànqí 8	shēn(biǎo)16	qùshì 35	shòuhàizhě 13	zhèngfǔ 38	bēitòng 19
jiàng bànqí 8		yùhài 17	yùhàizhě 12	zǒngtǒng 37	dàoniàn 9
yàndiàn 31		bìngshì 17		zhǔxí 24	huáiniàn 8
fāngshì 45		shēnwáng 12		lǐngdǎorén 17	
xíngshì 14		xīshēng 10		zǒnglǐ 10	

convey the whole nation's sadness about someone's death, via *jiàng bànqí/xià bànqí* (flying the flag at half mast). National leaders usually communicate their sadness about a very important person's death or a big group of people killed in other countries via telegram (*yàndiàn, (zhì)diàn*). So it is mainly a matter of *xíngshì* (form) and done in certain *fāngshì* (ways). The second column lists its premodifiers, such as *shēnqiè/shēn(biǎo)* (deep/deeply), *chéntòng* (with grief) and *chéngzhì* (sincere). The third column gives the causes for *āidào*, such as *yùnàn/yùhài/shēnwáng* (be killed), *shìshì/qùshì* (die), *búxìng* (misfortune), *bìngshì* (die of a disease). The fourth column is concerned with the objects of *āidào*, like *sǐzhě* (deceased) and *sǐnànzhě/línànzhě/yùhàizhě/shòuhàizhě* (victim). The subjects of *āidào* include *quánguó* (the whole nation), *rénmín* (people), *tóngbāo* (compatriot), *zhèngfǔ* (government), *zǒngtǒng* (president), *zhǔxí* (chairman), *zǒnglǐ* (prime minister), *lǐngdǎorén* (leader), etc. The final column gives its other collocates, such as *qīnshǔ/jiāshǔ* (family members), *wèiwèn* (condolence), *bēitòng* (grief), etc. *Āidào* is often conducted together with *wèiwèn*. The corpus data listed here are more related to a public mourning, associated more with a nation for the victims of a disaster. All of the objects of *āidào* listed here are killed because the CCL corpus contains a lot of newspaper articles, which often report social tragedies. Actually, *āidào* is also used to talk about privately mourning a family member, as exemplified in the following example from the CCL corpus:

(114) 人死后亲属和亲戚中的晚辈或平辈穿孝服, 表示[**哀悼**] (*āidào*)
       'After someone dies, his/her family members and relatives of the same or junior generation will wear *mourning* clothes to show *āidào*.'

Comparison

Different from *mourn*, *āidào* is a word used only to show one's sorrow about someone's death, based on the social or communal practice. *Āidào zhě* (*mourner*) is often *shāngxīn* or *bēitòng*, but not necessarily so. *Mourn* can be used to talk about one's feeling of sadness and showing of sadness. In addition, it can be used in a metaphorical way to talk about the feeling of loss of something, which is absent in *āidào*'s meaning. *Āidào* is predominantly used to talk about the showing of someone's sorrow or regret about the death of someone. Chinese words distinguish clearly between feeling and showing of sadness. English words, however, do not differentiate them sharply. Contexts have to be depended on to decide whether you are talking about communal or culturally mediated behaviour or someone's internal feeling.

7.1.7 *Depression* & Melancholy** and their Chinese equivalents

Depression & Melancholy**

Depression*

This sub-section will look at *depress, depression, depressing* and *depressingly,* leaving the discussion of *depressed* to the next sub-section, where it can be compared and contrasted with *melancholy* (adj.). For the discussion of *depress,* let us start with its dictionary definitions:

> LDCE: 1. to make someone feel very unhappy 2. to prevent an economy from being as active and successful as it usually is 3. *formal* to press something down, especially a part of a machine 4. *formal* to reduce the value of prices or wages

> OALECD: 1. (sb) sad and without enthusiasm 使(某人)忧愁, 消沉, 沮丧 2. press, push or pull (sth) down 将(某物)压下, 推下, 拉下 3. make (esp trade) less active 使(尤指贸易)不活跃, 不景气, 萧条:

> COBUILD: 1. If someone or something *depresses* you, they make you feel sad and disappointed. 2. If something *depresses* prices, wages, or figures, it causes them to become less.

LDCE's definition 'to make someone feel very unhappy' offers nothing valuable. OALECD says that *depress* implies 'without enthusiasm' and COBUILD uses 'disappointed' instead.

For its corpus data, its top 50 collocates based on 4,745 hits (inclusive of *depressing* and *depressed*) show that *be (1,361)* tops the collocate list, which is because, in most cases, *depress* is used as a past participle (some of them are actually adjectives, but the tagging tool of the BOE tags them as VBN). It has a strong colligation with prepositions, mainly *by (252), about (129), for (100)* and *at (76).* Its word sketch reveals that most of its subjects are associated with its feeling sense, such as *prediction (23), thought (11), feeling (9), war (7), event (6), death (5), news (5), fact (4) memory (4), alcohol (4).* Its modifier sketch tells us that *depress* is often related to *clinically (52), chronically (11), suicidally (7)* and *terminally (4),* which are all associated with its unhealthy condition. Its modifiers show that '*depress(ed/ing)*' could be very serious since it can be intensified by *severely (50), profoundly (19), deeply (57), terribly (8), thoroughly (10), utterly (8), seriously (22), extremely (18), very (143), incredibly (4),* and less serious because it can also be modified by *somewhat (7), slightly (12)* and *mildly (4),* and that it could happen *frequently (7), temporarily (6)* or *permanently (4).*

Now let us look at its nominal form *depression*, whose dictionary entries are shown as follows:

LDCE: 1. (a) a medical condition that makes you very unhappy and anxious and often prevents you from living a normal life (b) a feeling of sadness that makes you think there is no hope for the future 2. **the (Great) *Depression*:** the period during the 1930s when there was not much business activity and not many jobs 3. a long period during which there is very little business activity and a lot of people do not have jobs →*recession* 4. a part of a surface that is lower than the other parts 5. *technical* a mass of air under low pressure, that usually causes rain

OALECD: 1. being depressed; low spirits 忧愁; 沮丧; 消沉 2. hollow sunken place in the surface of sth, esp the ground; dip 凹陷处;(尤指)洼地, 坑: 3. period when there is little economic activity, and usu poverty and unemployment 经济萧条期. 4. (a) (winds caused by a) lowering of atmospheric pressure 气压降低(形成的气流). (b) area where this happens 低气压区.

COBUILD: 1. *Depression* is a mental state in which you are sad and feel that you cannot enjoy anything, because your situation is so difficult and unpleasant. 2. A *depression* is a time when there is very little economic activity, which causes a lot of unemployment and poverty. 3 A *depression* in a surface is an area which is lower than the parts surrounding it. 4. A *depression* is a mass of air that has a low pressure and that often causes rain.

For the meaning associated with the mental state, LDCE breaks it down into two senses: one refers to 'a medical condition that makes you very unhappy and anxious and often prevents you from living a normal life' and the other is 'a feeling of sadness that makes you think there is no hope for the future', which is quite similar to OALECD's 'without enthusiasm' and 'low spirits', or COBUILD's 'disappointed' and 'you cannot enjoy anything'. Now let us turn to its collocates based on 14,247 instances in the BOE. Its top 50 collocates reveal that it has strong colligations with the definite article *the (1,602)*, prepositions, predominantly *of (1,910)*, *in (660)*, *for (503)*, *from (454)*, *into (156)*, *by (122)*, *about (86)*, and *be (857)*. Based on its word sketch, the verbs of *depression* include *suffer (185)*, *treat (146)*, *cause (110)*, *alleviate (32)*, *associate (23)*, *diagnose (20)*, *lift (19)*, *trigger (17)*, *underlie (17)*, *worsen (16)*, *deepen (15)*, *combat (15)*, *cure (12)*, suggesting semantic preferences for causing, suffering, worsening, lessening or curing *depression*. Although some of them can be used in a metaphorical sense, most of them are associated with a medical condition. This is supported by its modifiers: *post-natal/postnatal/Post-natal (148/111/15), postpartum (126), manic (161), clinical (180), ST (38), tropical (61), chronic (72), maternal (26), suicidal (22)*. Its degree modifiers include *severe (288), deep (208), moderate (29), shallow (23)*. *Deep* and *shallow* show that *depression* is understood in terms of the metaphorical image: A FLUID IN A CONTAINER, with its depth correlated with its intensity. Table 7.24 shows the words frequently used in the 'and/or' pattern for *depression* (the figures following the word show the frequencies and the figures after the frequency indicate the salience):

Table 7.24 And/or pattern for *depression* in the BOE

and/or	Fr	Salience	and/or	Fr	Salience	and/or	Fr	Salience
anxiety	596	9.78	stress	134	7.24	headache	47	6.65
irritability	52	8.18	loneliness	36	7.22	anger	82	6.62
schizophrenia	75	8.17	lethargy	26	7.22	sadness	27	6.42
alcoholism	40	7.51	self-esteem	39	7.06	nausea	20	6.4
fatigue	64	7.48	despair	47	7.01	exhaustion	21	6.35
mania	32	7.36	anorexia	20	6.79	addiction	30	6.33
insomnia	31	7.35	paranoia	23	6.76	diabetes	32	6.32
psychosis	30	7.34	asthma	31	6.7	dementia	17	6.29
disorder	153	7.28						

From Table 7.24, it is clear that the list includes a lot of diseases or disease-related terms, such as *schizophrenia, alcoholism, mania, insomnia, psychosis, disorder, anorexia, paranoia, asthma, headache, nausea, addiction, diabetes, dementia*, etc. It further supports the earlier claim that *depression* as a noun is more used as 'a medical condition'. Other words in the list are mostly related to feelings, such as *anxiety, irritability, stress, loneliness, lethargy, despair, anger, sadness*. One noteworthy word is *self-esteem*, which means 'good opinion of one's own character and abilities' (OALECD). It occurs 39 times in this pattern, probably suggesting that *depression* is a condition that makes one lose one's self-esteem and have a low opinion of one's own character and abilities. We find *fatigue* and *exhaustion* in the list. *Fatigue* is 'a feeling of extreme physical or mental tiredness' (OALECD). So this might allude to the fact that *depression* arises from mental tiredness. *Anxiety* tops the list, so we have reason to argue that the mental tiredness might result from anxiety. Of course, the feeling of *depression* might also incorporate other feelings, such as *anger, sadness, despair, loneliness*. Consider the following paraphrases of *depression* extracted from the BOE:

(115) Remember that **depression is** merely anger turned in against yourself, instead of being directed outwards.

(116) ... for others the **depression is** a symptom of problems with life rather than an illness, and thus not curable by drug treatment. **Depression is** a painful experience ...

(117) Psychologists have sometimes argued that **depression is** more concerned with our feelings about the past, while anxiety is to do with fears for the future, which when you think about it, seems to make a lot of sense. DEPRESSION? Life events (for a list of these see the Holmes-Rahe scale in the section on stress). Psychological factors. Some psychologists **attribute depression to** 'learned helplessness', when we feel so out of control of our lives and it seems pointless to even try. Others **attribute depression to** 'faulty thinking', i. e. the way we view the world affects our moods. Psychoanalytical theories **see depression as** being a result of aggression being turned inwards upon ourselves.

(118) 'For me, the **depression is** connected to the gap between our expectations and our views of what matters in life, and the frustration which comes with never really achieving those.'

Depression is a well-researched topic in psychology, which explains why we can find many paraphrases in the corpus. According to the above examples, *depression* seems to be anger turned against oneself and this supports the earlier claim that it has to do with poor self-esteem; it is correlated with disappointment or despair, depending on its seriousness. Example (117) tells us that members of a discourse may disagree about what a discourse object might mean. For some psychologists, *depression* is more concerned with the feelings about the past, but the corpus data appear to show that it is not quite the case because anxiety, which is to do with fears about the future, tops the list in Table 7.24.

In the corpus, 2,418 hits of *depressing* as an adjective are found. Its word sketch shows that *depressing* can be modified by amplifiers, such as *very (91), deeply (25), really (22), profoundly (9), thoroughly (8), terribly (7), utterly (5) extremely (5), downright (5), totally (5), immensely (5),* and downtoners, like *pretty (25), rather (27), little (8), merely (4), quite (11),* etc. For the words it modifies, almost all of them are related to the sense of feeling: *account (62), reading (40), effect (39), news (30), picture (30), thought (28), experience (26), finale (26), run (22), statistic (14), aspect (12), defeat (16), sight (14), reality (9), spectacle (9), reminder (8), conclusion (7), truth (7), tale (7), prospect (6), regularity (6), scenario (5), episode (5), lack (5), storylines (5).* It seems that many of these words can be modified by *sad*, and *depressing* is, in many cases, only a stronger version of *sadness* in the sense of 'making one feel unhappy'.

For *depressingly* (310 hits), its top 50 collocates show that it semantically prefers neutral or even positive adjectives that have no obvious negative inclinations, like *familiar (56), predictable (12), similar (9), clear (5), large (5), inevitable (4), long (4)*. It seems that *depressingly* has lost its 'making sad' flavour and developed into a complete degree adverb, without negative tendency. This is referred to as 'delexicalisation' (Sinclair 1996). Similar cases would be *awfully, terribly, woefully*, etc.

Melancholy*

This sub-section will present a comparative analysis of *melancholy* and *depressed*, followed by the discussion of *melancholic*. To begin with, let us look at the dictionary entries of *depressed* and *melancholy*:

LDCE:

depressed 1. (a) very unhappy (b) suffering from a medical condition in which you are so unhappy that you cannot live a normal life 2. an area, industry etc that is depressed does not have enough economic or business activity 3. *formal* a depressed level or amount is lower than normal
melancholy *adj* very sad
n formal a feeling of sadness for no particular reason

OALECD:

depressed sad and without enthusiasm 忧愁的; 消沉的; 沮丧的:
melancholy *n* (tendency towards) deep sadness which lasts for some time; *depression* 忧郁; 抑郁. *adj* (a) very sad; depressed 悲哀的; 沮丧的 (b) causing sadness 使人忧郁的

COBUILD:

depressed 1. If you are *depressed*, you are sad and feel that you cannot enjoy anything, because your situation is so difficult and unpleasant.
2. A *depressed* place or industry does not have enough business or employment to be successful.
melancholy 1. [ADJ] You describe something that you see or hear as *melancholy* when it gives you an intense feeling of sadness.
2 [N] *Melancholy* is an intense feeling of sadness which lasts for a long time and which strongly affects your behaviour and attitudes. (LITERARY)
3 [ADJ] If someone feels or looks *melancholy*, they feel or look very sad. (LITERARY)

For *depressed* as a feeling, LDCE's explanation of 'very unhappy' is meaningless. OALECD's 'without enthusiasm' and COBUILD's 'you cannot enjoy anything' can show that getting *depressed* means one has lost the keen interest in life. For *melancholy*, LDCE claims that it is 'a feeling of sadness for no particular reason'. OALECD says the salient feature for *melancholy* is 'deep sadness which lasts for some time' and it uses *depression* to define *melancholy*. COBUILD defines *melancholy* as 'an intense feeling of sadness which lasts for a long time and which strongly affects your behaviour and attitude'. So what is shared by all three dictionaries is 'a feeling of deep/intense sadness'. 'A feeling which lasts for some time' is only shared by OALECD and COBUILD.

To determine their other distinguishing features, we need to look at their collocates. As mentioned earlier, many instances of *depressed* that are actually adjectives are tagged as VBN. However, we cannot differentiate them from the real past-participle cases using a corpus technology and merge them into this group, so we can only analyse what the BOE software program provides for us, albeit its incompleteness. In the BOE, *melancholy* occurs only 16 times as a noun, including *melancholies*. There are too few instances to make a claim, so I will focus my discussion on *melancholy* as an adjective.

The BOE contains 3,700 hits of *depressed* (*adj.*) and 1,772 hits of *melancholy* (*adj.*). For the sake of space, I only summarize the relevant findings as follows:

Depressed (3,700):
    Colligations:
        (a) link verbs: *be (171), feel (183), become (191), get (151), remain (49), look (30), seem (31)*
        (b) preposition: *about (55)*
    Semantic preferences:
        (a) feeling-related: *patient (76), mood (43), person (78), mother (54), state (54)*
        (b) non-feeling: *market (97), area (87), price (75), economy (29)*
Melancholy (1,772):
    Colligations:
        (a) link verbs: *feel (13), sound (10)*
        (b) preposition: *about (25)*
    Semantic preferences:
        (a) thinking: *thought (11), musing (3), reflection (3)*
        (b) music: *music (13), song (11), note (7), tone (5), vocal (3), melody (3)*

(c) things making one sad: *ending (6), tale (5), occasion (5), sight (4),
truth (8), task (6), reading (4)*

(d) things related to feeling or showing sadness: *mood (14), soul (5),
smile (5), expression (4)*

The above figures reveal that *depressed* has a much stronger colligation with link verbs, especially *feel* (49‰ > 7‰, taking their total numbers of occurrences in the corpus into consideration) than *melancholy*. In terms of semantic preferences, *depressed* tends to modify a person or an emotional state, while *melancholy* is more likely to modify words related to thinking or music. The above statistics seem to suggest that '*depressed*' focuses more on the inner emotional state (*feel, 183*), but it is also often outwardly manifested (*look, 30; seem, 31*) and is likely to be perceived. The use of 'sound melancholy' and the semantic association of music as mentioned above seem to suggest that a *melancholy* feeling tends to be outwardly manifested, especially via voice or music. Its semantic association with thinking shows that it is a typical inner state as well. In addition, *melancholy* also modifies positive words, such as *comedy (6)* and *pleasure (4)*. Significant collocates for these two words in other patterns include:

Unique patterns:

Depressed:

Modifier: *economically (25), clinically (21), severely (34), deeply (21), seriously (11), extremely (11), terribly (6), mildly (6)*

And/or: *anxious (110), angry (44), lonely (38), tired (23), miserable (21), irritable (17), lethargic (12), frustrated (10), frightened (10)*

Melancholy:

Modifier: *deep (8)*

And/or: *romantic (10), sweet (8), profound (8), beautiful (7), morbid (5), gentle (5), exquisite (4)*

Common patterns (*depressed/melancholy*):

Modifier: *little (7/10); rather (12/11)*

Obviously, *economically* and *clinically* come from the non-feeling senses of *depressed*. It is clear from the above list that *melancholy* is only modified by *deep*, (a) *little* and *rather*, unlike *depressed*, which is intensified by *severely, deeply, seriously, extremely, terribly, mildly, rather* and (a) *little*. It is interesting that all the words used in the 'and/or' pattern for *depressed* are negative, especially the highly frequent ones, i.e. *anxious, angry, lonely* and *tired*, which constitute the core meaning of *depressed*. In contrast, almost all the words in the list for *melancholy*

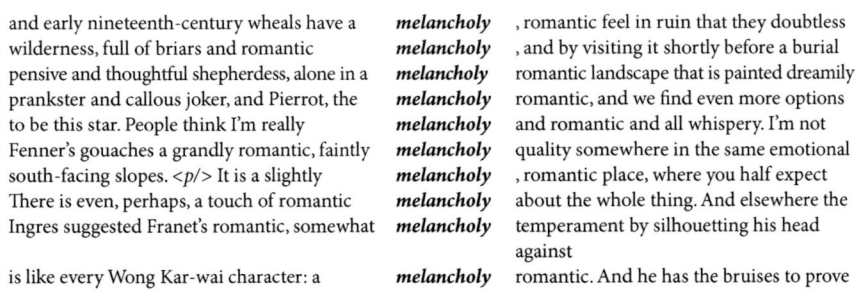

and early nineteenth-century wheals have a	*melancholy*	, romantic feel in ruin that they doubtless
wilderness, full of briars and romantic	*melancholy*	, and by visiting it shortly before a burial
pensive and thoughtful shepherdess, alone in a	*melancholy*	romantic landscape that is painted dreamily
prankster and callous joker, and Pierrot, the	*melancholy*	romantic, and we find even more options
to be this star. People think I'm really	*melancholy*	and romantic and all whispery. I'm not
Fenner's gouaches a grandly romantic, faintly	*melancholy*	quality somewhere in the same emotional
south-facing slopes. <p/> It is a slightly	*melancholy*	, romantic place, where you half expect
There is even, perhaps, a touch of romantic	*melancholy*	about the whole thing. And elsewhere the
Ingres suggested Franet's romantic, somewhat	*melancholy*	temperament by silhouetting his head against
is like every Wong Kar-wai character: a	*melancholy*	romantic. And he has the bruises to prove

Figure 7.4 Concordance listing of *melancholy*

are positive, except *morbid*. The concordance listing[10] in Figure 7.4 can show that all of the instances of *melancholy* come from the 'and' rather than the 'or' pattern, indicating that *melancholy* has a positive flavour in meaning and is thus less negative in terms of its semantic prosody.

My inspection of its other positive collocates in their concordances confirms this claim, though, in some instances, it is used as a noun rather than an adjective. Due to the inaccurate tagging, they are misplaced here. However, it does not affect our observation that *melancholy* is less negative. Look at the following example:

(119)   His mind was not political, only contemplative. That contemplation is pessimistic; perhaps ***melancholy is*** a better word.

(120)   In Iran and Sri Lanka for example a degree of ***melancholy is*** taken as an indication of a person's depth.

The above examples suggest that *melancholy* is closely associated with contemplation, which can be taken as an indication of a person's depth. The correlation of contemplation with depth should also apply in the English culture, not only in Iran and Sri Lanka, as shown in Example (120).

For *melancholic*, the dictionaries offer the following:

LDCE: *literary* feeling very sad

OALECD: (having a tendency to be) melancholy 忧郁的; 抑郁的

COBUILD: If you describe someone or something as *melancholic*, you mean that they are very sad. (LITERARY)

Both LDCE and COBUILD say that *melancholic* is literary, which seems to be the very thing that differentiates it from *melancholy*. In the corpus, 209 hits of *melancholic* as an adjective are found. Due to its low frequency in the corpus, we can only find a few meaningful words it modifies in its top 50 collocates, like *tone (5), song (4), mood (3)* and *music (3)*. It appears, from its collocates, that *melancholy* and *melancholic* are very much similar, only differing in that the latter is more literary. *Sanguine (8)* is particularly prominent in the collocates of the 'and/or' pattern, suggesting the antonym of *melancholic* seems to be 'hopeful, optimistic'. *Melancholic temperament (3)* is also found in its word sketch, showing that *melancholic* has a long-lasting quality, which may constitute one's character. *Gorgeously, majestically, beautifully, sweetly* and *wonderfully* in its modifiers seem to show that *melancholic*, albeit it means 'sad' or 'pessimistic', is not a completely negative word since it can be modified by words with clearly positive connotations.

Chinese equivalents of depression* & melancholy*

Sixty hits of *depress** and 54 hits of *melancholy** are found in the BPC. Their most frequently occurring Chinese translation equivalents are given in Table 7.25.

Table 7.25 Top three Chinese equivalents of *depression** & *melancholy** in the BPC

	Depression*	Melancholy*
Chinese translational equivalents	jǔsàng: 15	yōuyù: 21
	yāyì: 5	shānggǎn: 3
	qíngxù dīluò: 4	bēishāng: 3

Table 7.25 presents their top Chinese equivalents: *jǔsàng, yāyì, qíngxù dīluò* for *depression** and *yōuyù, shānggǎn, bēishāng* for *melancholy**. We have discussed *bēishāng* in Section 7.1.1 and will focus on the other five items here.

Jǔsàng

Jǔsàng occurs 1,904 times in the CCL corpus and its top collocates are presented in Table 7.26.

What we can see from the collocates in the first column in Table 7.26 is that *jǔsàng* is an emotion both experienced as an inner state, as shown in *gǎndào/ gǎn/juéde/gǎnjué* (feel), *xīnlǐ/xīnzhōng* (in the heart), *jīngshén* (spirit), *qíngxù* (mood), *xīnqíng* (frame of mind), and involving outward manifestations, as indicated in *biǎoqíng/shénqíng/shénsè/liǎnsè* (facial expression), *liǎn/mǎnliǎn/*

Table 7.26 Significant collocates of *jǔsàng* in the CCL corpus

Introversion/extroversion	Modifier	Feeling	Others
gǎndào/gǎn 164/25	*hěn 106*	*shīwàng 41*	*lìng 135*
juéde/gǎnjué 41/12	*shífēn 66*	*tòngkǔ 24*	*lìngrén 63*
xīnlǐ/xīnzhōng 21/17	*fēicháng 55*	*fènnù 21*	*shì 118*
jīngshén 45	*wànfēn 23*	*juéwàng 18*	*shuō 168*
qíngxù 85	*jí/jíle 16/17*	*xiāochén 13*	*xiǎng 58*
xīnqíng 77	*jídù/jíwéi 11/11*	*yōuyù 13*	*shībài 30*
xiǎnde 25	*yīdiǎn/yǒudiǎn 13/11*	*bēiāi 13*	*xiāoxī 22*
shénqíng 95	*yǒuxiē/yīxiē 22/11*	*gūdú 12*	*yīzhèn 10*
shénsè 16		*shāngxīn 11*	
liǎnsè 14		*jiāolǜ 10*	
biǎoqíng 13			
liǎn/liǎnshàng 27/10			
mǎnliǎn 11			
shēngyīn 10			

liǎnshàng (face/full face/on the face), *shēngyīn* (voice). It can be modified by *hěn/ shífēn/fēicháng* (very), *wànfēn/jíle/jí/jídù/jíwéi* (extremely), *yīdiǎn/yǒudiǎn/ yīxiē/yǒuxiē* (a little). It often co-occurs with *shīwàng* (disappointment), *tòngkǔ* (auguish), *fènnù* (indignation), *juéwàng* (despair), *xiāochén* (low-spirited), *yōuyù* (melancholy), *bēiāi* (sorrow), *gūdú* (loneliness), *shāngxīn* (sadness), *jiāolǜ* (anxiety) and *bùān* (uneasiness). It also tends to co-occur with *lìng/lìngrén/ shǐ* (cause/make), *shuō* (say), *xiang* (think), *shībài* (failure), *xiāoxī* (news) and *yīzhèn* (lasting for a short time). *Shuō* and *xiǎng* seem to support the claim I made earlier that *jǔsàng* is both extroverted and introverted. *Shībài* is the main cause for *jǔsàng*. *Yīzhèn* (lasting for a short time) seems to suggest that *jǔsàng* might come suddenly and go quickly. It is an immediate reaction to what has just happened, such as failure. It is specific because it has a definite reason. It may affect somebody for a long time, depending on how serious it is, but, more often, it is a strong emotion that only lasts for a short time and fades away soon.

Yāyì

Yāyì is formed by two synonymous verbs: *yā* and *yì*, both meaning 'press down'. In XHCBL, it is glossed as:

对感情、力量等加以限制, 使不能充分流露或发挥 (of feelings, strength, etc.) constrain; inhibit; depress; hold back

This is only its definition as a verb and its sense as a feeling is not included in it. Its meaning as a feeling has become vivid in the CCL corpus and 2,581 hits of *yāyì* are found there. Its top collocates are given in Table 7.27. The *introversion* column in Table 7.27 reveals that *yāyì* is a word predominantly denoting an inner emotional state: *gǎndào/gǎn/gǎnjué/juéde* (feel), *gǎnqíng/qínggǎn* (feeling/ emotion), *xīnqíng* (frame of mind), *qíngxù* (mood), *nèixīn/xīnlǐ/xīnzhōng/xīntóu* (in the heart), *sīxiǎng* (thought) and *xīnlíng* (mind). The *modifier* column shows that it is often intensified by amplifiers, typically *yánzhòng* (severely), *fēicháng* (very), *jídù* (extremely), and mitigated by downtoners, predominantly *yīdiǎn/dài* (slightly). It co-occurs with other negative feelings like *chénzhòng* (heaviness), *tòngkǔ* (anguish), *kǔmèn* (gloominess), *chénmèn* (dreariness), *kǒngjù* (fear) and *jiāolǜ* (anxiety). The last column reveals that *yāyì* is closely related to one's life (*shēnghuó*) and society (*shèhuì*), and that it is semantically associated with *qìfēn* (atmosphere), *rénxìng* (human nature), *zìwǒ* (self), *gèxìng* (personality) and *xìnggé* (character). From its semantic association with *gèxìng* and *xìnggé*, we can argue that it has become a temperament that affects a person's way of thinking, feeling and behaving or part of the human nature. *Chángqī* (for a long time) and *yīzhí* (always/all the time) show that it is a state extended in time. In

Table 7.27 Significant collocates of *yāyì* in the CCL corpus

Introversion	Modifier	Feeling	Others
gǎndào/gǎn 140/84	*yánzhòng* 19	*chénzhòng* 44	*shèhuì* 51
gǎnjué/juéde 35/31	*jídù* 11	*tòngkǔ* 39	*shēnghuó* 43
gǎnqíng/qínggǎn 71/17	*fēicháng* 20	*fènnù* 31	*qìfēn* 40
xīnqíng 71	*dài* 11	*kǔmèn* 22	*rénxìng* 40
qíngxù 63	*yīdiǎn* 8	*chénmèn* 18	*zìwǒ* 39
nèixīn 68		*kǒngjù* 18	*gèxìng* 36
xīnlǐ/xīnzhōng 47/42		*jiāolǜ* 14	*xìnggé* 11
xīntóu 25			*yīzhí* 33
sīxiǎng 21			*chángqī* 47
xīnlíng 13			*niǔqū* 20
			shūfù 19
			bàofā 16

the modern society, people are usually chained (*shùfù*) by duties, customs or traditions. Their desires and impulses are suppressed, and life like this is distorted (*niǔqū*), but finally they might explode (*bàofā*). Therefore, *yāyì* is an unpleasant feeling when one is not satisfied with the present situation and wants to change it, but one cannot do so due to some constraints from society or somewhere else.

Qíngxù dīluò

Qíngxù dīluò literally means '*qíngxù* (mood) is low'. Chinese conceptualizes that, if one feels low-spirited, one's *qíngxù* will get lower. It occurs 252 times in the CCL corpus. The corpus data shows that it often collocates with *jīngshén*/mental (13), *yīn*/because (13), *kùnnán*/difficulty (7), *gǎndào*/feel (5), *yàngzi*/appearance (5), *jǔsàng*/dejected (5) and *yìyù* (depressed). Its collocates tell us that *qíngxù dīluò* is usually caused by difficulty. It is a word describing one's mood, so it is experienced more as an inner emotional state, as shown in *jīngshén* and *gǎndào*. However, it also collocates with *yàngzi*, which seems to suggest that one tends to have some outwardly manifested behaviour or facial expressions when one is *qíngxù dīluò*. It is a mild word to describe a person's sadness, disappointment and frustration. *Kùnnán* is the usual and typical cause for the lowering of one's *qíngxù*. Sometimes, a failure or setback will also lead to *qíngxù dīluò*, but usually the consequence will be more serious than that.

Yìyù

As mentioned in Section 6.1.3, the parallel corpus used for this research is not a contemporary one, which cannot reflect the recent linguistic change. Hence, the researcher's intuition should come into play in identifying the closest equivalent in the other language. For *depression*, there is a modern translation equivalent—*yìyù* or *yìyùzhèng* (medical condition). *Yìyù* is formed by two words: *yì* (press down) and *yù*. The XHCBL's glosses for *yù* and *yìyù* are given as follows:

> *yù*: (忧愁、气愤等) 在心里积聚不得发泄 [(of sorrow, anger etc.) accumulate in the heart, but cannot release] (of sorrow, anger, etc.) pent-up; gloomy; depressed

> *yìyù*: 心有愤恨, 不能诉说而烦闷 [People will feel annoyed if they cannot reveal their feelings to others when they bear resentment towards something] depressed; despondent; gloomy

The real meaning of *yìyù* is far more than is defined in this dictionary. It is a quite modern concept, which has been coined to refer to a very serious unhealthy state that affects a person's normal life, including behaviour, thinking or feeling. It can be said to be a very strong version of *depression* in the sense of 'feeling sad or unhappy'. In practice, *yìyù* is also used to talk about one's intense feeling of sadness. The collocates from the CCL corpus can help capture its semantic subtleties. In the corpus, 778 hits of *yìyù* are found and its top collocates are shown in Table 7.28. What is revealed from the first column in Table 7.28 is that *yìyù* collocates predominantly with words of introversion, such as *jīngshén* (mental), *qíngxù* (mood), *xīnqíng* (frame of mind), *gǎndào* (feel) and *xīnzhōng/xīnlǐ* (in the heart). However, it also has physical manifestations, like *shénqíng* (facial expression). The negative feelings it co-occurs with include *jiāolǜ* (anxious), *zào/fánzào* (agitated), *búkuài* (unhappy), *gūdú* (lonely), *jǐnzhāng* (nervous), *tòngkǔ* (anguished), *xiāochén* (low-spirited), *bēiguān* (pessimistic), *kǔmèn* (gloomy) and *bēishāng* (sorrowful). Among them, *jiāolǜ* and *zào/fánzào* stand out, suggesting that *yìyù* is mainly caused by anxiety and agitation. The last column lists its other collocates, which may contribute to unravelling its meaning. *Huànzhě/bìngrén* (patient), *huàn* (contract/suffer from), *zhìliáo* (treatment), *zhèngzhuàng* (symptom) and *jíbìng* (disease) are all related to its sense as a medical condition. *Shénjīng* (nerve) might suggest that *yìyùzhèng* is to do with a nerve problem. *Shīmián* (insomnia) is one of its main symptoms. *Yìyù* may lead to *sǐ* (death), usually by *zìshā* (commit suicide). The

Table 7.28 Significant collocates of *yìyù* in the CCL corpus

Introversion/extroversion	Feeling	Others
jīngshén 68	*jiāolǜ 33*	*huànzhě/huàn 23/23*
qíngxù 57	*zào/fánzào 13/13*	*zhìliáo 17*
xīnqíng 52	*búkuài 13*	*zhèngzhuàng 16*
gǎndào 14	*gūdú 12*	*bìngrén 10*
xīnzhōng/xīnlǐ 10/9	*jǐnzhāng 10*	*jíbìng 10*
shénqíng 13	*tòngkǔ 9*	*shénjīng 10*
	xiāochén 8	*shīmián 9*
	bēiguān 7	*sǐ 17*
	kǔmèn 7	*zìshā 12*
	bēishāng 7	

following paraphrase from the CCL seems to be a very good summary of this emotion:

(121) 抑郁是一种过度忧愁和伤感的情绪体验，一般表现为情绪低落，心境悲观 ...

'*Yìyù* is an emotional experience of excessive worry and sadness, characterized by a low mood and pessimism' ...

Yōuyù

Yōuyù is a combination of *yōu* (worry) and *yù*, which was discussed in the last sub-section. XHCBL glosses it as follows:

忧伤, 愁闷 [worry + sadness, worry + closed] melancholy; heavyhearted; dejected

Yōuyù occurs 2,288 times in the CCL corpus and its top collocates are presented in Table 7.29.

Table 7.29 Significant collocates of *yōuyù* in the CCL corpus

Introversion/extroversion	Modifier	Feeling	Others
xīnqíng 78	*hěn 83*	*gūdú/gūjì 28/8*	*zhèng 150*
qíngxù 38	*fēicháng 23*	*jìmò 13*	*bìng 29*
jīngshén 37	*shífēn 17*	*tòngkǔ 25*	*huàn 44*
xīnzhōng 15	*lüèdài 19*	*bēishāng 21*	*huànzhě 16*
gǎndào/gǎnjué 45/15	*xiē/yǒuxiē 17/19*	*bēiāi 16*	*zìjǐ 51*
gǎn 21	*diǎn 31*	*shānggǎn 20*	*chénmò 25*
liǎnshàng/liǎn 33/26	*yīdiǎn 14*	*fánnǎo 13*	*chénsī 24*
liǎnsè/shénsè 25/20	*dàndàn de 18*	*jǔsàng 13*	*cāngbái 22*
shénqíng 74	*sī 17*	*kǒngjù 12*	*sǐ 20*
biǎoqíng 25		*juéwàng 12*	*qìzhì 9*
yǎnjing 77		*jiāolǜ 12*	*xìnggé 16*
mùguāng/yǎnshén 37/37		*chóuchàng 11*	*xiào/wēixiào 20/18*
xiǎnde 27		*xiāochén 11*	*měilì 14*
liúlù 19		*kǔmèn 14*	*làngmàn 9*
lòuchū 18		*chénmèn 13*	*wángzǐ 9*
shēngyīn 21			*wēnróu 9*
			chōngmǎn 30

The first column in Table 7.29 shows that *yōuyù* is both introverted, as revealed in its collocates related to introversion, characteristically *xīnqíng* (frame of mind), *qíngxù* (mood), *jīngshén* (mental), *xīnzhōng* (in the heart) and *gǎndào/gǎn/gǎnjué* (feel), and extroverted, as indicated in its following collocates: *liǎnshàng/liǎn* (on the face/face), *liǎnsè/shénsè/shénqíng/biǎoqíng* (facial expression), *yǎnjing* (eyes), *mùguāng/yǎnshén* (expressions in one's eyes), *xiǎnde* (appear), *liúlù/lòuchū* (reveal), *shēngyīn* (voice). The second column lists its modifiers: *hěn/fēicháng/shífēn* (very), *lüèdài/yǒuxiē/xiē/diǎn/yīdiǎn* (a bit/slightly), *dàndàn de* (faint) and *sī* (a minute quantity). The negative feelings it often co-occurs with include *gūdú/gūjì/jìmò* (loneliness), *tòngkǔ* (anguish), *bēishāng/bēiāi* (sorrow), *fánnǎo* (vexation), *jǔsàng* (dejection), *kǒngjù* (fear), *juéwàng* (desperation), *jiāolü* (anxiety), *shānggǎn/chóuchàng* (sentimentality), *xiāochén* (low-spiritedness), *kǔmèn* (gloom) and *chénmèn* (dreariness). For the last column, *zhèng/bìng* (disease), *huàn* (contract) and *huànzhě* (patient) clearly show that *yōuyù* is also associated with an unhealthy condition. *Zìjǐ* (33 + 18) co-occurs with *yōuyù* 51 times, which seems to suggest that *yōuyù* is something one bears alone. *Chénmò* (silence) and *chénsī* (contemplation) reveal that *yōuyù* is associated with quietness. *Cāngbái* (pale) might mean that *yōuyù* is related to a pale face. *Yōuyù* may also lead to death (*sǐ*) if it is a serious condition that needs medical treatment. It is more an emotional state closely related to the less active attitude towards life and the world, slightly fatalistic. A *yōuyù* person may be resigned to an unpleasant situation or fact and think s/he cannot change the situation, and therefore there is no point in trying. *Yōuyù* might be the basic nature and is shown in the way in which one reacts to situations or other people, so it is often linked with *xìnggé* (character) or *qìzhì* (temperament). Look at the following examples in which *yōuyù* as a temperament or character is mentioned:

(122) 不知道你自己发现没有, 你的气质里有一种忧郁 (*yōuyù*) 的东西。我 喜欢 忧郁 (*yōuyù*), 我这个人也常常忧郁 (*yōuyù*)

  'I don't know whether you've found that there is a vein of *melancholy* in your **temperament**. I like *melancholy* and I often feel *melancholy*.'

(123) 从幼小时就失去了家庭的温暖, 一生穷愁潦倒, 形成了他忧郁 (*yōuyù*) 孤独、愤世嫉俗和敏感的个性

  'He has lost the warmth from family and been very poor since he was very young, which helped to form his **melancholy**, lonely, cynical and sensitive **character**.'

Yōuyù is often semantically associated with *xiào/wēixiào* (smile), *měilì* (beautiful), *làngmàn* (romantic), *wēnróu* (gentle) and *wángzǐ* (prince), suggesting that sometimes it is totally positive. Consider the following examples:

(124) '好啊,' 他还是忧郁 (*yōuyù*) 地   笑笑

'"Ok," he gave a *melancholy* smile.'

(125) 而最漂亮的还是她那双忧郁 (*yōuyù*) 的嫣然动人的眼睛

'What is the most beautiful is her *melancholy* and enchanting eyes.'

In the above examples, *yōuyù* co-occurs with 'good' words, such as *smile* in Example (124) and *enchanting eyes* in Example (125). Like *yōushāng*, the reason why *yōuyù* is less negative is probably because it contains the character *yōu*, a concept closely associated with intellectuals who were so intelligent and knowledgeable that they could foresee what would happen to the people and country in the future, usually something bad. They were not happy about enjoying the temporarily peaceful life, but were always worried about the future of the country. Therefore, *yōu* was a Chinese concept correlated with knowledge, wisdom, thinking, farsightedness and worry. Its positive flavour still remains in some Modern Chinese words, of which *yōuyù* is one. A degree of *yōuyù* is seen as an indicaton of a person's depth.

Chōngmǎn (be filled with) is a typical verb that is used to describe *yōuyù*, as well as many other emotions. This is similar to the description of English emotions. In English, if you are filled with an emotion, or if it fills you, you feel it very strongly. We can say someone is filled with *admiration/joy/ happiness/horror/fear/anger/doubt/remorse*, etc. Therefore, Chinese and English are quite similar in the way emotions are conceived of, but they differ in specific conceptualizations. For example, in Chinese, *chōngmǎn* is only related to some emotions, not all. As discussed earlier in Section 7.1.1, in Chinese, we use *chénjìn* (be immersed into) to describe *bēitòng* with great intensity and we never use *chōngmǎn* to describe *gāoxìng* (delight) or *shēngqì* (annoyance). Sometimes, we need to add some other words to express the idea, such as 'chōngmǎn jìngpèi zhī qíng' (be filled with admiration), where *zhī* (particle, used between attribute and head) and *qíng* (feeling) are added to make the expression more like Chinese. Therefore, it seems that, even if the two languages are similar in the metaphorical mapping between the source domain and the target domain, they differ in specific linguistic manifestations/ expressions and details. We will return to the metaphorical issue in detail in Section 7.2.

Shānggǎn

For *shānggǎn*, XHCBL offers the following:

因感触而悲伤 [feel sad due to emotional stirrings] sentimental; sick at heart: 对景思人, 无限伤感。 Feel extremely sorrowful to see the sight and think of one's people

Shānggǎn is a specific kind of sadness particularly when you see the same place and find that the people you are close to do not stay there any longer. Things will change with time, but people tend to mourn those that used to exist. Hence, *shānggǎn* is the sadness brought about by emotional stirrings. In the CCL corpus, 1,240 hits of *shānggǎn* are found and its top collocates are shown in Table 7.30.

Table 7.30 Significant collocates of *shānggǎn* in the CCL corpus

Introversion/extrovsion	Modifier	Feeling	Others
qíngxù 41	*hěn 63*	*yōuyù 21*	*zìjǐ 34*
xīnzhōng 18	*shífēn 23*	*tóngqíng 9*	*chōngmǎn 19*
gǎndào/juéde 16/14	*fēicháng 15*	*gūdú 7*	*lìng/shǐ/jiào 39/39/12*
shēngyīn 12	*xiē/yǒuxiē 38/25*	*bēi 7*	*yīnwèi 30*
yǎnjing 10	*yīxiē 11*		*yǐnqǐ 16*
yàngzi 10	*diǎn 23*		*xiǎng 41*
shénqíng 8	*dài/lüèdài 37/13*		*qǐlái 24*
liúlù 10	*sī 10*		*biàn 19*
kàn 31			*zuòpǐn 14*
			huáijiù 12
			gùshì 11
			huíyì 11

In Table 7.30, we find *qíngxù* (mood), *xīnzhōng* (in the heart) and *gǎndào/juéde* (feel), showing that *shānggǎn* is an emotion experienced as an inner state; we also find *shēngyīn* (voice), *yǎnjing* (eyes), *shénqíng* (facial expression), *yàngzi* (appearance), *liúlù* (reveal), *kàn* (see), suggesting that *shānggǎn* is easily visible and perceivable. We also find that its modifiers include *hěn/shífēn/fēicháng* (very), *xiē/yǒuxiē/yīxiē/diǎn/dài/lüèdài* (slightly/a little) and *sī* (a minute quantity). It often co-occurs with *yōuyù* (melancholy), *tóngqíng* (sympathetic), *gūdú* (lonely) and *bēi* (sad). Of them, *yōuyù* is the salient one that shares a lot in common with *shānggǎn* in the sense that both are associated with people who are easily affected by sadness. For the last column, *chōngmǎn* suggests that, like many other emotions, *shānggǎn* is also conceptualized and understood in terms of gas or liquid. *Zìjǐ* seems to suggest that *shānggǎn* is a feeling often confined to oneself. Things that can arouse a feeling of *shānggǎn* include *zuòpǐn* (work of art), *gùshì* (story) and *huíyì* (memory). From *lìng/shǐ/jiào* (cause/make), *yīnwèi* (because) and *yǐnqǐ* (give rise to), it can be seen that *shānggǎn* is definitely triggered by something. *Qǐlái* (used after a verb or adjective to indicate the beginning or continuation of an action) and *biàn* (thus/so) show that *shānggǎn* is caused by something that has just happened. *Xiǎng* (think) shows that *shānggǎn* is often the outcome of thinking of something. It is associated with *huáijiù* (nostalgic) because one feels affectionately about the experiences one had in the past. Actually, *shānggǎn* is a feeling someone will have when s/he thinks of something worth recalling but gone. S/he wants to have it again or wants to change it back to its original condition, but s/he feels so helpless. Like *bēishāng*, *shānggǎn* is also a concept associated with the fatalistic view, characterized by a sense of powerlessness due to the laws of nature and society.

Comparison

So far, we have discussed, in great detail, *depressed** & *melancholy** and their Chinese equivalents. It seems that *depressed* has a wider range, covering the Chinese words *yìyù*, *jǔsàng*, *yāyì* and *qíngxù dīluò*. Of course, strictly speaking, *qíngxù dīluò* is not a word but a phrase into which modifying elements, like *fēicháng/shífēn* (very), can be inserted. This phrase is similar to *low-spirited* in the sense that both are conceptualized in terms of DOWN. *Depressed* can be preceded by modifiers indicating various degrees, showing that it has a broad semantic coverage. Among its Chinese translation equivalents, *qíngxù dīluò* is the least intense and *yìyù* the most. *Jǔsàng* and *yāyì* emphasize different aspects respectively. The former focuses on disappointment, frustration and hopelessness and the latter on the difficulty or impossibility of untying the knots and the incompetence to release one's sad feelings. *Depressed* and *yìyù* correspond to each other in the sense that they both denote a serious emotional state of sadness and a medical condition. The same applies to *melancholy* and *yōuyù*. Both *yōuyùzhèng* and *yìyùzhèng* can refer to a medical condition and may be preferred by different groups of people. *Yìyùzhèng* seems to be more formal, more academic and therefore occurs more frequently. Although OALECD relates *melancholy* to both *yōuyù* and *yìyù*, I would argue that *melancholy* is closer to *yōuyù* because they are both associated with a temperament or character, lasting long and sometimes can be used with a positive flavour. However, *yōuyù* is even more positive because it is a temperament admired and sought by many people. *Shānggǎn* is similar to *melancholy* in that a *shānggǎn de* person is also easily affected by emotions such as sadness. S/he tends to feel sad when s/he sees or thinks of something, which often seems incomprehensible to other people. It is quite close to *melancholy* in 'feeling of sadness for no particular reason'.

7.1.8 *Dejected*, disheartened* & despondent** and their Chinese equivalents

This section will look at *dejected*, disheartened*, despondent** and their Chinese near-equivalents.

Dejected, disheartened* & despondent**
Dejected*

Let us start with *dejected*, for which the dictionaries provide the following:

LDCE: unhappy, disappointed, or sad

OALECD: depressed; sad 沮丧的; 垂头丧气的; 情绪低落的; 郁郁不乐的

COBUILD: If you are *dejected*, you feel miserable or unhappy, especially because you have just been disappointed by something.

The dictionaries use 'unhappy', 'sad', 'depressed', 'disappointed', 'miserable' to define *dejected*. OALECD uses four words, three of which are four-character words, to express its meaning: *jǔsàng de, chuítóusàngqì de, qíngxù dīluò de, yùyùbúlè de*, in which the last one seems to be far from the semantic core of *dejected* and instead closer to *gloomy*. No entry of *deject* is found in the three dictionaries. The BOE generates only 226 hits of *deject* (v). A simple glance at its concordance reveals that in most cases it is used in the -*ed* form. So I just search for the form of *dejected*, regardless of word class tag. Six hundred hits of *dejected* are found in the corpus. Its top 50 collocates show that it colligates with the article-determiners *a (92), the (45)*, link verbs, predominantly *be (32), look (32), feel (11)*, verbs, like *sit (4), stand (3), leave (3)*, nouns, such as *face (4), tone (3)*, and prepositions, mainly *about (6), over (3)*. Its more frequent occurrence with *be* and *look* than with *feel* seems to suggest that *dejected* is more extroverted than introverted. In other words, it is more associated with an outward manifestation than an internal state. Its intensifiers cover a wide range of degree and include *very (12), utterly (7), totally (6), rather (5), little (5), somewhat (3), quite (3)*.

One hundred and seven hits of *dejectedly* are found in the corpus and its top 50 collocates show that the actions which are often done in a *dejected* manner include *say (12), sit (10), walk (8), stand (4)*, etc., showing that a *dejected* emotion is often manifested outwardly. In its top collocates, we do not find any verb that is related to an inner thought or a feeling, which further supports my earlier claim that *dejected* is more characterized by extroversion.

For *dejection*, I find the following in OALECD and COBUILD:

OALECD: sad or dejected state; depression 忧郁; 沮丧; 情绪低落

COBUILD: *Dejection* is a feeling of sadness that you get, for example, when you have just been disappointed by something.

As can be seen from the above definitions, the two dictionaries use the same words as for its stem to define or explain *dejection*, such as *sadness, depression* and *disappointed*, therefore telling us nothing more about its meaning. Turning to its corpus data, 139 hits of *dejection* are found in the BOE. From its top collocates, it can be seen that *dejection* has colligations with prepositions, predominantly *of (33), in (21), into (4)*, modifiers, typically *utter (5), deep (4)*, and possessive adjectives, like *his (4), her (4)*. From its word sketch, I cannot find any word that contributes significantly to its meaning due to its low frequency. So I choose not to make a claim about it. This is why I emphasize again and again throughout the book that a large corpus is needed to retrieve reliable and useful data.

Disheartened*

Now let us move on to look at the *dishearten* family. Of the three dictionaries used for this research, only OALECD includes an entry for *dishearten*:

cause (sb) to lose hope or confidence 使 (某人) 失去希望或信心; 使 (某人) 灰心

However, the other two dictionaries offer an entry for *disheartened*, rather than *dishearten*:

LDCE: *formal* disappointed, so that you lose hope and the determination to continue doing something

COBUILD: If you are *disheartened*, you feel disappointed about something and have less confidence or less hope about it than you did before. = discouraged

According to OALECD and LDCE, *disheartened* is characterized by disappointment and losing hope or confidence. However, COBUILD has a mild explanation, i.e. 'disappointed about something and have less confidence or less hope about it than you did it before', thus synonymous with 'discouraged'. Which definition is more adequate? I turn to the BOE, where all forms of *dishearten* are tagged as a verb. Only 718 instances of *dishearten* (v), including *disheartened* and *disheartening*, occur in the corpus. Its top 50 collocates reveal that *be (529)* tops the list, showing that in most cases *dishearten* is used in the participle form, either *disheartening* or *disheartened*. After inspecting the corpus, I find that *dishearten*, mostly in its participle form, colligates mainly with *get* and *feel*, suggesting that *disheartened* is predominantly inward. From the word sketch for *dishearten* (as a lemma), it can be seen that getting *disheartened* is most frequently caused by *drop (5), lack (3), defeat (3), criticism (2)* and *failure (2)*. The collocates listed in the 'and/or' pattern include *frustrate (4), disillusion (2), discourage (2), stun (2), confuse (2), shock (2)* and *disappoint (2)*, suggesting that feeling *disheartened* is triggered by something that has just happened and it is often related to unexpectedness as well. Further, *disheartened* has a broad range of modifiers: *very (31), rather (7), somewhat (6), pretty (5), extremely (4), especially (4), particularly (4), terribly (3), completely (3), totally (2), utterly (2), deeply (2)* and *profoundly (2)*. They can be reorganized according to its degree of losing hope or confidence as follows (in roughly ascending order): *somewhat, pretty, rather, very, especially/particularly, deeply, terribly, completely, utterly*. We may therefore argue that COBUILD's definition for *dishearten* 'disappointed about something and have less confidence or less hope about it than you did before' is closer to its meaning.

The only five instances of *dishearteningly* from the corpus are presented in Figure 7.5.

The concordance lines in Figure 7.5 seem to suggest that *dishearteningly* usually co-occurs with words with a negative connotation, like *elusive, low, difficult, ineffectual*, thus acquiring a negative semantic prosody. It seems that it is still an adverb indicating an emotional manner.

Frontier House (Channel 4, Sundays at 8pm).	**Dishearteningly**	, this is an American show (PBS) inspired
of her passing. Those traces were anyway	**dishearteningly**	elusive. After viewing the exterior (as
I think I sensed a great deal more-more	**dishearteningly**	than Papa did-how ineffectual we really
conviction of batterers until recently was	**dishearteningly**	low. <p/> There are simple solutions to
search for a bone-marrow-transplant donor	**dishearteningly**	difficult, Rob Howard says. So the family

Figure 7.5 Concordance listing of *dishearteningly*

Despondent*

This sub-section will explore the *despondent* family. No entry of *despond* is found in the three dictionaries. It occurs only 40 times in the BOE, so we will focus on *despondent*, for which the dictionaries say:

> LDCE: [Language: Latin; Origin: despondere *'to give up, lose hope'*, from spondere *'to promise'*] extremely unhappy and without hope

> OALECD: (about sth) having or showing loss of hope; wretched 失望的; 沮丧的; 消沉的; 苦恼的

> COBUILD: If you are *despondent*, you are very unhappy because you have been experiencing difficulties that you think you will not be able to overcome.

LDCE says that *despondent* originates from the Latin word '*despondere*', meaning 'to give up, lose hope', and implies 'extremely unhappy and without hope'. OALECD claims *despondent* means 'having and showing loss of hope'. Like the definition for *disheartened*, COBUILD's explanation for *disheartened* is also milder than the other two: 'If you are *despondent*, you are very unhappy because you have been experiencing difficulties that you think you will not be able to overcome'.

Turning to its corpus data (578 hits), its top collocates show that its colligational properties include link verbs, typically *be (103)*, *become (19)*, *feel (22)*, *look (15)*, *get (9)*, *grow (5)*, *seem (5)*, and prepositions, particularly *over (33)*, *about (29)*, *at (16)*. Its collocation with *feel*, *look* and *seem* seems to show that *despondent* is both outward and inward. In other words, it is both realized as an emotion involving external manifestations and mentally experienced as an internal emotional state. For its premodifiers, its word sketch shows the following: *increasingly (12)*, *irrationally (2)*, *thoroughly (2)*, *deeply (2)*, *totally (2)*, *apparently (2)*, *somewhat (2)*. From the above premodifiers, it can be seen that *despondent* is a serious emotional state that might be undergoing a gradual process since it is frequently modified by *increasingly*, which modifies neither *dejected* nor *disheartened*. Its co-occurring negative feelings in the 'and/or' pattern include *angry (6)*, *depressed (3)*, *desperate (3)*, *frightened (3)*, etc. *Angry* seems to suggest that *despondent* is not a totally passive feeling accepting peacefully the unpleasant reality. We will return to this later when we discuss its Chinese equivalents.

The BOE contains 84 occurrences of *despondently* and a randomly selected list of concordance lines is presented in Figure 7.6.

earth can I fight that?' Michelle pointed	*despondently*	at the television screen, which was showing
could not remember what it was. He looked	*despondently*	up at the window, which seemed large and
favour. 'I'll co-operate,' Toure replied	*despondently*	. 'What do you want to know?' Philpott
be dodging the flak, buddy,' Graham said	*despondently*	. 'We've blown our one real chance of
moved to the edge of the clearing and stared	*despondently*	at the twisted remains of the Audi which
was no longer working. So, somewhat	*despondently*	, we journeyed to Aberdaron, the nearest
getting through them,' Andrei summed up	*despondently*	. <*p/*> 'Why not?' Ilmari, the only one who
can tell me what to do?' the girl thought	*despondently*	as she exchanged her house-shoes for
'But I'll never do it,' she told herself	*despondently*	. 'I think of such mad things to do and
in the darkness of the rutted track. <*p/*>	*Despondently*	he started the car. <*p/*> His clothing was
moved, swung, wavered and then dipped,	*despondently*	. The head behind them drooped.
. In a corner the television set blinked	*despondently*	without a sound. The blinds were down and
and no mistake,' said Sam Gamgee. He stood	*despondently*	with hunched shoulders beside Frodo, and
tide overtakes you. Farewell!' <*p/*> And so	*despondently*	Merry now stood and watched the
Why had she ruined herself, Trudie thought	*despondently*	, as though finally coming out of a stupor
life. What's the good of it, he thought	*despondently*	, what's the point? Even if I win against
hoping it was Bunner, but Lucci's voice said	*despondently*	, 'Meers did it, Dave. He met the press
How did last night go?' ''kay,' said Holly	*despondently*	. 'What's wrong?' demanded Joan.
eleven, she'd realised he wasn't coming.	*Despondently*	, she switched off the TV, blew out the

Figure 7.6 Concordance listing of *despondently*

From the concordance listing in Figure 7.6, we can find 'pointed', 'looked', 'replied', 'said', 'stared', 'told', 'stood', etc., showing that *despondently* is still a pure adverb indicating an emotional manner, unlike many emotional adverbs, which have undergone or are undergoing the 'delexicalization' process.

OALECD defines *despondency* as 'loss of hope or misery ((泄气; 沮丧; 失望; 苦恼)'. The observation of its corpus data reveals that *despondency* (302 hits) has colligations with prepositions, particularly *of (65), among (10), into (9), about (9), by (9), with (8)*, and possessive adjectives, like *his (8), her (5)*. Its word sketch tells us that *despondency* collocates with negative feelings, such as *gloom (17), despair (9), apathy (2), sadness (2)* and *helplessness (2)*. Its frequent co-occurrences with *gloom* and *despair* show that *despondency* is more a feeling focusing on what is going to happen in future rather than an emotional reaction to what has happened.

Chinese equivalents of dejected*, disheartened* & despondent*

The BPC contains only six instances of *dishearten**, which are all shown below:

(126) 她只觉得寒冷、**沮丧** (*jǔsàng*) 和绝望。
　　　She was chilled and **disheartened** and desperate.

(127) 他仍旧愁眉不展，**灰心丧气** (*huīxīnsàngqì*)。
　　　He was still gloomy and **disheartened**.

(128) 傍晚, 当她精疲力竭**垂头丧气** (*chuítóusàngqì*) 地回到家时, 她发现杜洛埃来过了。

When she arrived at the house at the end of the day, weary and
disheartened, she discovered that Drouet had been there.

(129) 每当她发现他的知识那样丰富, 她心中的见解又是那样浅薄的时候,
要是同他的像安地斯山一样的智力相比, 她就不禁自惭形秽, **心灰意
冷** (*xīnhuīyìlěng*), 再也不愿作任何努力了。

As such she compared him with herself; and at every discovery of the
abundance of his illuminations, and the unmeasurable, Andean altitude
of his, she became quite ***dejected***, ***disheartened*** from all further effort on
her own part whatever.

(130) 他 毁谤亡人, 以谰言玷污其美名, 用这种下流手段来达到政治上的
成功, 使有道德之人甚为沮丧 (*jǔsàng*)。

It is ***disheartening*** to virtuous men to see such shameful means resorted
to achieve political success as the attacking of the dead in their graves
and defiling their honoured names with slander.

(131) 那些经过烟熏火燎的房基是黑糊糊的烟囱 (如今叫做谢尔曼的哨兵)
令人失望 (*lìng rén shīwàng*) 地不断出现。

Smoked foundations and the lonesome blackened chimneys, now
known as 'Sherman's Sentinels,' appeared with ***disheartening*** frequency.

All the Chinese words used to translate *dishearten** are marked in bold: *jǔsàng*
(2), *huīxīnsàngqì (1)*, *chuítóusàngqì (1)*, *xīnhuīyìlěng (1)* and *lìng rén shīwàng (1)*.
We have discussed *jǔsàng* earlier. *Lìng rén shīwàng* is an interpretative translation,
meaning 'disappointing'. We will skip this word and focus on the other three.
*Despondent** occurs 16 times in the parallel corpus. Among them, five instances
are translated as (*lìngrén*) *jǔsàng* and two as *chuítóusàngqì*. Fifteen occurrences
of *deject** are found in the BPC. Of them, five hits are translated as *jǔsàng* and
three hits as *chuítóusàngqì*. Taking all of them into consideration, we will examine
chuítóusàngqì, *huīxīnsàngqì*, *xīnhuīyìlěng*, *sàngqì* and *huīxīn*. *Huīxīnsàngqì* and
chuítóusàngqì both consist of *sàngqì*, thus they are quite similar. *Sàngqì* and
huīxīn are very important Chinese concepts that constitute *chuítóusàngqì*,
huīxīnsàngqì and *xīnhuīyìlěng*.

Sàngqì

Sàngqì is glossed as '因事情不顺利而情绪低落 [mood is low because things
have not proceeded smoothly] downhearted; dejected; crestfallen' in the XHCBL.
It is a verb-object structure formed by *sàng* (lose) and *qì* (gas). *Qì* is a Chinese-
specific notion from the traditional Chinese medicine. It refers to *néngliàng*
(energy) that exists in the form of gas that flows through the body. If a person

has less *qì*, s/he will be less energetic. It has developed many senses, such as spirits/morale/vigour, so *sàngqì* means 'losing vigour or spirits'. The CCL corpus contains 904 occurrences of *sàngqì*, out of which 493 hits come from *chuítóusàngqì* and 170 from *huīxīnsàngqì*. Only in 241 hits does it occur on its own or as a constituent of another phrase, like *lìng rén sàngqì (10)*. *Sàngqì* co-occurs with *juéwàng*/despair (11), *cuòzhé*/setback (9), *shībài*/failure (8) and *kùnnán*/difficulty (7). It may be argued that the latter three are the main causes for *sàngqì*. It seems that *sàngqì* is, for the most part, caused by the loss of or less confidence, enthusiasm and determination to go on doing something due to setbacks, failure and difficulties. Hence, it is an emotional reaction to what has happened, similar to *dejected* in this sense. *Sàngqì* is found to collocate with *juéde*/feel (10), *xiǎnde*/ appear (11), *shénqíng*/facial expression (6), *xīnlǐ*/in the heart (7). Eighteen occurrences of *sàngqì de yàngzi* (appearance) and nine instances of *shuō* (say) *sàngqì huà* (words) are found in the corpus. These all suggest that *sàngqì* is characterized by both extroversion and introversion.

Chuítóusàngqì

Chuítóusàngqì is a phrase formed by two words: *chuítóu* (with one's head drooped) + *sàngqì*. Therefore, we can claim that it is an expression mainly describing someone's outward manifestation when s/he feels *dejected*. It occurs 492 times in the CCL corpus. Its top collocates include *shuō*/say (42), *yàngzi*/ appearance (17), *kàn*/look (14), *xiǎnde*/appear (9), *shénqíng*/facial expression (6), *yīnwèi*/because (9) and *biàn*/thus (8), etc. *Shuō, yàngzi, kàn, xiǎnde* all clearly show that *chuítóusàngqì* is predominantly used to describe the external manifestations when s/he is *dejected*. It co-occurrence with *yīnwèi* (because) and *biàn* (thus) shows that *chuítóusàngqì* has a clear reason for this feeling.

Huīxīn

Another similar fixed expression is *huīxīnsàngqì*. Before discussing *huīxīnsàngqì*, let us look at *huīxīn*, which literally means 'grey heart'. In the Chinese culture, 'a grey heart' is conceptualized as the feeling of 'discouraged' or 'losing heart'. *Huīxīn* occurs 685 times in the CCL corpus and its top collocates are given in Table 7.31.

The first column in Table 7.31 gives the collocates that are related to its extroversion or introversion. It can be seen that introversion dominates the picture, as shown in *gǎndào*/*juéde* (feel), *qíngxù* (mood). *Shuō* (say) also occurs frequently with *huīxīn*, but it is not a typical verb characterizing extroversion in

Table 7.31 Significant collocates of *huīxīn* in the CCL corpus

Introvertion/extrovertion	Modifier	Feeling	Others
gǎndào 35	*hěn 28*	*shīwàng 45*	*shǐ 44*
juéde 11	*wánquán 6*	*juéwàng 20*	*lìng 14*
qíngxù 8	*yīdiǎn/diǎn 10/15*	*qìněi 15*	*ràng 12*
shuō 33	*yǒuxiē 5*	*jǔsàng 8*	*shībài 15*
		shāngxīn 5	*cuòzhé 15*
		xiāochén 5	*kùnnán 14*
		shīyì 5	*yīnwèi/yīn 12/12*
			xīwàng 8
			fàngqì 7

comparison to other apparent extroversion-verbs like *look, appear*, etc. It is usually preceded by *hěn* (very), *wánquán* (totally), *yīdiǎn/diǎn* (a bit), *yǒuxiē* (slightly), which shows that it is not a very intense emotional state because its modifiers display various degrees. The feelings it co-occurs with include *shīwàng* (disappointed), *juéwàng* (desperate), *qìněi* (discouraged), *jǔsàng* (dejected), *shāngxīn* (sad), *xiāochén* (low-spirited), *shīyì* (frustrated), etc. Its frequent causative collocates, such as *shǐ/lìng/ràng* (make), show that it strongly colligates with causative patterns. Its other significant collocates include *shībài* (failure), *cuòzhé* (setback), *kùnnán* (difficulty), *yīnwèi/yīn* (because), *xīwàng* (hope), *fàngqì* (give up), etc., suggesting that *huīxīn* is frequently caused by failure, setback, difficulty and less or loss of hope. The act of giving up might be the result of *huīxīn*. *Yīnwèi/yīn* appears to show that *huīxīn* has a clear reason and therefore is quite specific. *Huīxīn* is an emotional reaction to what has happened, which directly leads to one's less or loss of confidence about what one is going to do, so it is a feeling relating the past to the future. It is more inward, as compared with the more outward emotion *sàngqì*. It is close to *disheartened* in the above respects.

Huīxīnsàngqì

The CCL corpus generates 170 hits of *huīxīnsàngqì*, which often co-occurs with *shǐ*/make (17), *lìng*/cause (5), *gǎndào*/feel (12), *shuō*/say (9), *kùnnán*/difficulty (7), *cuòzhé*/setback (6), *shībài*/failure (5), *qíngxù*/mood (5), etc. From its collocates *gǎndào* and *qíngxù*, we can see that, in comparison to *chuítóusàngqì*, it is more experienced as an inner state. It is also mainly caused by *kùnnán*, *cuòzhé* and *shībài*.

Xīnhuīyìlěng

The last word I am going to discuss in this section is *xīnhuīyìlěng*, which is formed by *xīnhui*, an inverted form of *huīxīn*, and *yìlěng* (intention-cold), literally meaning 'one's desire is cold'. We can see that sadness in Chinese can also be conceptualized in terms of colour and temperature. The CCL corpus contains 226 occurrences of *xīnhuīyìlěng*, which co-occurs with *xiǎng*/think (12), *shēnghuó*/life (9), *gǎndào*/feel (7), *xiāochén*/low-spirited (6), *biàn*/thus (6), *xīwàng*/hope (5) and *yǒuxiē*/a bit (5), etc. From its constituent *xīnhuī* and its collocates *gǎndào*, *xiǎng*, *xiāochén*, it can be inferred that it is a word focusing on the inner emotional state. Another salient feature is that, like *xīnsuì*, it noticeably colligates with causative constructions, as shown by its collocates: *shǐ*/make (24), *ràng*/make (11) and *lìng*/make (8).

Comparison

We have discussed *dejected**, *despondent** and *disheartened** and their Chinese near-equivalents, i.e. *chuítóusàngqì*, *huīxīnsàngqì*, *xīnhuīyìlěng*, *sàngqì* and *huīxīn*. We will include *jǔsàng*, which was explored earlier, into the present discussion. Table 7.32 summarizes their respective features.

Table 7.32 Comparison of *dejected**, *despondent** and *disheartened** and their Chinese equivalents

	dejected* (past) (state) (more outward)	disheartened* (past-future) (state) (more inward)	despondent* (future) (process) (inward-outward)
jǔsàng (past-future) (process) (inward-outward)	√	√	√
huīxīn (past-future) (state/inward)		√	√
sàngqì (past) (state/outward)	√		
xīnhuīyìlěng (past-future) (process/inward)		√	√

It is obvious from Table 7.32 that *dejected* is more inward and *disheartened* more outward, while *despondent* is both experienced as an inner feeling and realized as an emotion involving physical manifestations. For the Chinese equivalents, both *huīxīn* and *xīnhuīyìlěng* focus on the inner emotional state and *sàngqì* emphasizes the external manifestations, while *jǔsàng* is characterized by both. Among the words in question, *despondent, jǔsàng* and *xīnhuīyìlěng* are conceptualized as a gradual process that may change, while all the others are understood as an emotional state that does not change much. *Dejected* focuses on the response to what has just happened and *despondent* describes the emotional state due to the gloomy prediction of what is going to happen in the future, while *disheartened* centres on both. If you are *sàngqì*, you feel very disappointed about the outcome and *dejected* about it; if you feel *huīxīn*, you feel *disheartened* about it and have less or lost the confidence and determination to keep doing it; if you feel *xīnhuīyìlěng*, you feel totally *despondent* about it and want to give it up. *Chuítóusàngqì* and *huīxīnsàngqì* are stronger versions of *sàngqì* and *huīxīn* respectively; they are similar in terms of the extent of losing hope, but the former highlights more the accompanying behaviour, namely 'drooping one's head', while the latter focuses more on the internal emotional state. *Jǔsàng* covers a wide semantic range; it is both extroverted and introverted; it relates what has happened to what is going to happen; it is conceptualized as a dynamic process. Therefore, it corresponds to all three English words.

7.1.9 *Gloom** and their Chinese equivalents

The words to be examined in this section consist of *gloom, gloomy, gloomily* and their Chinese equivalents—*yīnyù* and *mènmènbúlè*. The discussion will start with the examination of the English words.

*Gloom**

Let us first look at *gloom*, for which the three English dictionaries provide the following:

LDCE: 1. *literary* almost complete darkness 2. a feeling of great sadness and lack of hope

OALECD: 1. near darkness 昏暗; 阴暗: 2. feeling of sadness and hopelessness 忧郁; 忧愁; 失望

COBUILD: 1. The *gloom* is a state of near darkness. 2. *Gloom* is a feeling of sadness and lack of hope.

The three dictionaries all agree that *gloom* has two meanings: the original meaning of 'darkness' and the metaphorical meaning of a feeling, which is basically described as 'sadness', 'hopelessness' or 'lack of hope'. The Chinese equivalents for this feeling sense provided by OALECD are *yōuyù*, *yōuchóu* and *shīwàng*. Actually, *yōuyù* is the closest in meaning, while *yōuchóu* emphasizes worries and *shīwàng* is simply disappointment. For a deeper understanding of *gloom*, we need to look at the corpus data.

In the BOE, 3,439 hits of *gloom* are found. From its top 50 collocates, it can be seen that *gloom* colligates predominantly with prepositions, characteristically *of (526)*, *in (149)*, *for (91)*, *over (67)*, *into (43)*, *about (33)*, and the definite article *the (1219)*. Its word sketch shows that *gloom* is semantically associated with:

Object_of: (a) *pierce (22)*, *lift (94)*, *deepen (20)*, *lighten (11)*, *penetrate (6)*, *cast (16)*, *encircle (4)*, *spread (8)*, *gather (6)*, *settle (95)*, *surround (4)*
             (b) *predict (10)*, *forecast (5)*
             (c) *dispel (14)*, *relieve (7)*
Subject_of: *descend (20)*, *hang (17)*, *surround (12)*, *deepen (11)*, *loom (10)*, *envelop (7)*, *spread (7)*, *lift (6)*, *settle (5)*, *pervade (5)*

From the collocates in the (a) group of the 'object_of' pattern, it is clear that *gloom* is conceptualized as something like cloud, fog, gas or light that can be gone into or through and can rise or disperse, go around, move outwards in all directions, come together and remain in the air. The verbs in the (b) group are to do with the future and those in the (c) group are used in a non-metaphorical way. The subject_of collocates are very much like those in the (a) group of the object_of pattern. Although some of the above collocates are used to describe 'darkness', in most cases, according to the BOE, *gloom* is used in its metaphorical sense, as illustrated in Example (132):

(132)   When the *gloom* finally lifts, the pessimists will be surprised at how much has been going right.

Its word sketch shows that its modifiers include *economic (46)*, *deep (33)*, *stygian (18)*, *global (9)*, *grey (8)*, *unrelieved (6)*, *financial (5)*, *dusty (5)*, *unrelenting (4)*, *oppressive (4)*, *pervasive (4)*, *heavy (4)*, etc. It can be seen that many of them are related to its abstract meaning, like *economic*, *global* and *financial*. *Gloom* is modified by *heavy* to indicate a great degree. The abstract collocates of *gloom* used in the pattern 'and/or' include *doom (452)*, *despondency (17)*, *despair (17)*, *pessimism (5)*, *depression (7)*, etc. *Doom* occurs highly frequently due to the fixed phrase 'doom and gloom/gloom and doom', meaning 'when there seems to be no hope for the future'. As expected, all the other negative-feeling collocates have to do with 'lack of hope'.

Let us move on to examine *gloomy*, which is described as the following in the three dictionaries:

> LDCE: 1. making you feel that things will not improve = *depressing*
>
> 2. sad because you think the situation will not improve = *depressed*
>
> 3. dark, especially in a way that makes you feel sad

> OALECD: 1. dark or unlighted, esp in a way that is depressing or frightening 阴暗的, 黑暗的 (尤指使人沮丧或恐惧) 2. (that makes people feel) sad and depressed (使人感到) 忧愁的, 沮丧的

> COBUILD: 1. If a place is *gloomy*, it is almost dark so that you cannot see very well. 2. If people are *gloomy*, they are unhappy and have no hope. = *despondent* 3. If a situation is *gloomy*, it does not give you much hope of success or happiness. = *grim*

All the dictionaries divide the meaning of *gloomy* as a feeling into two categories: one is 'sad' and the other is 'making sad'. OALECD lists it as one meaning and only puts 'that makes people feel' in brackets. The Chinese equivalents it provides include *yōuchóu de* and *jǔsàng de*. The former focuses on 'worries' and the latter on 'frustration'. For a deep understanding of its meaning, we should look at its corpus data. In the BOE, 2,824 hits of *gloomy* are found. Its top collocates show that its colligational properties include the article-determiners *a (470), the (430)* and the preposition *about (64)*. Its word sketch reveals that it semantically prefers *picture (93), forecaster (72), prognosis (23), prediction (68), outlook (61), forecast (43), view (43), prospect (22), scenario (16)*, suggesting that *gloomy* is more hopeless about one's prospect or future than the outcome of a specific event. This is also reflected in the collocates of the 'pp_about_p' pattern: *prospect (15)* and *future (7)*. It seems that *gloomy* is more outward than inward as we can find *look (73), sound (12), seem (11)* and *appear (5)* in the collocates of the pattern 'adj_comp_of'. *Feel* occurs only 22 times in this pattern.

For *gloomily (382)*, let us look at its word sketch directly. Its 'verb' pattern tells us that *gloomily* is semantically associated with verbs that can be done in an emotional manner, typically *say (65), stare (20), think (10), sit (6), reply (6)* and *nod (6)*, out of which only *think* is an introverted verb, so we may argue that *gloomily* is more outward than inward. For its adverb premodifier, I only find *rather (9)*. The verb it frequently premodifies is *predict (11)*.

Chinese equivalents of gloom*

Now let us move on to look at the Chinese equivalents for the *gloom* family. *Gloom** occurs 151 times in the BPC and its top Chinese equivalents are shown in Table 7.33.

Table 7.33 Chinese equivalents of *gloom** in the BPC

Feeling	Original meaning
yōuyù: 11	*yīn'àn*: 11
yīnyù: 10	*yōuàn*: 10
mènmènbúlè: 7	*hēiàn*: 7
yīnchén: 8	*àn*: 7
yōu (chóu/lǜ): 7	

For Table 7.33, we will focus on the expressions in the first column as the words in the second column are related to its original meaning of 'darkness'. Since *yōuyù* has been discussed in Section 7.1.7 and *yīnchén* is a word describing countenance rather than expressing feelings directly, we will focus on *yīnyù* and *mènmènbúlè* here. Seven hits of *gloom** are translated as *yōu (chóu/lǜ)*, showing that *gloom* is linked with the Chinese concept of *yōu*, which means worry or concern. It is not the focus of this research, so we will exclude it from our discussion. Example (133) seems to show that *gloom* is a more serious state than *depression*:

(133) 不断地将他过去的处境和现在的处境相对比, 表明平衡正向坏的一面
       倾斜, 于是产生了一种终日忧郁 (*yōuyù*) 或者至少是消沉 (*xiāochén*)
       的心态。
       Constant comparison between his old state and his new showed a
       balance for the worse, which produced a constant state of ***gloom*** or, at
       least, ***depression***.

Yīnyù

The significant collocates of *yīnyù* (667 hits) are shown in Table 7.34.

The first column in Table 7.34 shows the collocations that are related to physical manifestations, either via expressions or voice, including *liǎnsè* (countenance), *shénqíng/biǎoqíng/shénsè* (facial expression), *kàn* (look), *mùguāng/yǎnshén* (expression in one's eyes), *xiǎnde* (appear), *yǎnjing/yǎn* (eyes), *liǎnshàng/liǎn/miànkǒng* (on one's face/face), *shēngyīn* (voice). It seems to

Table 7.34 Significant collocates of *yīnyù* in the CCL corpus

Extroversion	Modifier	Feeling	Others
liǎnsè 27	*hěn 13*	*chénzhòng 10*	*tiānqì 8*
shénqíng/biǎoqíng 27/16	*shífēn 8*	*bēiāi 5*	*qìfēn 21*
shénsè 13	*fēicháng 7*	*jǔsàng 5*	*lǒngzhào 13*
kàn 26	*dài 15*	*tòngkǔ 5*	*chénmò 13*
xiǎnde 19			*chénsī 12*
mùguāng/yǎnshén 18/17			*chénmèn 7*
yǎnjing/yǎn 16/7			*xìnggé 5*
liǎnshàng/liǎn 13/11			*xīnqíng 16*
miànkǒng 9			*qíngxù 14*
shēngyīn 10			

suggest that *yīnyù* is experienced more as an emotion with physical manifestations than as an inner feeling. Its modifiers include *hěn/shífēn/fēicháng* (very) and *dài* (slightly). It also co-occurs with other sad feeling words, such as *bēiāi* (sorrowful), *jǔsàng* (dejected) or *tòngkǔ* (anguished). In XHCBL, *yīnyù* is glossed as:

1. (天气) 低沉郁闷; (气氛)不活跃 (of weather) gloomy; dismal; (of atmosphere) not lively 2. 忧郁, 不开朗 depressed; closed and gloomy

This explains why we find *tiānqì* (weather), *qìfēn* (atmosphere) and *lǒngzhào* (shroud) in the last column. The frequent expression would be some place is 'lǒngzhào zài *yīnyù* de qìfēn zhōng' (lit. *yīnyù* hangs over), where *lǒngzhào* is a typical Chinese word to describe cloud, fog or shadow. Therefore, it is similar to *gloomy* in terms of collocating with words describing cloud or fog. This is because emotions and feelings are often understood metaphorically in terms of various forms of substance—gaseous, fluid and solid (see Kövecses 2000, Chapter 5). *Chénmò* (silence), *chénsī* (contemplation) and *chénmèn* (dreariness) are often associated with *yīnyù*, suggesting that *yīnyù* has a quality of quietness. It is also used to talk about a person's character, so we can say *yīnyù* could be extended in time. Another feature is that it frequently co-occurs with *xīnqíng* (frame of mind) or *qíngxù* (mood), but seldom with *gǎnqíng* or *qínggǎn*, which is more believed to be the Chinese counterpart of *feeling*. This feature is also shared by most of the Chinese sadness words discussed. It probably shows that in the Chinese culture sadness is more understood as a *xīnqíng* or *qíngxù*, rather than a *gǎnqíng* or *qínggǎn*; it also confirms the idea suggested in Zhang and Ooi (2008) that *gǎnqíng* and *qínggǎn* are not exact equivalents of *feeling*.

Table 7.35 Significant collocates of *mènmènbúlè* in the CCL corpus

Extroversion	Introversion	Others
shuō/shuōdào 51/7	*xīnlǐ/xīnzhōng 14/6*	*zìjǐ 13*
zǒu 10	*juéde 10*	*biàn 10 qǐlái 9*
xiǎnde 7	*gǎndào 8*	*yīzhí 17 zhěngtiān 11*
liǎn 5	*xīnqíng 7*	*zǒngshì 10 chángcháng 7*
biǎoqíng 5	*qíngxù 5*	*wèishénme 11*
	xiǎng 26	*yīnwèi 6*

Mènmènbúlè

The CCL corpus contains 435 hits of *mènmènbúlè* and its top collocates are presented in Table 7.35, where it can be seen that *mènmènbúlè* is frequently used to describe an outward action that is done in an unhappy manner, like *shuō/shuōdào* (say) or *zǒu* (leave). In the first column, we also find *xiǎnde* (appear), *liǎn* (face), *biǎoqíng* (facial expression), which all point to its characteristic of extroversion. However, we can also find *xīnlǐ/xīnzhōng* (in the mind), *juéde/gǎndào* (feel), *xīnqíng* (frame of mind), *qíngxù* (mood) and *xiǎng* (think), which are closely related to its feature of introversion. Therefore, *mènmènbúlè* is a combined feeling of both extroversion and introversion. The collocates in the last column give us some ideas about its other features. *Zìjǐ* (oneself) suggests that it seems to be a feeling confined to oneself. *Biàn* (change) and *qǐlái* (used after a verb to indicate the beginning of an action) appear to show that *mènmènbúlè* starts at a certain point of time. *Yīzhí/zǒngshì* (all the time/always), *chángcháng* (often) and *zhěngtiān* (all the day) seem to show it often lasts for a rather long time. *Wèishénme* and *yīnwèi* (because) tell us that usually such a feeling has a clearly identified reason. It is post-modified by *hěn* (very/10). Another semantically similar four-character idiom is *yùyùguǎhuān*, which is more formal and literary. The original meaning of *mèn* in Chinese is 'tightly closed or sealed'. If someone bottles up all his/her unhappy feelings or worries in the mind and does not lessen them by sharing them with others, s/he will get *mènmènbúlè*.

Comparison

In this section, we will compare *gloom** with *yōuyù*, *yīnyù* and *mènmènbúlè*. *Yōuyù* is often semantically associated with positive words, such as *xiào* (smile), *měilì* (beautiful), *làngmàn* (romantic), *wēnróu* (gentle) and *wángzǐ* (prince); *mènmènbúlè* semantically prefers *zǒngshì/yīzhí* (always/all the time); *yīnyù* is more associated with words indicating or related to outward manifestations; *gloomy* has a totally different set of collocates that are associated with the future, such as *prospect, future, outlook, forecast,* etc.

None of these three Chinese equivalents corresponds exactly to *gloomy*. *Yōuyù* is more an inward feeling that is extended in time rather than a momentary occurrence and has no specific reason. However, sometimes it is also viewed as something very beautiful. *Yīnyù* is manifested more outwardly and could last for a short or long time. Both *yōuyù* and *yīnyù* can be related to a person's character. *Yōuyù* is closer to *melancholy*, though they differ in many aspects. *Yīnyù* is similar to *gloomy* in that they are both outwardly manifested. However, *gloomy* can be used to modify a sad situation. *Mènmènbùlè* is more specific because it has a definite reason. In comparison with *yōuyù*, it does not last so long. It will fade away with the gradual disappearance of the cause. It is a combination of extroversion and inversion. *Mènmènbùlè* is the least intense in the Chinese *gloomy* group. If people are *gloomy*, they think the situation will not improve. *Mènmènbùlè* is a feeling when things are not going as wished. If people are *mènmènbùlè*, they are not satisfied with what has happened and they are thinking about the past. When people are *gloomy*, they are pessimistic about the future.

7.1.10 *Upset** and their Chinese equivalents

*Upset**

This section will investigate *upset*, for which the dictionary definitions relevant to feeling are presented below:

> LDCE: **adj.** 1. unhappy and worried because something unpleasant or disappointing has happened 2. if you are upset with someone, you are angry and annoyed with them **v.** 1. to make someone feel unhappy or worried **n.** 1. worry and unhappiness caused by an unexpected problem

> OALECD: **v.** distress the mind or feelings of (sb) 使 (某人) 苦恼或心烦: **n** upsetting or being upset 翻倒; 扰乱; 不安

> COBUILD: 1. If you are *upset*, you are unhappy or disappointed because something unpleasant has happened to you. *Upset* is also a noun. 2. If something *upsets* you, it makes you feel worried or unhappy.

From the above emotion-related definitions in LDCE and COBUILD, we can see that the determinants of *upset* are worry, unhappiness and disappointment. OALECD uses *distress*, a more difficult word, to define *upset*, and thus gives no valuable information. LDCE's explanation of the phrase 'be upset with somebody' as 'be angry and annoyed with somebody' seems to introduce anger into its composition. Now let us look at the corpus data. In the BOF, 3,866 hits of *upset* (n) are found and its top collocates reveal that *upset* as a noun, as expected, colligates with the articles *the (342)*, *an (582)*, and prepositions, typically *of (454)*, *by (81)*, *at (72)*, *over (65)*. According to its word sketch, its significant adjectival modifiers include *big (243)*, *major (150)*, *stunning (58)*, *emotional (45)*, *huge (37)*, *first-round (28)*, *minor (16)*, *shocking (14)*, *potential (13)*, and its nominal modifiers are predominantly *stomach (125)* and *tummy (28)*. Interestingly, *upset* is often modified by *stunning* or *shocking*, showing that *upset* is much to do with unexpectedness. This confirms that disappointment is a main factor of getting *upset*. *Major* and *minor* are deployed to intensify or mitigate its degree. From *big* and *huge*, it can be discerned that *upset* is also conceptualized as something that can change in size to indicate varying intensity. Despite the big difference in frequency between *emotional* and *stomach/tummy (45: 153[125+28])*, there is no obvious inclination that *upset* without a modifier might refer to an emotional or stomach *upset* because both occur quite frequently. Contexts have to be relied on to decide what it is. The words used in the pattern of 'and/or' include *diarrhoea (10)*, *rash (5)*, *nausea (4)*, *headache (6)*, *cold (6)*, *streak (8)*, *controversy (6)*, *anger (5)*, *pain (7)*, *trouble (4)*. Only the last four words have to do with an emotional *upset*.

Now let us look at *upset* as an adjective. In the corpus, 4,070 hits are found and its top collocates tell us that *upset* (adj.) colligates strongly with prepositions, particularly *about (221)*, *with (106)*, *by (83)*. According to its word sketch, it is predominantly associated with link verbs, typically *be (570)*, *get (448)*, *become (101)*, *feel (75)*, *look (56)*, *seem (47)*, *sound (25)* and *appear (14)*, suggesting that it is both extroverted and introverted, because *sound*, *appear*, *seem* and *look* are closely related to outward manifestations. It frequently collocates with amplifiers, predominantly *very (191)*, *really (64)*, *extremely (27)*, *terribly (19)*, *deeply (14)*, emphasizers, mainly *particularly (11)*, *genuinely (10)*: and downtoners, typically *pretty (20)*, *quite (22)* and *little (4)*. However, we can see that it collocates much more frequently with amplifiers than downtoners.

Its word sketch shows that the emotion words it co-occurs with in the 'and/or' pattern include *angry (153)*, *distressed (14)*, *confused (14)*, *tired (17)*, *nervous (18)*, *sad (14)*, *unhappy (10)*, *anxious (9)*, *mad (9)*, *stunning (9)*, *frightened (9)* etc. From the above collocates, it is clear that *angry* is the most frequent collocate of *upset*, co-occurring with it 153 times in this pattern, much higher than other negative emotion words. This seems to suggest that being *upset* is closely related to *anger* and they are two co-existent feelings stimulated by unpleasant and unexpected events.

In the BOE, 17,124 hits of *upset* as a verb are found and its top 50 collocates show that *upset* as a verb strongly colligates with *be (4,335)*, and prepositions, typically *to (1,664)*, *by (1,146)*, *about (1,009)*, *at (631)*, *with (512)*, *over (224)*. This is because (a) it is often used in passive voice and (b) in many instances, a verb tag is mistakenly assigned to an adjective. Its word sketch reveals that its frequent objects include *balance (216)*, *applecart/apple-cart/cart (64)*, *stomach (34)*, *seed (38)*, *resident (31)*, *everyone/everybody (24)*, *rhythm (17)*, *neighbour (15)*, suggesting its metaphorical usage is more common. Its subjects include *something (29)*, *news (21)*, *death (19)*, *decision (19)*, *incident (16)*, *comment (14)*, *criticism (12)*, *attack (12)*, *remark (11)*, *teenager (10)*, *fact (10)*, *event (10)*. It seems that most of them, if not all, are very likely to be connected to emotions. Some of them have obvious negative inclinations themselves, such as *death, criticism, incident, death, violence, attack* and *risk*, which are prone to *upset* people, while others may need to be preceded by negative modifiers to make people sad, like *remark, comment, news, decision, fact, event*, etc. Its predominant intensifiers include amplifiers, such as *very (1,044)*, *really (468)*, *deeply (122)*, *extremely (102)*, *greatly (25)*; emphasizers, like *particularly (108)*, *genuinely (27)*; and the downtoner *mildly (5)*. A simple glance of their frequencies will show that *upset* (v) is much more likely to be intensified by amplifiers than downtoners. Its word sketch shows that the words used in the 'and/or' pattern are closely related to emotions, such as *shock (61)*, *hurt (49)*, *disappoint (32)*, *worry (27)*, *offend (19)*, *depress (14)*, *frustrate (18)*, *surprise (18)*, *annoy (17)*, *embarrass (16)*, *anger (15)*, *frighten (14)*, *disturb (11)*, *concern (11)*. These negative emotion words reveal that an *upset* feeling might be mixed with one or more of these shown feelings, especially those highly frequent ones, like *shock, hurt, disappoint, worry*. The fourth sense of *hurt* in LDCE is glossed as 'insult somebody: to make someone feel very upset, unhappy, sad etc'. The following example from LDCE illustrates well the *worry* component of *upset*:

(134) If you are the victim of a burglary, the emotional *upset* can affect you
        for a long time.

One might find what has happened *unexpected*, and become *sad* and *disappointed*. Based on what has happened unexpectedly, the experiencer might become *worried* about the future and become *angry* about why this happened. This might be the most typical case for *upset*. It almost covers the whole process. So far, we seem to be able to conclude that *upset* is a mixed feeling of *unexpectedness*, *unhappiness, disappointment, worry* and *anger*. In specific situations, some factors might be less significant and others may become dominant.

Chinese equivalents of upset*

OALECD defines *upset* as 'distress the mind or feelings of (sb) (使 (某人) 苦恼 或心烦', where the Chinese equivalent concepts used to translate *upset* are *kǔ'nǎo* (worried) and *xīnfán* (perturbed). Let us look at the parallel corpus data. *Upset** occurs 60 times in the corpus and its top four Chinese equivalents are *fánnǎo (5)*, *nánguò (5), shēngqì (4)* and *zháojí (3)*. The most frequent Chinese translations of *upset* include *fánnǎo* (worry) and *nánguò* (sad), *shēngqì* (annoyed) and *zháojí* (anxious/worried). *Fánnǎo* is the closest in meaning to the Chinese equivalents provided by OALECD—*kǔ'nǎo* and *xīnfán*. However, the parallel corpus tells us that the other three are also its equivalents. Actually, none of these is the exact or close equivalent to the English *upset*. It seems that no single Chinese word qualifies as its equivalent, because all of the above-mentioned elements constitute the feeling of *upset*. However, in translating a certain text segment, the translator focuses only on one of the aspects based on the context and uses a semantically similar word to convey the intended meaning prominent in that context. Consider the following examples:

(135) 'Well, almost everything,' Frank amended hastily, disturbed by the expressions on their faces. He tried to look cheerful, for he did not believe in **upsetting** ladies.

'唔, 差不多全烧光了,' 弗兰克显然对她们脸上的表情感到有点为难, 才连忙纠正说。他想要显得愉快一些, 因为他不主张叫小姐太太们 **烦恼** (*fánnǎo*) 。

(136) The blush was not difficult for she was breathless and her heart was beating like a drum. 'Rhett, I'm so sorry about what I—I said to you that night—you know—at Rough and Ready. I was—oh, so very frightened and **upset** and you were so—so—' She looked down and saw his brown hand tighten over hers. 'And—I thought then that I'd never, never forgive you! But when Aunt Pitty told me yesterday that you—that they might hang you—it came over me of a sudden and I—I—'. She looked up into his eyes with one swift imploring glance and in it she put an agony of heartbreak. 'Oh, Rhett, I'd die if they hanged you!'

她脸上的红晕是不难做到的, 因为她已经喘不过起来, 心也似敲鼓般的 怦怦直跳。' 瑞德, 我很抱歉, 我对你----我那天晚上对你说的----你知 道----在拉尤雷迪。那时我----啊, 我多么害怕和着急 (*zháojí*), 而你又是那么----那么----' 她眼睛朝下,看见他那只褐色的手把她的手腕抓得更紧了。' 所以----那时我想我永远永远也不饶恕你! 可是昨天皮蒂姑妈突然告诉我说, 你----说他们可能会绞死你----这真把我吓倒了, 所以我----我—' 她抬起头来,用急切祈求的目光注视着他的眼睛,她的目光中还含着揪心的痛苦。'啊, 瑞德, 要是他们把你绞死了, 我也不想活了!

(137) 'What will Mother say when she hears?' He looked up in sudden anguished apprehension. 'You wouldn't be telling your mother a word and **upsetting** her, now would you?'

'妈听到了会怎么说呢? ' 他忽然惊慌失措地抬起头来。'你总不至于向你妈透露让她难过 (*nánguò*) 吧, 会吗?'

(138) She picked up the cologne bottle and took a large mouthful, carefully rinsed her mouth and then spit into the slop jar. She rustled down the stairs toward the two who still stood in the hall, for Pittypat had been too **upset** by Scarlett's action to ask Rhett to sit down. He was decorously clad in black, his linen frilly and starched, and his manner was all that custom demanded from an old friend paying a call of sympathy on one bereaved. In fact, it was so perfect that it verged on the burlesque, though Pittypat did not see it. He was properly apologetic for disturbing Scarlett and regretted that in his rush of closing up business before leaving town he had been unable to be present at the funeral.

她拿起香水瓶,往嘴里倒了一大口,漱了半天,吐在了痰盂里。她赶紧下了楼,看见他们还在过厅里站着,朝他们二人走去,皮蒂姑妈正为思嘉举动而生气 (*shēngqì*), 没顾上请瑞德坐下。瑞德郑重其事地穿着一身黑衣服,衬衫上镶着褶边,而且是浆过的,一切举止也都符合一位老朋友向失去亲人的人表示慰问的样子,一切都是那么周到,甚至到了可笑的地步,但皮蒂姑妈并没有察觉,他这么晚前来打扰,一本正经地向思嘉表示了歉意。

In Example (135), Frank modified his previous remark by saying 'almost everything' and tried to look cheerful in order not to make ladies worried. The translation focuses on the constituent meaning part of *fánnǎo* (worry). In (136), when Scarlett heard that Rhett would be hanged, she got frightened and anxious. *Zháojí* (anxiety) was emphasized in this context. Example (137) shows that he did not want to make his mother *nánguò* (sad) by hiding the secret. The situation for (138) was a bit complicated. Scarlett drank a lot of brandy on the funeral day of her husband and her behaviour was unacceptable at that time. Aunt Pitty was so *shēngqì* (annoyed) that she forgot to ask Rhett to take a seat when he visited her to show his sorrow.

It can be seen that different words denoting quite distinct Chinese concepts are used to convey the meaning of *upset* in these translations. It seems to support the claim that the congruence between languages is a more textually valid type of equivalence (González *et al.* 2008). Seen in isolation, *upset* is an emotion word that expresses a mixture of several feelings, i.e. *sadness, worry, anxiety* and *annoyance*. Chinese does not encode so many emotional and semantic components into one single lexical word. It seems that Chinese emotional concepts tend to be more discrete, with each emphasizing one emotional component or aspect.

7.1.11 *Bitter*, agony*, anguish* and *tòngkǔ*

In English, *anguish* and *agony* are synonymous, both meaning 'extreme mental or physical suffering or pain'. *Bitter* is something different. However, they are all connected to the feeling of *tòngkǔ* in Chinese. To find out how they differ from each other and why they are all related to *tòngkǔ*, we need to examine them in the corpus.

*Bitter**

Below are the entries for *bitter* as an adjective from the three dictionaries, with appropriate omissions:

LDCE: 1. feeling angry, jealous, and upset because you think you have been treated unfairly 2. making you feel very unhappy and upset 3. a bitter argument, battle etc is one in which people oppose or criticise each other with strong feelings of hate and anger 4. having a sharp strong taste like black coffee without sugar 5. unpleasantly cold

OALECD: 1. having a sharp taste like aspirin or unsweetened coffee; not sweet 苦的; 有苦味的 2. difficult to accept; causing sorrow; unwelcome 难以忍受的; 引起悲伤的; 不受欢迎的 3. caused by, feeling or showing envy, hatred or disappointment 引起、感觉或显示出嫉妒、憎恶、怨恨或失望的 4. piercing cold 严寒

COBUILD: 1. In a *bitter* argument or conflict, people argue very angrily or fight very fiercely. 2. If someone is *bitter* after a disappointing experience or after being treated unfairly, they continue to feel angry about it. 3. A *bitter* experience makes you feel very disappointed. You can also use *bitter* to emphasise feelings of disappointment. 4. . . . extremely cold. 5. A *bitter* taste is sharp, not sweet, and often slightly unpleasant.

From the above definitions, it can be seen that the original meaning of *bitter* as a bad taste has been extended to different domains and developed different meanings. This analysis will focus on the senses to do with feelings. What is shared by these three dictionaries is that it denotes an unpleasant feeling or it is used to modify something that can cause such a feeling. LDCE defines *bitter* as 'feeling angry, jealous, and upset because you think you have been treated unfairly' and 'making you feel very unhappy and upset'. OALECD says that *bitter* is 'difficult to accept; causing sorrow; unwelcome' and 'caused by, feeling or showing envy, hatred or disappointment'. COBUILD claims that 'If someone is *bitter* after a disappointing experience or after being treated unfairly, they continue to feel angry about it.' To sum up, *bitter* as a feeling is associated with 'angry/resentful', 'jealous/envious', '*upset*' and 'disappointed'.

Now let us look at how *bitter* behaves in the BOE, which yields 13,274 hits of *bitter* as an adjective. An inspection of its top 50 collocates reveals that *bitter* colligates with the articles *a (3,027)*, *the (2,043)*, prepositions, predominantly *about (307)*, *with (189)*, link verbs, typically *be (813)*, *feel (124)*, and nouns it modifies. Its collocates show clearly that *bitter* is more often used in its metaphorical sense: *rival (435)*, *dispute (259)*, *blow (226)*, *disappointment (201)*, *experience (198)*, *battle (177)*, *memory (163)*, *row (146)*, *feud (139)*, *enemy (135)*, *war (120)*, *rivalry (95)*, *attack (103)*, *fight (100)*, *debate (92)*, *divorce (85)*, *fighting (82)*, *division (82)*, *conflict (78)*, *irony (76)*, *struggle (76)*, *argument (68)*, etc. *Taste* occurs only 272 times. *End (264)* and *pill (205)* occur frequently in the corpus due to the fixed phrases *to the bitter end* and *a bitter pill*. In the sense of 'piercing cold', it collocates frequently with words related to coldness, such as *cold (222)*, *wind (65)* and *winter (63)*. In the sense of 'caused by, feeling or showing envy, hatred or disappointment' (LDCE), it has a semantic preference for things involving opposition, antagonism or hostility, such as *rival/rivalry, dispute, debate, conflict, fight/fighting, feud, struggle, attack, blow, row, war, division, divorce, argument, enemy, irony*. It also semantically prefers things that cause people to be unhappy and *upset*, typically *experience, memory, disappointment*. Its word sketch shows that its adverbial modifiers include *extremely (19)*, *increasingly (125)*, *particularly (42)*, *rather (18)*, *quite (13)*, *slightly (30)*, *little (22)*, *somewhat (10)*, etc. It also shows that *bitter* often co-occurs with *resentful (40)* and *angry (104)*, as exemplified in the following examples:

(139)   It is vital for the bereaved person to express their grief, for grief cannot be suppressed. The feelings must go somewhere. Sometimes unexpressed grief may turn inwards, festering into a **bitter** and **resentful** outlook on life, or it may manifest as chronic physical tension.

(140)   Labour groups have consulted only organizations from their own
        constituency, treating these as the representatives of a genuine
        community, and in doing so ignoring representatives of local business or
        excluding the often **bitter** and **resentful** local white working class. This is
        a strategy for subverting dialogue while appearing to encourage it and is
        not part of the process of open corporatism advocated here.

(141)   Either the system of justice has not operated properly and you've been
        unjustly punished, or it has operated properly and you've got what you
        deserve. If you choose the first you become **angry, bitter** and **resentful**.
        Our society is full of **angry, bitter** and **resentful** people. Some of them
        appear in the media, voicing their complaints about women priests, or
        homosexuals, or the youth of today . . .

(142)   Mr Cooper said a secret survey of prison staff revealed they were
        severely stressed and their morale was devastatingly low. 'Across the
        board, the findings reveal staff are **angry, bitter**, sunk in cynicism and
        apathy, isolated, ignored, badly treated, seriously stressed. It is simply
        appalling that prison staff are so shabbily treated.' But Queensland
        Corrective Services Commission director-general Keith Hamburger said
        the situation was not as bad as indicated. Moves had been made to
        reduce stress on staff in the State's prisons.

(143)   We saw how Helen (Chapter 2) died **angry** and **bitter** at the man who
        jilted her, only to ruminate continually on this theme in her novels
        today.

Bitter is associated with *outlook* in (139), *working class* in (140), *people* in (141),
and *prison staff sunk in cynicism and apathy* in (142). It seems to suggest that
bitter could be a long-term feeling or an attitude towards life. Example (143)
shows a typical case of *bitter* in which the feeling, like angry, is aiming more at
someone else, such as the man who jilted her, rather than oneself.

Turning to *bitterly* (3,715 hits), its word sketch[11] shows that, roughly speaking,
it semantically prefers three semantic groups of words: one is to do with
opposition, typically verbs, such as *complain (280), divide (161), oppose (182),
contest (104), fight (77), resent (73), criticise/criticize (58), dispute (26), comment
(17), quarrel (14), argue (16), retort (5)*, etc. Some verbs may not be prototypical
opposing verbs, like *comment*, but they still assume an opposing side. The second
one is related to verbs showing or feeling sad emotions, such as *regret (87), weep
(37), sob (14), remark (10), smile (23), laugh (35), cry (17)*. The third group include
adjectives denoting unpleasant feelings, such as *disappointed (426), disappointing*

(63), unhappy (15), angry (10), resentful (6), showing opposing feelings, such as *ironic (12), hostile (11), critical (18)*, or relating to coldness, like *cold (331)*. It seems that, if its feeling-related sense involves an opposition, it tends to be related to hatred or anger; if it describes a passive feeling one suffers mentally, it is likely to be an unacceptable and unwelcome feeling, more like '*upset*' and '*unhappy*'.

Let us move on to look at *bitterness*, which is the nominal form of *bitter*, mainly in the senses of 'difficult to accept; causing sorrow; unwelcome' and 'caused by, feeling or showing envy, hatred or disappointment'. The corpus yields 2,684 hits of *bitterness*. Its top 50 collocates and its concordance show that it has a strong colligation with prepositions, typically *of (604), with (94), toward(s) (71), between (42), over (54), about (44), at (53), without (38), against (21)*. The preposition *toward(s)* confirms my earlier claim that *bitter* is often a quite active feeling, aiming at someone else in an unfriendly way. *Bitter* also colligates with verbs, typically *express (20), cause (14), create (12), feel (10)*, modifiers, like *great (26), deep (7)* and quantifiers, typically *much (27), little (11)*. Its word sketch reveals that it frequently co-occurs with negative feelings, such as *anger (117), resentment (55), hatred (42), frustration (26), despair (20), rage (14), jealousy (13), envy (10), hostility (8)*, etc.

Now let us turn to its Chinese counterparts. Two hundred and eighteen instances of *bitter** occur in the BPC. Its original meaning as a *bitter* taste occurs only 13 times. Another clearly discernible translation equivalent is *lěng* (cold) (12). It is interesting that *bitter/bitterly* is often used to indicate a degree and its Chinese translations for this sense include a wide range of adjectives (18) and adverbs (25, including 13 instances of *hěn*). The translations of its other metaphorical uses are summarized in Table 7.36.

As was mentioned earlier, *bitter* has been extended to many domains and developed dozens of meanings, which basically can be classified into two categories, i.e. 'unpleasant' or 'causing an unpleasant feeling'. Chinese has many words to describe such situations, so it can be translated as a variety of words

Table 7.36 Chinese equivalents of *bitter** in the BPC

Feeling	Others
tòngkǔ: 44	*kǔ (kǔ/kǔ'nàn/shòukǔ/kùnkǔ): 10*
xīnsuān: 9	*jiānkè/kēkè/kèbó: 8*
xiào: kǔxiào 8 + lěngxiào 1	*nánguò/jiānnán/zāo/láosāo/*
kǔ'nǎo/fánnǎo/àonǎo: 6	*yuànshēngzǎidào: 7*
nánshòu/nánguò/bēishāng/bēitòng: 6	*others: 42*

that convey such meanings. Table 7.36 shows that the most frequent translation is *tòngkǔ* (44). It is also associated with other feelings. In nine instances, it is translated as *xīnsuān* (heart-sour). In nine instances, it is used to modify laugh/smile, where the Chinese translations are *kǔxiào* (bitter-laugh) and *lěngxiào* (cold-laugh), as exemplified in Example (144) (*bitter* is translated as *lěngxiào*):

(144) 如果从构成这一群人中的每一个男人、每一个女人和每一个尖嗓门
　　　 的孩子的口中爆发出轰笑, 海丝特·白兰或许可以对他们所有的人报
　　　 以桀傲的冷笑 (*lěngxiào*) 。 ...
　　　 Had a roar of laughter burst from the multitude—each man, each
　　　 woman, each little shrill-voiced child, contributing their individual
　　　 parts—Hester Prynne might have repaid them all with a **bitter** and
　　　 disdainful **smile**.

Six of the translations are close to 'annoyed and worried', such as *fánnǎo, kǔ'nǎo, àonǎo*, each with a distinct emphasis. Five of them are to do with sadness, such as *nánshòu, nánguò, bēishāng* and *bēitòng*. For the non-feeling translations, ten of them are associated with *kǔ* (bitterness) in its metaphorical sense, such as *kǔnàn* (distress), *shòukǔ* (suffering), *kùnkǔ* (hardship). This is because, in Chinese, the taste of *bitter* is also conceived of as something unpleasant or unacceptable, like hardship, suffering and pain. Eight of them are connected with *kè* (acrimonious) like *jiānkè, kēkè* and *kèbó*. *Kè* roughly means 'harsh, unpleasantly stern or unkind', often linked with envy or hatred. Five of them are associated with a difficult life, including *nánguò* (hard-live), *jiānnán* (hard), *zāo* (bad), *láosāo* (complaint) and *yuànshēngzǎidào* (complaints are heard everywhere). From the above analysis, it can be seen that the taste of *bitter* in English can be mapped onto many domains, resulting in various metaphorical meanings. Some of them are shared by Chinese, such as *kǔnàn* (bitter-difficulty), *shòukǔ* (suffer-*bitterness*), *kùnkǔ* (difficulty-bitterness). It seems that the closest Chinese equivalent for *bitter* in the sense of feeling is *tòngkǔ*, with the taste of *bitterness* mapped onto the domain of feeling, as exemplified in the Examples (145)–(147):

(145) 然后, 他又恢复了冷静 、 痛苦 (*tòngkǔ*) 的感觉 。
　　　 Then he came down to cold, **bitter** sense again.

(146) 他抬起头来这个冷酷、痛苦 (*tòngkǔ*) 的现实,使他猛地清醒了。
　　　 He raised his head, and the cold, **bitter** reality jarred him into
　　　 wakefulness.

(147) 在他最需要的时候失去她, 使他加倍痛苦 (*tòngkǔ*) 。
　　　 His loss seemed all the more **bitter** now that he needed her most.

In Example (148), *nánshòu* was used to translate *bitter* because *tòngkǔ* is a relatively strong word to denote a feeling of pain:

(148) 就 像大人们的烦恼也是烦恼一样,他忘记烦恼并不是因为他的烦恼
不怎么沉重和难受 (*nánshòu*),而是因为--种新的、更强烈的兴趣暂时
压倒并驱散了他心中的烦恼--就像大人们在新奇感受的兴奋之时, 也
会暂时忘却 自己的不幸一样。

Not because his troubles were one whit less heavy and **bitter** to him than a man's are to a man, but because a new and powerful interest bore them down and drove them out of his mind for the time—just as men's misfortunes are forgotten in the excitement of new enterprises.

Agony* & anguish*

In this section, I will compare and contrast *agony** and *anguish**. Look at their dictionary entries:

agony:

> LDCE: [Origin: from *Greek, 'trouble, great anxiety'*] 1. very severe pain 2. a very sad, difficult, or unpleasant experience
>
> OALECD: extreme mental or physical suffering (精神或肉体的) 极大痛苦
>
> COBUILD: *Agony* is great physical or mental pain.

anguish:

> LDCE: *written* mental or physical suffering caused by extreme pain or worry
>
> OALECD: severe physical or mental pain (肉体的或精神的) 极度痛苦 **anguished** feeling or expressing *anguish*
>
> COBUILD: *Anguish* is great mental suffering or physical pain. (WRITTEN)

From the above definitions, we can see that *agony* has one basic meaning, namely 'great/extreme mental or physical suffering/pain'. LDCE breaks it down into two senses: 'very severe pain' and 'a very sad, difficult, or unpleasant experience'. According to the dictionary definitions, *anguish* is extremely similar to *agony*, except that *anguish* is 'caused by extreme pain or worry' (LDCE).

For its corpus data, for the sake of space, I will not offer a detailed analysis, but only summarize the relevant research findings. First, their colligational properties are summed up as follows:

agony (5,299):

    preposition: *in (1,188), of (1,112), over (56)*
    definite article: *the* (1,166)
    adjectival possessive: *his (110), our (45), her (58), their (41), own (16)*
anguish (2,592):

    preposition: *of (619), in (245), over (77)*
    definite article: *the (495)*
    adjectival possessive: *his (100), her (87), their (62), my (20), its (13)*

It can be seen that their colligational patterns are almost the same. Turning to their sketch difference, their common patterns can be summarized as follows (*agony*/*anguish*, only significant collocates are listed):

  Object_of: *suffer (103/27), express (5/18), experience (8/14), cause (12/36), feel (16/27), ease (11/12)*
  And/or: *ecstasy (54/5), despair (5/16), grief (4/19), pain (37/102), frustration (4/13), anger (5/22), fear (7/20)*
  A_modifier: *mental (20/92), sheer (18/5), terrible (18/8), emotional (8/14), physical (12/4), deep (3/14), personal (11/17), private (7/14), great (26/34)*

Considering their occurrences (5,299/2,592) in the corpus, *anguish* co-occurs much more frequently with other negative feelings, such as *despair, grief, pain, frustration, anger* and *fear*. What is also remarkable from the above listing is that *anguish* occurs much more frequently with *mental* (35‰ > 3.8‰) and less frequently with *physical* (1.5‰ < 2.3‰) than *agony*. This difference might suggest that *anguish* without any modifier tends to denote a physical pain. Its more frequent co-occurrence with *emotional* than *agony* (5.4‰/1.5‰) also supports this claim. For *agony*, its collocating frequencies with *mental/physical* (20/12) do not show a striking difference, so it can be argued that *agony* is quite neutral in isolation. Both tend to be modified only by amplifiers, such as *sheer, terrible, deep*, rather than downtoners. The *anguish-only* patterns show that its possessor is all in the family circle, i.e. *family (19), mother (7), father (3)*, probably because it is often caused by worry, and that it is also often associated with other negative feelings, like *fury (8), isolation (7), heartache (5), loneliness (4), hurt (3), desperation (3)*. The *agony-only* patterns reveal that it is semantically associated with *prolong (44), endure (34), inflict (12), shorten (3)*, etc., which might imply that *agony*, unlike *anguish*, is more conceptualized as a dynamic process rather than a static state. Its unique adjectival modifiers are mainly *excruciating (12)* and *absolute (31)*, suggesting that *agony* tends more to be intensified by amplifiers. In addition, it is often used in the pattern 'agony of X'. Its concordance shows that in this pattern an enormously wide range of words can occur as a cause of *agony: failure, hunger, heat, homesickness/seasickness, helplessness, expectation, impatience, grief, guilt, shame, remorse, repentance, loss, separation, jealousy, fear, regret, worry, poverty, unhappiness, embarrassment, fright, indecision, irresolution, uncertainty*, etc. This seems to suggest that in terms of causes *agony* covers a broader range in the scale of seriousness. An inspection of its concordance reveals that it occurs much more frequently with mental causes than physical causes in the BOE, which might be because we talk about our mental experiences much more than physical ones. Consider the following examples:

(149) His voice was hurried, nervous. 'For the first time in my life I wished
       I smoked,' he said, looking down at his feet in an ***agony*** of
       embarrassment. 'I like you, Trudie, I like you a lot.' 'I'm no good.' He
       shook his head. 'What's good when it's at home?' 'Respectable!'

(150) The cat sat in front of the bird cage in an *agony* of ***frustration*** at being
       so near and yet so far. 猫无可奈何 (*wúkěnàihé*) 地坐在鸟笼前，眼看着
       鸟儿近在咫尺，可怎么也够不着。 (http://dict.cn/frustration)

In Example (149), *embarrassment* is the cause of *agony* or the mental pain itself. But in Chinese, in such a situation, the experience of getting embarrassed is never associated with *tòngkǔ*. Similarly, in Example (150), the failure to reach the bird is far from being *tòngkǔ*. So we may argue that *agony* is not necessarily intense or severe.

Now let us move on to look at *agonize/agonise*. Before the corpus analysis, the relevant dictionary definitions are examined:

LDCE: to think about a difficult decision very carefully and with a lot of effort

OALECD: suffer great anxiety or worry intensely (about sth) **agonized,
-ised** expressing agony **agonizing, -ising** causing agony

COBUILD: If you *agonize over* something, you feel very anxious about it and spend a long time thinking about it.
     agonizing/agonising: 1. Something that is *agonizing* causes you to feel great physical or mental pain. 2. *Agonizing* decisions and choices are very difficult to make.
     agonized/agonised: *Agonized* describes something that you say or do when you are in great physical or mental pain.

A close inspection of the above dictionary entries seems to reveal that *agonise/agonize* as a verb has quite a different meaning from its nominal form. It has a pretty specific meaning, closely related to anxiety, worry and long-time thinking. However, OALECD's explanations of its –*ing* and –*ed* forms, i.e. 'causing agony' and 'expressing agony', show that these two forms are still close in meaning to its nominal form. COBUILD's paraphrases of them confirm this hypothesis.

The corpus can tell us whether this is true. The BOE generates 1,195 hits of *agonize* and 1,399 hits of *agonise*. I examined them together for their top 50 collocates. As expected, *agonise/agonize* strongly colligates with *over (489)* and *about (92)*. Its collocates show that the possible reasons to *agonize/agonise* include *wait (93), death (64), decision (60), pain (46), choice (20), question (17), dilemma (8), defeat (9), slowness (12), loss (11)*, etc. Out of the 2,594 instances in total, 1,753 hits are in the –*ing* form and 612 in the –*ed* form, leaving only 229 hits of other forms. The collocates of *agonizing/agonising* suggest that it semantically prefers words indicating a time period, predominantly *day (33), moment (26), hour (17), minute (18), time (17), month (16), week (16), year (13)* and *night (12)*, revealing that to *agonise/agonize* is a dynamic *process (14)*, which could be as short as a moment or as long as a year. Its other nominal collocates include *wait (89), death (62), decision (58), pain (44), choice (20), question (16), slowness (12), detail (12), loss (11), defeat (9), dilemma (8), experience (8)* and *reappraisal (8)*. Among them, *decision, choice, dilemma* and *reappraisal* are concerned with judgement or evaluation and the other collocates are all associated with physical or mental pain.

Now let us move on to compare *agonized/agonised* and *anguished*. The frequencies of their collocates are summarized as follows:

> *anguished (849): cry (48), look (17), voice (11), tone (7), expression (6), eye (6), moan (4), wail (4), howl (3), scream (3)*
> *agonized/agonised (612): scream (10), cry (9), face (8), expression (6), sound (6), look (6)*

It can be seen that both are semantically associated with words to do with visible or audible manifestations, such as *cry, scream, look, voice, expression, sound.* However, it appears that, compared with *agonized/agonised*, *anguished* is more frequently associated with physical pain, as indicated in its collocates, such as *cry, scream, moan, wail, howl*, etc., which apparently denote physical pain. From the discussion so far, it is clear that *agonized/agonised* and *agonizing/agonising* diverge considerably in meaning from their stem *agonize/agonise*, but go towards their root.

Turning to their Chinese equivalents, 88 hits of *agony** are found in the BPC. A summary of the search findings is given in Table 7.37.

Table 7.37 Chinese equivalents of *agony** in the BPC

Feeling	*tòngkǔ 44, zhémo 3, jùtòng 3, nánwéiqíng 2, nánshòu 2, tòngchǔ 2*
Idiom	*zhuānlán 5*
Left out	2
Others	25
Total	88

Table 7.37 shows that, in half of the instances, *agony** is translated as *tòngkǔ*. Its other translations include *zhémo* (a stronger version of *tòngkǔ*), *jùtòng* (lit. severe physical pain), *tòngchǔ* (another formal word for pain), *nánshòu* (a less formal word for pain), *nánwéiqíng* (from *agony of embarrassment*), *zhuānlán* (from *agony column*), etc. In still many other cases, it is translated in various ways because it has an extraordinarily wide semantic scope, with causes ranging from very minor to very serious matters.

For *anguish*, the BPC yields only 46 hits. The search result is shown in Table 7.38.

Table 7.38 Chinese equivalents of *anguish** in the BPC

Feeling	*tòngkǔ 21 (jídù tòngkǔ 5), tòngchǔ 1,*
	zhémo 3, xīnzhōng . . . jùtòng/xīnlǐ . . . jítòng 5
	bēitòng/fènwài nánguò 4
	kǔ'nǎo/kǔmèn 5
Physical pain	3
Others	4
Total	46

From Table 7.38, it can be clearly seen that, although *anguish* can mean both physical and mental pain, it is used in its physical sense only three times in the corpus. This might be attributed to the composition of the parallel corpus since fiction talks much more about feelings than about physical pains. Among the feeling group, 21 instances are translated as *tòngkǔ*, including five instances of *jídù tòngkǔ* (extremely *tòngkǔ*); one instance is translated as *tòngchǔ*, which is highly similar in meaning to *tòngkǔ* but more formal; in three of them, *zhémo*, which roughly means 'torture', is used. Five of them are translated by using split constructions 'xīnzhōng . . . jùtòng' and 'xīnlǐ . . . jítòng', which are understood in terms of metaphorical images of what is physically happening in one's heart. What they depict is more or less the same as *tòngkǔ* does, but this means of description exhibits a more vivid picture. *Anguish* is also associated with *grief*, because *bēitòng* or *fènwài* (extremely) *nánguò* is used in four translations. Consider the following example:

(151) 这种不正常比邦妮的死还要严重, 因为邦妮死后初期的悲痛 (*bēitòng*) 现在已逐渐减轻, 她觉得那个惨重的损失可以默默地忍受了。

This wrongness went even deeper than Bonnie's death, for now the first unbearable **anguish** was fading into resigned acceptance of her loss.

Five of the translations are associated with *kǔ'nǎo*/*kǔmèn* (vexation/gloom). Obviously, *anguish* focuses more on the pain or suffering, regardless of reason. This is quite different from the Chinese *tòngkǔ*, which is more specific. So, from the above analysis, it seems that *anguish*, defined as 'great mental or physical pain or suffering', consists of similar semantic components to *tòngkǔ*. However, it covers a wider range of pain than *tòngkǔ* does because, as noted earlier, it is also associated with *grief, vexation, gloom* or *worry*.

Tòngkǔ

This section will discuss the Chinese counterpart shared by this group of words based on the BPC, i.e. *tòngkǔ*. For *bitter*, as was presented earlier, OALECD does not include *tòngkǔ* in its Chinese explanations. What it offers for *anguish* and *agony* are both *jídù tòngkǔ* (extremely + *tòngkǔ*). It seems that, according to this dictionary, no English word is equivalent to *tòngkǔ* itself. XHCBL defines *tòngkǔ* as follows:

> 身体或精神感到非常难受: pain; suffering; agony; physical suffering or mental pain: ～的生活 painful life | 得了这种病, 非常～。 The disease causes great pain and suffering.

Interestingly, it lists neither *anguish* nor *bitter* here. Let us look at how it behaves in the CCL corpus, where 17,259 hits of *tòngkǔ* occur. Its significant collocates, classified into five categories, are shown in Table 7.39.

The collocates in the first column are relevant to the characteristic of extroversion: *liǎn*/*liǎnshàng* (face/on the face), *biǎoxiàn* (manifest), *biǎoqíng* (facial expression), *kàn*/*kàndào* (look/see), *yǎnjing* (eyes), *yàngzi* (appearance). *Gǎndào*/*gǎnjué*/*gǎnshòu* (feel), *nèixīn* (inner heart), *xīnzhōng*/*xīnlǐ* (in the heart) and *xīn* (heart) point to its attribute of introversion. So *tòngkǔ* could be a facial expression (*biǎoqíng*), frame of mind (*xīnqíng*) or feeling (*gǎnqíng*/*gǎnshòu*). The verbs in the second column show that *tòngkǔ* has semantic preferences for words of causation, typically *ràng*/*lìng*/*shǐ*/*jiào* (cause/make), *zàochéng*/*dàilái*/*dài*/

Table 7.39 Significant collocates of *tòngkǔ* in the CCL corpus

Introversion/extroversion	Verb	Classifier and modifier	Noun		Feeling
liánshàng/lián 161/109	shǐ/lìng 787/167	zhèzhǒng 423	shībài 73	jīngshén 299	āi 168
biǎoxiàn 83	ràng/jiào 326/119	nàzhǒng 132	máodùn 140	línghún 74	xìngfú 152
biǎoqíng 164	dàilái/dài 341/160	yíqiè/suǒyǒu 216/81	jiānnán 81	xīnlíng 93	xīwàng 153
kàn/kàndào 213/89	zàochéng 178	xǔduō 145	kùnnán 63	sīxiǎng 73	huānlè 268
yǎnjīng 85	chǎnshēng 61	dà/jùdà/jídà 426/153/84	bìng/jíbìng 74/72	guòchéng 162	kuàilè 166
yàngzi 71	chōngmǎn 185	shēn 111	zāinàn 71	jīnglì 294	bēishāng 114
xiànrù 137		hěn/fēicháng 663/210	zhémo 264	tǐyàn 62	bēiāi 101
gǎndào 684	rěnshòu/rěn 368/89	shífēn 180	zhèngzhá 169	jīngyàn 62	juéwàng 136
juéde 148	chéngshòu 128	bùkān 224	jiānáo 72	shēnghuó 312	fánnǎo 109
gǎnjué 144	zāoshòu 165	nányǐrěnshòu 69	sǐ/sǐwàng/sǐqù 222/123/67	rénshēng 119	shīwàng 92
gǎnshòu 97	jīngshòu 73	wànfēn 121	búxìng 129	jiātíng 63	kǒngjù 90
nèixīn 320	jiěchú 215	jí/jídù 101/103	shìqù 115	àiqíng 82	fènnù 84
xīnzhōng/xīnlǐ 184/127	jiětuō/bǎituō 89/75	yìdiǎn 93	ròutǐ/shēntǐ 140/73	shìqíng 96	bùān 78
xīn 157	jiǎnqīng 224		shēnyín 140	xiànshí 75	gūdú 70
xīnqíng 98	jiǎnshǎo 85			shèhuì 76	zhízhuó 196
gǎnqíng 87				lìshǐ 59	zhōng 992
				shēngmìng 129	zìjǐ 620
				rénlèi 117	cì 142
				huíyì/jìyì 152/56	

chǎnshēng (bring about/lead to), words related to a state (*chōngmǎn*/be filled with, *xiànrù*/get caught into), suffering (*zāoshòu/shòu*), enduring (*rěnshòu/rěn/chéngshòu/jīngshòu*), relieving (*jiěchú/jiětuō/bǎituō*) and lessening (*jiǎnqīng/jiǎnshǎo*). These verbs basically cover the whole process of *tòngkǔ*. The third column lists its classifiers, typically *zhǒng* (kind) in *zhèzhǒng* (this kind) and *nàzhǒng* (that kind), and modifiers, such as *dà/jùdà/jídà* (great/enormous), *nányǐrěnshòu/bùkān* (unbearable), *hěn/fēicháng/shífēn* (very), *shēn* (deep), *wànfēn/jí/jídù/jíqí* (extremely) and *yìdiǎn* (a little). It seems that *tòngkǔ*, in most cases, is intensified by amplifiers and only in a small number of cases by downtoners. Like English, Chinese uses the same word *tòngkǔ* to express both physical and mental pain. However, only three collocates (Table 7.39) are clearly associated with its physical sense: *ròutǐ/shēntǐ* (body) and *shēnyín* (groan); in contrast, we find a great number of occurrences of *jīngshén/xīnlíng* (mind), *línghún* (soul) and *sīxiǎng* (thought). *Tòngkǔ* is a *jīnglì/tǐyàn/jīngyàn* (experience) or a *guòchéng* (process), which composes *shēnghuó/rénshēng/shēngmìng* (life). As *rénlèi* (human kind), we have our *tòngkǔ*, which might be associated with *huíyì/jìyì* (memory), *jiātíng* (family), *shèhuì* (society), *shìqing* (event), *xiànshí* (reality) or *lìshǐ* (history). It may be caused by *shībài* (failure), *máodùn* (dilemma), *sǐ/sǐwáng/sǐqù* (die/death), *búxìng* (misfortune), *shīqù* (loss), *jiānnán* (hardship), *kùnnán* (difficulty), *bìng/jíbìng* (disease) or *zāinàn* (disaster). Suffering *tòngkǔ* is a *zhémo* (torment) or *jiān'áo* (torture). Some people may *zhēngzhá* (struggle) to get out of this situation. *Xīwàng* (hope) and *ài* (love) may mitigate *tòngkǔ*. Both *kuàilè* (joy) and *huānlè* (gaiety) are the antonyms of *tòngkǔ*. A life with less *tòngkǔ* is *xìngfú* (happy) *de*. *Tòngkǔ* is a close companion of *juéwàng* (desperation), *fánnǎo* (vexation), *bēishāng/bēiāi* (sorrow), *shīwàng* (disappointment), *kǒngjù* (fear), *fènnù* (indignation), *gūdú* (loneliness) or *bù'ān* (uneasiness). People often have mixed feelings of *tòngkǔ* and other negative feelings. If someone is said to be *tòngkǔ* and *juéwàng*, we can know that s/he is extremely *tòngkǔ*. If someone is *tòngkǔ* and *gūdú*, we may see that s/he is not very *tòngkǔ*. *Tòngkǔ* highly frequently occurs in the pattern '*tòngkǔ zhīzhōng / tòngkǔ zhōng*' (in *tòngkǔ*), which is similar to *agony* or *anguish*. *Tòngkǔ* is often a feeling confined to oneself (*zìjǐ*), suggesting that *tòngkǔ* is often something one has to digest on one's own.

Comparison

Now let us compare all these words. First, we will look at how *tòngkǔ* and *bitter* differ. *Bitter* as a feeling is a metaphorical extension of a taste, so it can only be used to express an inner emotional state. Unlike *tòngkǔ*, it does not have a semantic preference for words indicating outward manifestations, like (facial) *expressions, face, show, eyes,* etc. However, like *tòngkǔ,* it often collocates with experience or memories, which can cause a *bitter* feeling. *Bitter* can be a passive emotional reaction towards something unacceptable, unwelcome or sorrow-causing, but, if it is concerned with an opposition, i.e. 'I feel bitter towards someone else', it tends to be an active feeling mixed with *hatred, anger, rage, jealousy* or *hostility. Tòngkǔ* is a combination of metaphors, i.e. *tòng* (pain) and *kǔ* (bitter). It has developed into a word denoting *tòng,* both mental and physical, and the mental *kǔ,* with its original meaning of the physical taste of *kǔ* lost. It is mainly used to describe an internal state, but it is also semantically associated with outward manifestations. Both *bitterness* and *tòngkǔ* are conceptualized as something that is changeable in size, depth and amount, etc., so both can be preceded by modifiers such as *deep, great, much, little,* etc. Both semantically prefer *feel, express, cause,* and other negative-feeling words, like *despair, disappointment.* What differs between them is that *tòngkǔ* is a good companion of *fánnǎo* (vexation), *bēishāng* (sorrow), *bēiāi* (sorrow) *gūdú* (loneliness) and *fènnù* (indignation). Except *fènnù,* all the other feelings are quite passive. *Fènnù* may grow out of *tòngkǔ* in certain circumstances, but people are much more inclined to *shòu/rěnshòu/chéngshòu* (endure) *tòngkǔ.* In contrast, *bitterness* is more associated with *anger, resentment, jealousy, hatred, rage, envy, hostility,* which might be caused by the more frequent use of *bitter* in the sense of 'I feel bitter towards someone else'. If used in this sense, the sufferer is quite active because s/he is unsatisfied with the present situation and trying to get rid of it by turning the fire to other people. So, *bitter* is equivalent to *tòngkǔ* only in the non-opposition sense.

Now let us come to the comparison between *anguish* and *tòngkǔ.* Unlike *bitterness, anguish* implies extreme pain or suffering and can hardly be modified by downtoners, while *tòngkǔ* could be a less intense feeling and sometimes intensified by downtoners, such as *yǒuxiē* (slightly), *xiāngdāng* (fairly). *Anguish* and *tòngkǔ* both have a semantic preference for verbs like *suffer, feel, express, experience, cause, ease,* etc. They are both semantically associated with negative feelings, such as *despair, frustration, fear* and the like. *Anguish* has a semantic preference for family words, such as *family, father, mother,* suggesting that *anguish* is more associated with family. *Tòngkǔ* does not have such an inclination.

Agony often occurs in the pattern 'the *agony* of X', where X indicates the cause or accompanying behaviour, including *failure, hunger, heat, homesickness/ seasickness, helplessness, expectation, impatience, grief, guilt, shame, remorse, repentance, loss, separation, jealousy, fear, regret, worry, poverty, unhappiness, embarrassment, fright, indecision, irresolution, uncertainty,* etc. In terms of cause, *agony* covers a much broader range in the scale of seriousness. However, *tòngkǔ* hardly co-occurs with *impatience, grief, shame, remorse, repentance, fright, fear, worry, poverty, indecision, irresolution, uncertainty* or *embarrassment.* Compared with *agony, tòngkǔ* is a more specific emotion, emphasizing the unacceptability of what has happened to the sufferer and the inability to solve the problem or change the situation. It is a quite passive emotional state.

It can be seen that, from the above analysis, *tòngkǔ* is only partly equivalent to the three words, overlapping with each in certain aspects. *Bitter* indicates a less intense feeling than *tòngkǔ,* only denoting the inner emotional state. *Anguish* and *agony* are both extroverted and introverted, with the former more conceptualized as a static emotional state and the latter more understood as a dynamic process that could be *endured, prolonged, shortened.* In terms of the spectrum of causes, *agony* has the broadest range of coverage, followed by *anguish* and *bitterness. Anguish* and *agony* are translated as *tòngkǔ* only if they fall within its scope. Take 'agony of embarrassment' for example, it is an unpleasant feeling or mental pain in the general sense, but it is not what the Chinese *tòngkǔ* covers.

Tòngkǔ is a more introverted and more specific emotion. It is perceived as both a process and a state. It fulfils most of the functions of *anguish, agony* and *bitter* in its non-opposition sense, but it has a narrower semantic coverage than both *agony* and *anguish.* The typical case for *tòngkǔ* is that someone is suffering and not able to get out of it due to the incompetence to untie the mental knot. Just as the pattern 'xiànrù … tòngkǔ' conveys, *tòngkǔ* is like a pit someone is likely to fall into but is difficult to get out of. They may feel helpless or desperate before they free themselves from the trap. But people who have fallen in the trap are quite passive in the sense that they tend to accept what has happened to them and, in most cases, do not intend to take any action.

7.2 Metaphors in sadness expressions in Chinese and English

A systematic corpus-based comparison of sadness expressions between English and Chinese has been made in Section 7.1. Before embarking on an overall comparison of their commonalities and differences, it is necessary to talk about metaphors, as most of the examined items are metaphorical conceptualizations. Metaphor was regarded as merely a literary device and hence outside the scope of linguistics. It was brought to public attention in linguistics by Lakoff and

Johnson's pioneering *Metaphors We Live By* (1980), in which it is characterized as a conceptual phenomenon whereby a target domain is structured and understood with reference to a more basic source domain. It is in fact pervasive in human understanding. Based on Lakoff and Johnson's *Metaphors We Live By*, I summarize the metaphorical mappings between source domains and target domains of all the metaphorical sadness expressions examined in this research in Table 7.40.

From the inventory of the expressions shown in Table 7.40, we can find that Chinese seems to have more metaphorical sadness expressions at the lexical level (including prefabricated expressions) than English. This is due partly to the fact that Chinese words are composed of characters. If a word contains a character that is a metaphor, the whole word becomes a metaphor as well, like *(bēi)tòng*, where only *tòng* is metaphorical. What can also be seen from Table 7.40 is that they are quite similar in terms of metaphorical mappings, as both Chinese and English map the domains of physical injury, taste, container and spatial orientation onto the domain of feeling. Both cultures conceptualize mental experience (mental pain or feeling) in terms of physical experience (physical pain, injury or taste) and think of and talk about sadness as DOWN and happiness as UP. For example, in Chinese, there are *qíngxù dīluò* (mood + down), *yāyì* (press down), *yìyù* (press down + (of sorrow, anger, etc.) pent-up), *gāoxìng* (high + mood), as shown in Table 7.40. In English, we can find *depress* (press down), *deject* (cause to fall down), *upset* (overturn), as shown in Table 7.40, and *low/high-spirited* which are not discussed and therefore not shown in the table.

According to Lakoff and Johnson (1980), the mapping of attributes in the domain of spatial orientation onto other conceptual domains is referred to as orientational metaphors. They claim that these spatial orientations are based on the nature of the human body and the way the body operates in our physical environment. Lakoff and Johnson (1980) observe that HAPPY/GOOD IS UP and BAD/SAD IS DOWN in English linguistic expressions. They argue that human beings walk erect because they have the ability to overcome the gravitational force, so the erect body is associated with a positive connotation and the prostrate posture with a negative one. This is the reason why UP has positive connotations and DOWN has negative ones, which seems to be shared by Chinese (Lan 1999, 2002). The fact that Chinese and English cultures conceive of UP and DOWN in a similar way may be attributed to common human experience, among which walking erect is considered the essential one.

When we shift the attention from the node word (the examined items) to the wider context and look at the collocations shown in Section 7.1, we find that

Table 7.40 Comparison of metaphors in sadness expressions in Chinese and English

Chinese metaphorical sadness expression	Source domain	Target domain (feeling)	English metaphorical sadness expression	Source domain	Target domain (feeling)
(bēi)tòng/pain	physical injury (ontological)	grief			
tòngkǔ/painful and bitter	physical pain + bitter (ontological)	anguish	*bitter*	taste (ontological)	unhappy
(bēi)shāng/hurt	physical injury (ontological)	sorrow			
shāngxīn/heart is hurt	physical injury (ontological)	sad	*brokenhearted*	physical injury (ontological)	extremely sad
xīnsuì/heart is fragmented	physical injury (ontological)	extremely sad			
huīxīn/grey heart	colour (ontological)	disheartened			
xīnhuīyìlěng/grey heart + cold intention	colour + temperature (ontological)	despondent	*deject*/cause to fall down	spatial orientation	despondent
(yōu)yù/accumulate in a closed container (liver)	container	melancholy			
yāyì/press down + press down	spatial orientation	depressed	*depress*/press down	spatial orientation	very unhappy
yīnyù/cloudy + accumulate in a closed container (liver)	weather (ontological) + container	melancholy	*gloomy*	darkness (ontological)	sad and hopeless
yìyù/press down + accumulate in a closed container (liver)	spatial orientation + container	depression			
bù gāoxìng/not + high + mood	spatial orientation	unhappy	*upset*/overturn	spatial orientation	unhappy, annoyed, anxious and worried
mènmèn(bùlè)/tightly closed in a closed container (heart)	container	gloomy			
nánguò/hard + live	live a life (structural)	sad			
qíngxù dīluò/mood + low	spatial orientation	depressed			

both Chinese and English cultures metaphorically conceptualize emotions in terms of gaseous or fluid, so the image of 'being full' in a container is associated with a strong feeling. In English, if someone is filled with an emotion, s/he feels it very strongly. We can say someone is filled with *admiration/joy/happiness/ horror/fear/anger/doubt/remorse*, etc. This is similar to the description of Chinese emotions. *Chōngmǎn* (be filled with) in Chinese is a typical verb used to describe an intense emotion, such as *yōuyù, bēitòng, bēishāng, bēiāi, shānggǎn, tòngkǔ*. It is interesting to note that, in both cultures, metaphorical expressions are mainly used to describe strong feelings, while a modifier or quantifier is used instead to describe a less intense or weak feeling.

It is not surprising that there are similarities in metaphorical conceptualizations of emotions between these two cultures because metaphor is grounded in embodied experience, an idea that has been dominant in cognitive linguistic metaphor research from the very beginning (Lakoff and Johnson 1980, 1999). We construe our emotions in terms of our physical activities, so our emotional experience is closely related to our physical experience. We are all human beings and share a lot in common in human physical experience, which leads to similar metaphorical conceptualizations in the emotion domain. In fact, 'most of our normal conceptual system is metaphorically structured'; that is, 'most concepts are partially understood in terms of other concepts' (Lakoff and Johnson, 1980: 56). Metaphor is a cognitive tool for conceptualizing our world and it plays a central role in the construction of social reality; metaphor is rooted in cultures and pervasive in human languages. Actually, not only metaphors, but the whole human conceptual system emerges from everyday human experience (Sweetser 1990). This partly explains why all human languages share some similarities.

On the other hand, Table 7.40 shows that Chinese and English also display some differences in metaphorical sadness expressions. First, as mentioned earlier, some Chinese emotion words, like *bēishāng, bēitòng, yōuyù, mènmènbúlè* shown in Table 7.40, are composed of two parts and only one of them is metaphor (the Chinese characters in the brackets are not metaphors). Obviously, this does not apply to English. Secondly, both cultures have their own specific ways of perceiving sadness. The Chinese culture conceives of sadness in terms of weather, colour, temperature and living a life, such as *nánguò* (hard + live), *xīnhuīyìlěng* (grey heart + cold intention), *yīn(yù)* (cloudy). Chinese has a specific sadness concept *yù*, which has developed its meanings in the order of 'fánnǎo' (vexation), 'zǔzhì/bìsè' (block), 'yōuchóu/yōuyù' (sorrow and worry), 'yuànhèn' (resentment), 'bàonù' (rage) and the like (*Hànyǔ Dà Cídiǎn*: 858). In Modern Chinese, it is mainly used in disyllabic words, meaning (1) 'pent-up sorrow', as in *yīnyù, yìyù*,

(2) 'be held up and accumulate', as in (*yōu*)*yù, yùjié, yùjī*, and (3) 'luxuriant', as in *yùyùcōngcōng*. In the modern discourse, the meaning of 'pent-up sorrow' remains active, but the meanings of 'yuànhèn' and 'bàonù' have become rare. Its meaning of sadness is associated with a blocked image: the sad feeling in the form of *qì* is held up and accumulates gradually in one's body. *Gānqì yùjié* (liver + *qì* + block) is a typical expression to describe the situation when someone's sad feeling has been held up and accumulates in one's liver. The traditional Chinese medicine believes that, if *qì* is held up in the liver, it will lead to great sadness, i.e. *yù*. Another Chinese-specific concept is *mèn* (tightly closed), a less serious emotional state, as in *mènmènbúlè*. *Mèn* occurs when someone is thinking about something unhappy and does not share it with others. It seems to be understood in terms of a closed container, but it is specifically associated with the image of the heart. The typical expression is *mèn zài xīnlǐ* (tightly closed in the heart), because the heart is believed to be the locus of various emotions in the Chinese culture. In English, the conceptualization of emotions is also associated with a closed container, e.g. *pent-up anger/frustration/affection/feelings*. However, what makes the difference is that the Chinese concepts are specifically associated with the image of an organ as a container. Further, the Chinese culture associates them with specific sad feelings *yù* and *mèn*, and encodes these associations in its emotion lexicon; however, the English container conceptualization is quite general as any feeling, whether positive or negative, can be *pent-up*.

Thirdly, Chinese and English differ in linguistic manifestations or specific conceptualizations of sadness, though they are similar in certain conceptual mappings between domains. For instance, *tòngkǔ*, *agony* and *anguish* are all conceptualized in the image of 'be in/into something' as we can find 'chǔ yǔ *tòngkǔ* zhī zhōng' in Chinese, and 'in agony'/'in anguish' in English. However, Chinese *tòngkǔ* is also understood in terms of the 'falling into (*xiànrù*) something' image. These two images are quite close, and both are mapped from a container. The main difference between them is to do with the 'state' character of the former and the 'activity' character of the latter. Various kinds of emotional states may be conceptualized as containers (Lakoff and Johnson 1980; Machakanja 2008) in both cultures. We can find 'in love', 'in grief', 'in depression', 'in excitement' in English and their counterparts 'chǔyǔ liànài/bēitòng/yìyù/xìngfèn zhīzhōng' in Chinese. It is also common to say 'fall into depression' or 'fall in love'. But can we infer metaphors in a systematic way across cultures? We will still feel weird if we hear 'fall into agony or anguish'. Another example to illustrate this would be *upset*. Both cultures map the spatial orientation onto the feeling of sadness, but the association of the image of 'overturn' with sadness is English-specific.

Considering its metaphorical process, it is not hard to understand that *upset* is a complex concept characterized by a mixture of *sadness, annoyance, worry* and *anxiety*. There is no such Chinese word that incorporates so many emotional components into one simple concept just because there is no such metaphorical construal of sadness in Chinese. The issue relevant to metaphorical words is that the difference in word formation will lead to their difference in usage patterns, so many so-called translation equivalents are not truly correspondent to each other. For example, the association of the image of *chōngmǎn* (being filled with) with an intense feeling seems to be shared by English and Chinese, maybe also other languages, but Chinese never uses *chōngmǎn* to describe *gāoxìng* (happiness), *shāngxīn* or *nánguò*. They cannot be metaphorically understood in terms of 'a full container' probably because they are already metaphors that are associated with other images, so they cannot be used in this way.

Fourthly, even if sadness is related to the mapping between the same source domain and the same target domain in the two cultures, when it comes to the exact meaning it refers to, they exhibit some cultural differences. For example, although both cultures map the physical experience of injury onto the sad feeling, *shāngxīn* and *xīnsuì* in Chinese are both quite different from the English *heartbroken** in use and meaning. This can also be illustrated by the conceptualization of *bēitòng*. Apart from *chōngmǎn*, we also use *chénjìn* (be immersed into) to describe *bēitòng*. Although *chénjìn* also presents us an image of 'being full', the association of a strong emotion with the state of 'be immersed in' is rather specific to Chinese. So it can be argued that in distinctive cultures the specific associations arising from the same or similar conceptual mapping might be different and consequently lead to different linguistic manifestations. This seems to suggest that languages may display cultural variations and distinctiveness at varying levels of metaphorical conceptualizations. Therefore, cross-linguistic studies on metaphors should go deeper to look at their differences in specific conceptualizations, rather than stop at the level of mapping between domains.

Studies on emotions show that the metaphorical conceptualizations of emotions are closely related to the conceptualizations of body parts, which display considerable cultural variation (Ameka 2002; Enfield and Wierzbicka 2002; Turpin 2002; Ye 2002; Yu 2002, 2003, 2009), though human beings undergo similar bodily events or processes in our emotional experience. One typical example would be that in the Chinese culture the organ *dǎn* 'gallbladder' is related to courage because the gallbladder is thought to play a role in making judgements and decisions and therefore has to do with courage (Yu 2003).

Chinese has traditionally linked various emotions with internal organs, which can be traced back to traditional Chinese medicine. An overview is given below, with the metaphorical images evoked in the expressions given in the parentheses (Yu, 2009: 239).

(i)　　spleen: anger (gaseous energy of qi expanding)
(ii)　　liver: anger (fire burning)
　　　　sadness (split, ripped into pieces)
(iii)　　intestines: anxiety (knotted, twisted, hanged)
　　　　sadness (knotted, twisted, split, ripped into pieces)
(iv)　　stomach: anxiety (hanged)
(v)　　lungs: sadness (split)
(vi)　　gallbladder: fear (void, frigid, hanged, dropped, lost, trembling, split)
(vii)　　heart: anger (fire burning)
　　　　anxiety (troubled, hanged, lifted, suspended, pinched, scorched, fried, burned by fire)
　　　　sadness (pain, frigid, wounded, twisted, fragmented, pierced, torn apart, pounded)
　　　　fear (shocked, throbbing, frigid, lifted, split)
　　　　happiness (open, vast, bright, blooming)
　　　　relief (laid down, settled down, calm down, broad)
　　　　admiration (toppled, drunk)
　　　　vexation (closed up, blocked, messed up, troubled, pain)
　　　　disappointment (frigid, grey)
　　　　disgust (vomiting)
　　　　hatred (pain, rotten)
　　　　guilt (void, lost)

This list is based on dictionaries. These metaphorical images can roughly reflect how emotions are understood in the Chinese culture. We can see that the heart is especially rich in emotional associations, which explains why Yu (2009) makes a book-length analysis of *xīn*/heart metaphors, in which he points out that 'the dichotomies between body and mind, heart and head, in English do not exist in traditional Chinese thought' (p. 352) and the heart has been traditionally seen as the organ of thinking and feeling in the Chinese culture. All these associations have been encoded in the Chinese lexicon. One hundred and thirty-one words starting with *xīn* are found in the XHCBL and the great majority of them are metaphors, like *xīnshēng* (heart-voice/heartfelt wishes), *xīnbìng* (heart-disease/worry), *xīnyuàn* (heart-wish/wish) and *xīnxì* (heart-thin/cautious; careful). There are still numerous metaphorical *xīn*-words not starting with *xīn* that cannot be easily counted due to the searching method, such as *fàngxīn* (lay down-heart/rest assured), *jiāoxīn* (burnt-heart/anxious), *yíxīn* (suspicious-heart/suspicion), *guānxīn* (close-heart/concern/care), *nàixīn* (endure-heart/patience), *xìnxīn* (believe-heart/confidence), *juéxīn* (determine-heart/determination) and *xióngxīn* (masculine-heart/ambition). The illustration of the *xīn*-words might help understand why metaphors are pervasive in the Chinese lexicon as well as in the sadness lexicon (expressions).

Yu's analysis of *heart* is comprehensive and almost exhaustive, but, as he states in the conclusion of the book, he mainly leans on a qualitative approach, which will inevitably lead to some unsatisfactory findings. Consider the following quotes about *shāngxīn* from his book (p. 259):

(1) 心碎 *xīn-suì* (heart-fragmented) 'be heart-broken'
(2) 伤心 *shāng-xīn* (wound-heart) 'sad; grieved; broken-hearted'

From the above quotes, it is clear that he thinks both *shāngxīn* and *xīnsuì* are the same as *heartbroken* or *broken-hearted*. But my corpus-based analysis in Section 7.1.4 shows that neither *shāngxīn* nor *xīnsuì* is the same as *heartbroken**: *shāngxīn* as a word in modern discourse denotes a more outward but less intense emotion than *heartbroken*, and *xīnsuì* is a more intense feeling than *heartbroken* but sometimes it could be absolutely positive. This divergence seems to suggest that the subtle differences of conceptual metaphors between distinctive cultures can only be revealed by corpus-based analyses. Another thing that should be noted in his qualitative analysis is that he analyses many words that are hardly used in real language. For example, he discusses 心伤 and also glosses it as '*xīn-shāng* (heart-wounded) 'sad; grieved; broken-hearted' (p. 259). However, only 115 hits of *xīnshāng* are found in the CCL corpus and few of them are used as a word, as exemplified in the following lines:

她说:'我们的　心伤　透了', 我们之所以加入国大党
对130多万名伊拉克儿童所造成身　心伤　害远不止

It is clearly seen that in '心伤透了' (heart-pierced) and '身心伤害' (physical and mental hurt) in the above lines, 心 and 伤 happen to co-occur, but they do not serve as a word. A qualitative analysis like this attaches equal weight to the word which occurs more than 2,800 times and only a few times in a corpus, while a corpus-based analysis puts particular stress on frequency and real language use.

7.3 Summary

This section is a brief conclusion that sums up the major findings of this research, based on the contrastive analysis in Section 7.1. The steps my analysis followed can be schematically presented in Figure 7.7.

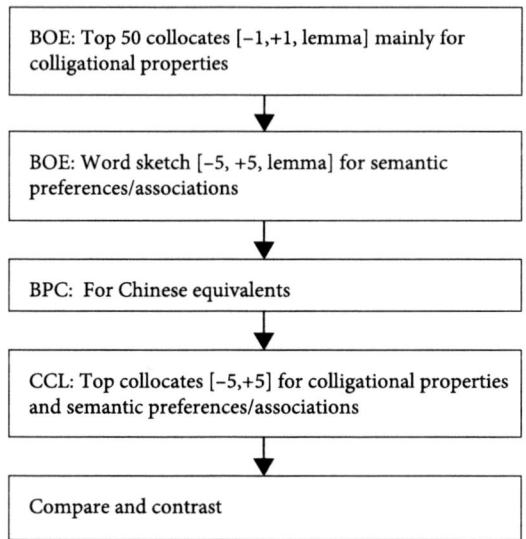

Figure 7.7 Diagram for contrastive corpus-based analysis

Basically, I followed these procedures. For some words, I also searched for their collocates in the span of −5 to +5. The research yields an equivalence network of sadness expressions between English and Chinese, which is presented in Figure 7.8. Looking at Figure 7.8, our first impression is that of chaos. This is an equivalence network principally based on a unidirectional parallel corpus, i.e. from English to Chinese. From it, we can see how these sadness expressions match up between English and Chinese. By carefully comparing the Chinese synonyms obtained from the parallel corpus, we have figured out the distinction dimensions so we can distinguish them from each other. At the same time, the semantic information of the original English lexical item has been revealed. My intuition has also served to complement the research findings. For example, I added *yìyù*, a quite modern word, to the equivalent group of *depression** to compensate for the lack of contemporary texts in the parallel corpus.

It is true that there are some common points in Chinese and English sadness expressions. For one thing, they are similar in certain metaphorical mappings through which sadness is conceptualized, as noted earlier. For another, sadness

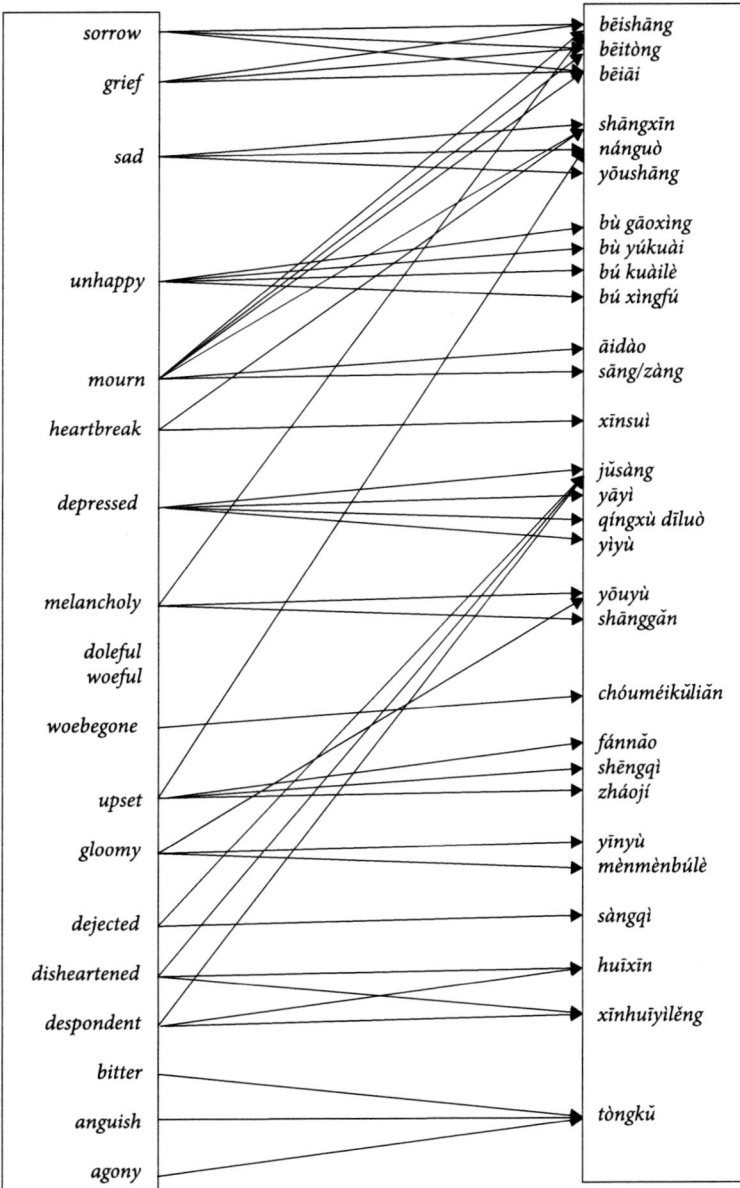

Figure 7.8 Equivalence network of sadness expressions between English and Chinese

expressions in both languages have strong colligations with modifiers and the verb *feel* (*gǎnjué/gǎndào/juéde/jué*); both are semantically associated with words related to its physical manifestations, like *eyes, voice, facial expression, appearance*. Nevertheless, their cultural/linguistic differences observed in attested data seem more prominent than their commonalities. Table 7.41 summarizes the major findings concerning the semantic differences of the examined lexical items.

Table 7.41 Major differences between English and Chinese sadness expressions

Words	English	Chinese
sorrow/grief *bēishāng/bēiāi/ bēitòng*	Lacking the dimension: altruistic or personal.	Altruistic—Chinese specific.
unhappy *bù gāoxìng/ bú kuàilè/ bù yúkuài/ bú xìngfú*	*Unhappy* covers the meanings of all four Chinese equivalents.	Dimensions: introversion/extroversion, specificity/generality, length.
sad *shāngxīn/ nánguò/ yōushāng*	*Sad* seems to be a generic term. It means 'feeling unhappy', 'showing unhappy' and 'making someone unhappy'.	No real generic term in Modern Chinese. Compared with *sad*, *shāngxīn* is more intense, specific and extroverted, *nánguò* is also more specific, and *yōushāng* is more intense, more literary, more introverted and less negative. *Nánguò* may be caused by oneself or someone else, while *shāngxīn* is more likely to emphasize the pain on 'ME' caused by other people or some external force.
heartbreak *shāngxīn/xīnsuì*	*Heartbreak* lies between *shāngxīn* and *xīnsuì* in terms of intensity.	*Shāngxīn* seems to be more extroverted and *xīnsuì* is mainly used in causative constructions and less negative.
mourn *bēishāng/ bēitòng/ bēiāi/ shāngxīn/ āidào*	*Mourn*: (1) feel sad and miss someone after his/her death, (2) show publicly one's bereavement that may or may not be sincere, based on ritualized or social practice, and (3) feel regret about the loss of something.	*Āidào*: show one's sadness about someone's death, based on ritualized or communal practice. *Bēishāng/bēitòng/bēiāi/ shāngxīn*: voluntary feeling of sadness.

doleful/woeful/ woebegone	Mainly showing one's sadness.	No exact equivalent. Chinese does not distinguish between feeling and showing sadness in the lexicon. It tends to combine emotion words and facial organs to describe emotional manifestations.
depressed/ melancholy jǔsàng/yàyì/ qíngxù dīluò /yìyù/ bēishāng/ yōuyù/ shānggǎn	*Depressed* has a wider semantic range, covering the meanings of *jǔsàng, yàyì, qíngxù dīluò* and *yìyù*. *Melancholy* and *yōuyù* are similar in that they are both related to a temperament or character and sometimes can be used in a less negative way. But it is closer to *shānggǎn* in feeling sadness for no particular reason.	Each equivalent emphasizes a different aspect. *Jǔsàng* focuses on disappointment, frustration and hopelessness and *yàyì* on the difficulty or impossibility of untying the knots and the incompetence to release one's sad feelings. *Yìyù* is closer to *depression*, but not *depressed*. *Yōuyù* is much less negative. *Shānggǎn* is the sadness invoked by emotional stirrings.
upset nánguò/fánnǎo /shēngqì/zháojí	*Upset* is a complex concept characterized by a mixture of several feelings, i.e. *sadness, worry, anxiety* and *annoyance*.	No exact Chinese equivalent. Chinese does not encode so many components into one single emotional concept. It seems that Chinese emotional concepts tend to be more discrete, with each emphasizing one emotional aspect.
gloomy yōuyù/yīnyù/ mènmènbùlè	*Gloomy* is more semantically associated with the future. The past vs future dimension is lacking in Chinese *gloomy* expressions.	*Yōuyù* is more an inward feeling without specific reasons. However, sometimes it is also viewed as something very beautiful. *Yīnyù* is manifested more outwardly. Both *yōuyù* and *yīnyù* can be related to a person's character. People will feel *mènmènbùlè* when things are not going as wished.
dejected/ disheartened/ despondent jǔsàng/sàngqì/ huīxīn/ xīnhuīyìlěng	*Dejected* focuses on the reaction to what has just happened, while *despondent* emphasizes the feeling due to the gloomy prediction about the future, and *disheartened* centres on both.	*Sàngqì* seems to focus on the emotional reaction to what has just happened, but no Chinese expression emphasizes the pessimistic thinking about the future; *huīxīn* and *jǔsàng* focus on both, with the former more introverted and the latter more extroverted.

(continued)

Table 7.41 Major differences between English and Chinese sadness expressions (Continued)

Words	English	Chinese
bitterness/ agony/ anguish tòngkǔ	*Bitterness* indicates an inner emotional state, and it is equivalent to *tòngkǔ* only in the non-opposition sense. *Anguish* implies extreme pain or suffering and is hardly modified by downtoners. *Anguish* is more conceptualized as a static emotional state, while *agony* is more understood as a dynamic process. Of these words, *agony* has the broadest range of semantic coverage, followed by *anguish* and *bitterness*.	*Tòngkǔ* has a narrower semantic coverage than *agony* and is less intense *anguish*. It talks about the suffering invoked by something specific, especially if one is not able to get out of it due to the inability to untie the mental knot.

Only the relatively important findings are presented in Table 7.41 because the semantic details are too rich to be listed here. I will sum up the broader linguistic/cultural differences revealed by the earlier contrastive analyses as follows:

(1) In terms of colligational patterns, first, Chinese sadness expressions, different from their English counterparts, have a strong colligation with prepositional phrases that indicate the perceived loci related to the inner emotional or outer physical activities, typically *xīnzhōng/xīnlǐ* (in the heart) and *liǎnshàng/mǎnliǎn* (on the face). This might be because Chinese does not distinguish between feeling and showing sadness in the lexicon. Instead, it uses the collocation with other words/items, typically prepositional phrases, such as 'in the heart', 'on the face', to express the difference. Secondly, they tend to be preceded by classifiers, such as *zhǒng* (kind), *fèn* (portion), *sī* (lit. silk/minute), *cì* (times) and *zhèn* (lasting for a short time). The Chinese classifier system is not only a system of linguistic categorization, but also reflects its underlying conceptual structure (Jiang 2004; Tai 1994; Tai and Chao 1990). For example, *sī* is an extension from the shape of long, thin silk to a slight intensity of feeling. Thirdly, unlike their English counterparts, Chinese sadness expressions strongly colligate with the particle *de*, but hardly with various forms of *be*, which, of course, is due to the typological differences between these two languages. Fourthly, unlike English, Chinese sadness expressions are predominantly preceded by causative constructions, such as *lìng/shǐ/ràng (rén)*, to express the meaning of 'making or causing someone to be sad', while such a meaning has been incorporated as a sense into the English sadness lexicon. This suggests that, in expressing causative meanings, Chinese sadness expressions rely more on analytic expressions. Further, this feature seems to be applicable to the whole language (cf. Xu 2002). So we can argue that, at least in terms of causative expressions, English has a higher degree of lexicalization than Chinese.

(2) In terms of collocations, first, Chinese sadness expressions are more semantically associated with *biǎoqíng/shénsè/shénqíng* (facial expression) and *yàngzi* (appearance), which are realized by link verbs in English, mainly *look, appear, seem*, etc. Secondly, although sadness expressions often collocate with their hypernyms in both Chinese and English, they collocate with different superordinates. In English, most sadness expressions, such as *sadness* (148, −5, +5), *grief* (83, −5, +5), *sorrow* (21, −5, +5), often co-occur with *feeling*; in contrast, in Chinese, most

sadness expressions frequently co-occur with *qíngxù* (mood) or *xīnqíng* (frame of mind), rather than the Chinese translation equivalents of *feeling—qínggǎn* or *gǎnqíng*. This is probably because *qínggǎn* or *gǎnqíng* is not truly equivalent to *feeling* (Zhang and Ooi 2008). It seems that in the Chinese discourse *sadness*, as well as other feelings, is more conceptualized or talked about as *qíngxù* or *xīnqíng*, rather than *gǎnqíng* or *qínggǎn*. Thirdly, Chinese sadness expressions collocate more frequently with their hypernyms—*qíngxù* or *xīnqíng*—than their English counterparts do with *feeling*.

(3) For metaphorical sadness expressions, Chinese and English differ in certain conceptual mappings between domains. For example, as noted earlier, Chinese maps the domains of colour, temperature, weather, living a life onto the domain of sadness, which English lacks; however, unlike English, Chinese does not associate sadness with darkness.

(4) Chinese and English differ in linguistic manifestations or specific conceptualizations of sadness, though they are similar in certain conceptual mappings between domains. A typical example for this is that both Chinese and English construe sadness as a container, but the English construal is rather general, and the Chinese understanding, by contrast, is based on a specific system relating various emotions to different organs. This is much to do with traditional Chinese medicine.

(5) Many Modern Chinese sadness expressions are still related to traditional fatalism, as many Chinese people, especially at the time of difficulties, still believe that events are decided by fate and there is nothing one can do to prevent them from happening. If someone feels that s/he cannot change or control fate, s/he thinks it is pointless to try. *Bēishāng, shānggǎn, yōushāng* and *yōuyù* are all relevant to the fatalistic view, to different extents.

(6) *Sad* is an umbrella term for all sadness expressions in English, while Modern Chinese lacks such a cover term. The closest one would be *shāngxīn* or *nánguò*, but neither of them fulfils the same function as *sad* does in English. We can also find that *unhappy* covers a broad semantic range and it incorporates into one single word the meanings of Chinese *bú xìngfú, bú kuàilè, bù yúkuài, bù gāoxìng, búxìng*. *Unhappy* has a wide semantic range because *happy* is also a cover term like *sad*. Modern Chinese lacks such a cover term probably because it is a mixture of Old Chinese characters and derived modern words. Each Old Chinese character has a distinctly clear meaning, such as *bēi* and *xǐ*. In Modern

Chinese, they can be used as a cover term, but often in combinations, like *bēi xǐ jiāojiā* (sorrow + joy + mingle) or *xǐ nù āi lè* (happiness + anger + sadness + joy). This might have hindered the modern cover terms in the emotion domain, probably in other domains as well, from its entry into Modern Chinese.

(7) Chinese and English apply different dimensions to distinguish sadness expressions. For instance, in Chinese, the dimension of voluntary vs ritualized is applied in distinguishing Chinese sadness expressions, in which *shāngxīn/nánguò/bēitòng/bēishāng* is voluntary and *āidào* is ritualized and culturally mediated. There is a quite clear division of labour between them for *āidào* is only used to mean 'show one's sadness' and is specifically used in ritualized situations. In English, there is no such clear dividing line. For example, *mourn* combines both voluntary and ritualized feelings into one word, though *mourning* seems to have a strong tendency to be more ritualized, but it covers three Chinese concepts *āidào*, *sāng* and *zàng*, which are also distinctly distinguished. This point can also be illustrated by the concept of *bēiāi*, which is unique for its altruistic characteristic. The dimension of *personal* (TO ME) vs *altruistic* (TO OTHERS) is Chinese-specific. Further, the Chinese *gloomy* group lacks the dimension of past vs future and so does the Chinese *dejected* group. Languages differ in ways to combine semantic components into lexical words; in other words, different languages differentiate their words or synonyms along different dimensions, which reflect the ways in which their speakers organize, classify and categorize the world.

(8) Some Chinese sadness expressions are often associated with a positive or less negative semantic prosody, as exemplified by *xīnsuì*, *yōuyù* and *yōushāng*. The case of *xīnsuì* shows that the same image can be understood in different ways in different contexts within the same language. The cases of *yōuyù* and *yōushāng* might be to do with the constituent character *yōu*, which was traditionally associated with wisdom, knowledge, contemplation, far-sightedness, etc. *Yōu* still keeps its less negative flavour in many Chinese words.

(9) It seems that English sadness expressions have a wider semantic space than their Chinese counterparts because quite a few English sadness expressions such as *depression*, *gloomy* are also associated with economy, but Chinese sadness expressions are confined only to emotions and seldom used to talk about economy or other things, except that they are used in their original senses.

I have discussed, in detail, the similarities and differences displayed in the English and Chinese sadness expressions. It seems that almost all of the above findings can be generalized to the whole emotion domain of these two languages. It is also possible for some of them, such as (3), (4), (6), (7), to be extended to other domains. The research findings appear to suggest that the cultural variations are best explored and described using corpus methodology as the subtle nuances of meaning between semantically similar expressions can only be discerned by looking at their colligations, collocations, semantic associations as well as a large number of examples. The corpus data can provide not only hard evidence for the analyser's introspection but also new findings that are less accessible to human intuitions.

8

Implications

The previous chapter contrasted the colligations, collocations and semantic associations of near synonyms in the emotion domain between English and Chinese by drawing on corpus data from two large monolingual corpora and a parallel corpus. This chapter will address potential applications of this methodology in the areas of psychology, contrastive lexical studies, bilingual lexicography and language pedagogy.

8.1 Psychology

As mentioned in the introduction of this book, the psychological approach to the study of emotions lacks objectivity for two reasons. For one thing, such an approach is merely based on introspection. For another, the subjects studied are unlikely to behave in a natural way under observation. The corpus-linguistic approach to the study of emotions, as illustrated in this research, does not have such problems. It is based on texts written independently of the study, so the results are less distorted by the subjects. Besides, accuracy and reliability can be achieved because the number of texts examined is much larger than could be looked at in psychological studies. So using corpora to study emotions has at least two advantages. First, the study bases its conclusions on actual usage rather than on mere introspection. Secondly, because a corpus is a collection of numerous opinions about the question under investigation, the corpus-based study can consider a large number of opinions without interviewing informants. The corpus-based contrastive research on emotions can reveal the multiple perspectives on human emotional experience reflected in 'emotion' terms in different languages and show human emotions are neither universal nor innate, which has been mistakenly claimed by many psychologists. In fact, the corpus-based approach can also be extended beyond emotions to other domains in psychology.

8.2 Contrastive lexical studies

Previous studies of cross-linguistic lexical semantics usually have been conducted in the field of traditional contrastive lexical semantics, cognitive linguistics, cultural linguistics or Natural Semantic Metalanguage. In this research, I have developed a unique theoretical approach to compare and contrast lexical meaning, which integrates corpus-linguistic theories on meaning (as a social construct, usage and paraphrase) (Teubert 2005, 2010; Teubert and Cermakova 2004) and corpus-linguistic categories, i.e. colligation, collocation and semantic preference/association (Sinclair 1996; Hoey 2005). A new complex methodology has also been developed to tease meaning out of corpus evidence.

It is a new attempt to extend the corpus-linguistic framework to the field of contrastive lexical studies. The research results suggest that this approach, compared with other approaches basing analyses mainly on inspection, qualitative reasoning and intuition, can present more details about word usage patterns and meaning. It seems to be a more viable way to distinguish the subtle nuances of meaning between synonyms within and across languages. The use of parallel corpora to establish the correspondence between linked expressions can offer quantitative information on the congruence between two languages. One reason for the revival of contrastive linguistics is the possibility of using large corpora (Altenberg and Granger 2002). The strength of using corpora in contrastive lexical semantics should not be underestimated. In addition, it is also possible to use the corpus-based methodology to contrast languages at other levels, such as phraseology, syntax, grammar.

8.3 Bilingual lexicography

The methodology of the present work can shed some new light on bilingual lexicography. Most old dictionaries were based on 'a mixture of citations, introspection, and what other dictionaries said' (Moon 2007: 7). Monolingual lexicography, since the first publishing of Sinclair's *Collins Cobuild English Language Dictionary* in 1987, has entered a new era, in which a dictionary has become 'a record of how language was actually used, not thought to be used, with this record constructed from corpus evidence' (Moon 2007: 7). Its birth had a massive impact on the practice of commercial dictionary-making, lexicographical theory and language description in general; the advent of corpora not only provides a more objective source of evidence, but also leads to a new look at language (Moon 2007).

Bilingual lexicography has lagged far behind monolingual lexicography in terms of the application of corpora. Take English–Chinese for example. After 27 years, no English–Chinese dictionaries comparable with COBUILD dictionaries have come out. The Longman and Oxford English–Chinese dictionaries have been revised several times, but they are still based on the old lexicographical theory and principles. As shown in Section 7.1, the Chinese definitions in those dictionaries are simply translations of their English parts. Therefore, there is a pressing need for the compilation of corpus-based bilingual, especially English–Chinese, dictionaries, in which the detailed information about synonyms in English should be included. Such information can make language learners aware of the distinctions between synonyms within and across languages. Of course, the implementation of such a project will pose some problems. One is that it is hugely time-consuming to analyse corpus data. Another is how to organize the analysis results, i.e. how to present the colligational and collocational patterns and the information on the semantic associations of words within limited space. An electronic dictionary might be a viable option.

As translational equivalents between L1 and L2 do not match up neatly, the traditional practice of glossing L2 words by offering single L1 words should be used with caution. Language learners wish to know more details about how to use a particular word in specific situations. It is impossible for learners to learn every word by reading concordances, albeit possible for some words. The details concerning repeated patterns, actual uses and exact meanings should be made available in the bilingual dictionary. It does not matter in what form the information on word use and meaning is presented. What does matter is that language learners can find such information somewhere. It will save learners a lot of effort and time.

8.4 Language pedagogy

This section addresses the potential uses of the corpus-based methodology in the English language classroom. It has two implications for language pedagogy, both related to vocabulary teaching, particularly the teaching of synonyms in L2. For one thing, translational equivalents across languages were assumed to be unproblematically 'the same', but the corpus-based analysis of this research reveals that apparently similar items in fact display appreciable differences.

Therefore, the traditional practice of using translational equivalents in L1 to explain L2 vocabulary should be used with caution. Relating one single word in L1 to another in L2 will mislead learners into believing they are the same. Language learners need to be made aware of the disparity between what a word exactly means and what can be found in its gloss in the textbook.

For another, inappropriate word choice arising from a partial understanding of its meaning is quite common in second/foreign language learning. In-depth knowledge about the distinctions between semantically similar words would be highly useful to L2 learners. Native speakers can detect the usage of words and use them correctly, based on their intuition, albeit they are less able to describe them. However, language learners have to rely greatly on the information from teachers or dictionaries to fully grasp them, especially synonyms. It is quite common that even teachers cannot tell how to distinguish them, although they have no difficulty in using them. If teachers can use corpora to analyse and contrast synonyms in L2 and their translational equivalents in L1, summarize their findings about the extent to which they are similar and how they differ, and show them to learners, their production errors will be greatly reduced.

Conclusions

9.1 Summing up

This concluding chapter will sum up the present work, discuss the limitations of the study and finally propose some further research topics. This research deals with a cross-linguistic contrast of sadness expressions between English and Chinese. An in-depth analysis has been made on the basis of the corpus data by applying corpus-linguistic theories on meaning (i.e. meaning is a social construct, usage and paraphrase) and by employing a corpus-linguistic lexical model (i.e. to describe lexical items in terms of colligations, collocations and semantic preferences/associations). The approach used is embedded in a corpus-theoretical framework. It incorporates the use of parallel corpora into this methodology to establish the lexical links across languages and provide illustrative examples.

This research extends the corpus-linguistic framework to the field of contrastive lexical semantics between English and Chinese. It gives fresh insight into how developments in corpus-linguistic theories and in the application of computer corpus technology can advance the field of lexical contrastive linguistics. It is a nuanced description of similarities and differences that epitomizes the descriptive potential of the corpus-based approach to contrastive lexical semantics.

Apart from a quantitative analysis of sadness expressions based on the corpus data, a qualitative analysis of metaphorical sadness expressions in English and Chinese has also been made. The analysis reveals some similarities in the way in which these two cultures conceptualize emotions metaphorically, as well as some remarkable differences in specific cultural conceptualizations and linguistic manifestations. The detailed corpus-based analysis shows that the cultural disparities reflected at the lexical level of language also come from two other sources. One is from the different ways in which two languages encode meanings in their lexicons and the different dimensions used to distinguish synonyms in distinctive cultures. The other is the influence from their traditional philosophies when meanings were encoded in the lexicon at the outset. A long time after the development, there are still discernible traces in their meanings.

The research findings clearly show that human emotions are neither innate nor universal, but culture-specific, which is contrary to previous psychological findings. It seems that this corpus-linguistic approach can open up new possibilities for psychological studies on emotions. Contrastive lexical studies can also benefit from this approach in that the subtle nuances of meaning can be captured and consequently semantically similar items within and across languages can be distinguished. Not only can what they share and how they differ be discovered, but also the impact of cultural differences on encoding meaning in the lexicon can be revealed. By analysing corpus data, cultural conceptualizations, whether metaphorical or literal, can be highlighted and the understanding of how emotions are understood in distinctive cultures can be greatly enriched. In addition, the application of this approach to bilingual lexicography and language pedagogy should not be underestimated.

9.2 Limitations

The methodology of corpus linguistics uses directly observable language data and computational tools for the detection and classification of linguistic phenomena. Both data and computer programs are open to scrutiny by the peer community. The results they produce are reproducible. However, we also have to be aware that corpus linguistics has its limitations. First, a corpus-based analysis is time-consuming, and consequently the number of linguistic items that can be handled in a study is limited. Secondly, it is true that corpus data are objective, but the interpretation of the data may not be totally so because, when the analyser interprets the data, s/he will unavoidably add a subjective point of view to the analysis. Even in corpus tagging or marking, human beings are reproducing their bias (Teubert, in Zhang 2009). This is why Sinclair (1991) was opposed to corpus annotation.

This research is concerned with cross-linguistic semantic contrast of sadness expressions in English and Chinese. For this research, there are several limitations. First, the monolingual corpora I used were not exactly comparable in size and composition. Secondly, the BPC used to establish the cross-linguistic congruence was made up of only fictional texts, so the Chinese equivalents retrieved from this parallel corpus might not be exactly the same as those from a general corpus. Thirdly, the size of the BPC is rather limited, containing a total of only 3,707,397 tokens. Similarly, the Chinese equivalents found based on this small parallel corpus might differ, maybe slightly, from those using a large parallel corpus. It is for the readers to decide to what extent the research findings would differ if a large general English–Chinese parallel corpus had been used. Fourthly, the Chinese data were not POS tagged. Although it is still arguable whether POS tagging is encouraged, whether Chinese has the same POS classification system as English, if we want to compare and contrast English and Chinese quantitatively, it seems to be better to have both POS tagged on the basis of function so that they can be comparable. Fifthly, the English collocates were produced by the Sketch Engine based on t-score, while the Chinese collocates were obtained on raw frequency because the whole CCL corpus was not available and I could only get the concordance lines I needed. Without the corpus, it was impossible to produce collocates according to t-score.

I hope that future contrastive lexical studies can be done on the basis of a large general English–Chinese[1] parallel corpus containing bilingual texts both produced after 1919 and two large monolingual corpora comparable in size[2] and composition[3]. It will be better if any Chinese POS tagging software based on a well-defined tagset becomes publicly available or any freely available online large Chinese corpus can generate data tagged by such a program. More reliable research findings will be achieved if the online concordancer of a large Chinese corpus can produce collocates based on t-score or even offer the Word Sketch and Sketch Diff functions as provided by the Sketch Engine. If all of these matters are resolved, we will get closer to the linguistic truth in the field of cross-linguistic lexical studies between English and Chinese.

9.3 Further research

This book has explored a new path in conducting contrastive lexical studies by adopting a corpus-linguistic approach, which combines corpus-linguistic structural categories with corpus-linguistic theories on meaning. The research findings suggest a number of starting points for further research. First, more in-depth studies on other emotions can be explored to discover more about cultural discrepancies reflected in the lexicon and to further support the claims made in this research. Secondly, studies on non-emotion words/items can be conducted to explore in depth about what the Chinese and English lexicons share and how they differ. As discussed earlier, for a particular language pair, the metaphorical mappings might be quite similar, but the linguistic manifestations and the exact meanings they refer to might not be so. Only after extensive research on words in more domains has been done can claims about specific differences be made and consequently can a more complete picture concerning the Chinese and English lexicons be drawn. The dimensions and metaphorical mappings used in this study may not apply to other domains, but they can serve as a reference for future researchers to find new dimensions and new mappings appropriate to their investigations. Thirdly, future focus can be extended from single words to bigger units, such as lexical items or (extended) units of meaning, so that Sinclair's (1996) lexical model, i.e. to investigate units of meaning in terms of colligation, collocation, semantic preference and semantic prosody, can serve as a viable tool to undertake this task. Fourthly, for other language pairs, it would be possible to proceed in a similar way. Fifthly, this corpus-linguistic approach to contrastive lexical studies can be further extended to language pedagogy as synonyms are of great importance in foreign/second language learning and teaching. As stated early in Section 6.6, this book did not devote very much to the analysis of colligational properties of the words/items because it focused more on meaning differentiation and comparison of sadness concepts within each language and across languages. A cross-linguistic comparison from the perspective of language pedagogy, with more emphasis on the syntactic properties and favoured synactic patterns and environments of the words/items, might be highly helpful for language learners.

Appendix
English glossing of Chinese words

	English glossing	Chinese pinyin	Chinese characters
Extro-version	facial expression	*biǎoqíng/shénqíng/shénsè/ liǎnsè*	表情/神情/神色/脸色
	on the face/face/ full face/face	*liǎnshàng/liǎn/mǎnliǎn/ miànkǒng*	脸上/脸/满脸/面孔
	look/see	*kàn/kàndào/kànjiàn/jiàn*	看/看到/看见/见
	appearance	*yàngzi*	样子
	appear	*xiǎnde*	显得
	eye	*yǎnjing*	眼睛
	expression in one's eyes	*yǎnshén/mùguāng*	眼神/目光
	cry/weep	*kū/kūqì*	哭/哭泣
	voice	*shēngyīn*	声音
	groan	*shēnyín*	呻吟
	tears	*yǎnlèi/lèishuǐ*	眼泪/泪水
	shed tears	*luòlèi/liúlèi*	落泪/流泪
	cry bitterly	*tòngkū*	痛哭
	say	*shuō/shuōdào*	说/说道
	express (deeply)	*(shēn)biǎo/biǎodá/biǎoshì*	(深)表/表达/表示
	convey	*zhuǎndá*	转达
	reveal	*liúlù/lòuchū*	流露/露出
	manifest	*biǎoxiàn*	表现
	telegram of condolence	*yàndiàn/(zhì)diàn*	唁电/(致)电
	form	*xíngshì*	形式
	way	*fāngshì*	方式
	fly the flag at half mast	*jiàng bànqí/xià bànqí*	降半旗/下半旗
Intro-version	feel	*gǎndào/gǎnjué/gǎnshòu/ gǎn/juéde/(shēn)gǎn*	感到/感觉/感受/感/觉得/(深)感
	inner heart/heart	*nèixīn/xīn*	内心/心

	English glossing	Chinese pinyin	Chinese characters
	in the heart	*xīnzhōng/xīnlǐ/xīntóu*	心中/心里/心头
	frame of mind	*xīnqíng*	心情
	mood	*qíngxù*	情绪
	emotion/feeling	*gǎnqíng/qínggǎn/qíng*	感情/情感/情
	mental	*jīngshén*	精神
	mind	*xīnlíng*	心灵
	soul	*línghún*	灵魂
	think	*xiǎng*	想
Verb	cause/make	*ràng/lìng/shǐ/jiào*	让/令/使/叫
	bring about	*zàochéng/dàilái/dài*	造成/带来/带
	induce/give rise to/lead to/invite	*rě/nào/yǐnqǐ*	惹/闹/引起
	occur/emerge	*fāshēng/chūxiàn/chǎnshēng*	发生/出现/产生
	be filled with	*chōngmǎn*	充满
	be filled in one's bosom/chest	*mǎnhuái*	满怀
	be immersed in	*chénjìn*	沉浸
	fall into/get caught into	*xiànrù*	陷入
	suffer	*zāoshòu/shòu*	遭受/受
	endure	*rěnshòu/chéngshòu/jīngshòu*	忍受/承受/经受
	(try very hard to) suppress	*(qiáng)rěn*	(强)忍
	relieve	*jiěchú/jiětuō/bǎituō*	解除/解脱/摆脱
	lessen	*jiǎnqīng/jiǎnshǎo*	减轻/减少
Modifier	extremely	*jí/jíle/jídù/jíqí/jíwéi/wúbǐ*	极/极了/极度/极其/极为/无比
	totally	*wánquán*	完全
	endlessly	*wúxiàn/bùyǐ*	无限/不已
	unbearable	*nányǐrěnshòu/bùkān*	难以忍受/不堪
	exceedingly	*guòdù*	过度
	utmost	*mòdà*	莫大
	enormous	*jùdà/jídà*	巨大/极大
	very	*hěn/fēicháng/shífēn/lǎodà/tǐng/hǎo*	很/非常/十分/老大/挺/好
	deep	*shēnshēn/shēnqiè*	深深/深切
	really	*zhēn/shízài*	真/实在
	particularly	*tèbié*	特别

	rather	*xiāngdāng*	相当
	extremely	*fènwài*	分外
	a little/slightly	*yīdiǎn/diǎn/yīxiē/xiē/yǒudiǎn/ yǒuxiē/lüèdài/dài*	一点／点／一些／些／有点／有些／略带／带
	faint	*dàndàn de*	淡淡的
	a minute quantity	*sī*	丝
	small amount	*jǐfēn*	几分
	severely	*yánzhòng*	严重
	heavy	*chénzhòng*	沉重
	with grief	*chéntòng*	沉痛
	sincere	*chéngzhì*	诚挚
	always/all the time	*zǒngshì/yīzhí*	总是／一直
	often	*chángcháng*	常常
	all the day	*zhěngtiān/zhěngrì*	整天／整日
	lasting for a short time	*yīzhèn*	一阵
	for a long time	*chángqī*	长期
	kind/this kind/ that kind	*zhǒng/zhèzhǒng/nàzhǒng*	种／这种／那种
	portion	*fèn*	份
	number of times	*cì*	次
Feeling	extremely sad	*bēitòngyùjué*	悲痛欲绝
	grief	*bēitòng*	悲痛
	sorrow	*bēishāng/bēiāi*	悲伤／悲哀
	sad	*bēi*	悲
	sad	*nánguò/nánshòu*	难过／难受
	sad	*shāngxīn*	伤心
	unhappy	*bù gāoxìng*	不高兴
	unhappy	*bú kuàilè*	不快乐
	unhappy	*bù yúkuài*	不愉快
	unhappy	*bú xìngfú*	不幸福
	immensely sad/ heartbroken	*xīnsuì*	心碎
	mourn	*āidào*	哀悼
	depression	*yìyù/yìyùzhèng/yōuyùzhèng*	抑郁／抑郁症／忧郁症
	unhappy	*búkuài*	不快
	nervous	*jǐnzhāng*	紧张
	melancholy	*yōuyù*	忧郁
	depressed	*yāyì*	压抑
	melancholy	*shānggǎn*	伤感

English glossing	Chinese pinyin	Chinese characters
melancholy	*yōushāng*	忧伤
gloomy	*yīnyù*	阴郁
gloomy	*mènmènbúlè*	闷闷不乐
dejected	*jǔsàng/sàngqì/chuítóusàngqì*	沮丧/丧气/ 垂头丧气
disheartened	*xīnhuīyìlěng/huīxīnsàngqì*	心灰意冷/灰心丧气
low-spirited	*qíngxù dīluò*	情绪低落
despondent	*huīxīn*	灰心
anguish	*tòngkǔ*	痛苦
low-spirited	*xiāochén*	消沉
discouraged	*qìněi*	气馁
frustrated	*shīyì*	失意
pessimistic	*bēiguān*	悲观
sad/sentimental	*shānggǎn/chóuchàng*	伤感/惆怅
sympathetic	*tóngqíng*	同情
indignation	*fènnù*	愤怒
grief and indignation	*bēifèn*	悲愤
annoyance/anger	*shēngqì/qì*	生气/气
agitated/perturbed	*fán/fánzào/zào/xīnfán*	烦/烦躁/躁/心烦
anxious/worried	*jiāolu/zháojí*	焦虑/着急
dreary	*chénmèn*	沉闷
worry	*yōuchóu/yōu/chóu/lǜ*	忧愁/忧/愁/虑
woebegone	*chóuméikǔliǎn/ chóuróngmǎnmiàn*	愁眉苦脸/愁容满面
gloomy	*kǔmèn*	苦闷
grievance/feel wronged	*wěiqu*	委屈
uneasiness	*bùān*	不安
vexation	*fánnǎo*	烦恼
worried	*kǔ'nǎo*	苦恼
fear	*kǒngjù/hàipà*	恐惧/害怕
shock	*zhènjīng*	震惊
despair	*juéwàng*	绝望
disappointment	*shīwàng*	失望
loneliness	*gūdú/jìmò/gūjì*	孤独/寂寞/孤寂
shame	*xiūkuì*	羞愧
regret	*hòuhuǐ*	后悔

	love	*ài*	爱
	happy	*xìngfú*	幸福
	joy	*huānlè*	欢乐
	gaiety	*kuàilè*	快乐
	delight	*gāoxìng*	高兴
	hope	*xīwàng*	希望
People	mother	*mǔqīn*	母亲
involved	father	*fùqīn*	父亲
	parents	*fùmǔ*	父母
	family (member)	*qīnshǔ/qīnrén/jiāshǔ*	亲属/亲人/家属
	wife	*qīzi*	妻子
	husband	*zhàngfū*	丈夫
	son	*érzi*	儿子
	deceased	*sǐzhě*	死者
	victim	*sǐnànzhě/lǐnànzhě/yùhàizhě/ shòuhàizhě*	死难者/罹难者/ 遇害者/受害者
	the whole nation	*quánguó*	全国
	people	*rénmín*	人民
	compatriot	*tóngbāo*	同胞
	government	*zhèngfǔ*	政府
	president/ chairman/prime minister/leader	*zǒngtǒng/zhǔxí/zǒnglǐ/ lǐngdǎorén*	总统/主席/总理/领导 人
	mourner	*āidàozhě*	哀悼者
Cause	because/why/ reason	*yīnwèi/yīn/wèishénme/ yuányīn*	因为/ 因/原因/为什 么
	news	*xiāoxī*	消息
	news about the death of a beloved person	*è'hào*	噩耗
	failure	*shībài*	失败
	difficulty	*kùnnán*	困难
	setback	*cuòzhé*	挫折
	hardship	*jiānnán*	艰难
	misfortune	*búxìng*	不幸
	loss	*shīqù*	失去
	disaster	*zāinàn*	灾难
	die/death	*sǐ/sǐqù/sǐwáng/shìshì/qùshì*	死/死去/死亡/逝世/ 去世
	die of disease	*bìngshì*	病逝

	English glossing	Chinese pinyin	Chinese characters
	be killed in a disaster	*lǐnàn/yù'nàn/yùhài/ shēnwáng*	罹难/遇难/遇害/ 身亡
	give one's life for/ die a martyr's death	*xīshēng*	牺牲
	loss/lose	*shīqù*	失去
	departure	*líkāi*	离开
	think of	*xiǎngqǐ/xiǎngdào*	想起/想到
	thought	*sīxiǎng*	思想
Modifies	past	*guòqù*	过去
	memory	*huíyì/jìyì*	回忆/记忆
	experience	*jīnglì/tǐyàn/jīngyàn*	经历/体验/经验
	process	*guòchéng*	过程
	thing/event	*shì/shìqing/shìjiàn*	事/事情/事件
	past events	*wǎngshì*	往事
	story	*gùshì*	故事
	work of art	*zuòpǐn*	作品
	atmosphere	*qìfēn*	气氛
	occasion	*chǎnghé*	场合
	temperament	*qìzhì*	气质
	personality	*gèxìng*	个性
	character	*xìnggé*	性格
Others	mourn/miss	*dàoniàn/huáiniàn*	悼念/怀念
	(of sorrow) be blocked	*yùjié/yùjī*	郁结/郁积
	silence	*chénmò*	沉默
	contemplation	*chénsī*	沉思
	calmness	*píngjìng*	平静
	pale	*cāngbái*	苍白
	smile	*xiào/wēixiào*	笑/微笑
	romantic	*làngmàn*	浪漫
	gentle	*wēnróu*	温柔
	prince	*wángzǐ*	王子
	beauty	*měilì*	美丽
	intestine + broken	*chángduàn*	肠断
	gall bladder + crack	*dǎnliè*	胆裂
	belly	*dùzi*	肚子
	body	*ròutǐ/shēntǐ*	肉体/身体

torment	*zhémo*	折磨
torture	*jiān'áo*	煎熬
struggle	*zhēngzhá*	挣扎
powerless/helpless	*wúkěnàihé*	无可奈何
sigh	*tànxī*	叹息
console	*ānwèi/wèiwèn*	安慰/慰问
persuade	*quàn*	劝
give up	*fàngqì*	放弃
human kind	*rénlèi*	人类
human nature	*rénxìng*	人性
family	*jiātíng*	家庭
work/job	*gōngzuò*	工作
society	*shèhuì*	社会
reality	*xiànshí*	现实
history	*lìshǐ*	历史
nation	*mínzú*	民族
life	*rénshēng/shēnghuó/ shēngmìng*	人生/生活/生命
dilemma	*máodùn*	矛盾
leave	*zǒu*	走
in mourning	*shǒuxiào*	守孝
mourning wreath	*huāquān*	花圈
mourning coach	*sòngzàngchē*	送葬车
mourning clothes	*sāngfú*	丧服
go into mourning	*fúsāng*	服丧
announce the death	*bàosāng*	报丧
patient	*huànzhě/bìngrén*	患者/病人
contract/suffer from	*huàn*	患
treatment	*zhìliáo*	治疗
symptom	*zhèngzhuàng*	症状
disease	*jíbìng/bìng/zhèng*	疾病/病/症
nerve	*shénjīng*	神经
insomnia	*shīmián*	失眠
suicide	*zìshā*	自杀
thus/so	*biàn*	便
not have	*méiyǒu*	没有
nostalgic	*huáijiù*	怀旧

English glossing	Chinese pinyin	Chinese characters
energy	*qì/néngliàng*	气/能量
point	*diǎn/chù*	点/处
desolate	*qīliáng*	凄凉
sad	*bēicǎn*	悲惨
bitter laugh	*kǔxiào*	苦笑
severely	*yánzhòng*	严重
weather	*tiānqì*	天气
shroud	*lǒngzhào*	笼罩
oneself	*zìjǐ/zìwǒ*	自己/自我
life/living	*rìzi*	日子
have a hard time	*nánguò (lit)*	难过
chained	*shùfù*	束缚
between	*zhījiān*	之间
in/in the middle of	*zhīzhōng/zhōng*	之中/中
exquisite	*yōuměi*	优美
calmness	*níngjìng*	宁静
gentle	*wēnhé*	温和
elegant	*yōuyā*	优雅
gentle and quiet	*wénjìng*	文静
moving	*chǔchǔdòngrén*	楚楚动人
innocence	*chúnzhēn*	纯真

Notes

1 Introduction

1 Cognitive linguistics in the book does not refer to Chomskyan linguistics, but a branch of linguistics that argues that language is only a part of human cognition, represented by Lakoff, Langacker, Fauconnier and others.

5 The corpus-linguistic framework

1 The original text makes a mistake in the year of the book, which should be 2001.

6 Methodology

1 According to its documentation available online, the CCL corpus contains 307,317,060 tokens and 9711 types. We may infer that it only counts Chinese characters as punctuation marks are not included in its list of character types.

2 Schachter uses 'nàgè nǚháizi liǎojiě/piàoliàng' and 'liǎojiě/piàoliàng de nǚháizi' to illustrate 'there is no consistent basis for distinguishing verbs with adjectival meanings from other verbs' (p. 18). But, in fact, in the above examples, *piàoliàng* (beautiful) and *liǎojiě* (know) are not the same. For one thing, 'nàgè nǚháizi liǎojiě' (that girl + knows, probably meaning 'I know that girl') is ungrammatical, while 'nàgè nǚháizi piàoliàng' (that girl is beautiful) is perfect Chinese. For another, 'liǎojiě de nǚháizi' (a girl I know) has to be embedded in the context to be understood, otherwise it is incomplete in meaning, while 'piàoliàng de nǚháizi' (a beautiful girl) is standard Chinese.

3 The original [Gon97] has been changed to (Gong 1997) to make it consistent with the citation format in this book.

7 Contrastive analysis of sadness expressions in English and Chinese

1 Part of the analysis in this section has been published in the paper entitled 'Analysing *sorrow* and *grief*: a contrastive-semantic perspective', in V. B. Y. Ooi, A. Pakir, I. S.

Talib and P. K. W. Tan (eds), *Perspectives in Lexicography: Asia and Beyond*, Tel Aviv: K Dictionaries Ltd. 2009, 51–68.

2 All the English data in the book were updated in September 2010.

3 Word Sketch only presents salient patterns and will lead to some unavoidable omissions, so sometimes I also extend the span to −5, +5 and search for other meaningful collocates. In such cases, I will mark them after the frequency.

4 The frequency generated by Wordsmith is not necessarily the same with the one by the CCL tool because the latter counts the number of lines containing the node word, regardless of how many times it occurs in the same line, while the former takes the real number of occurrences of a word as its frequency. For example, 伤感 in the line '我要对你说的是底下的话——这些话也许能安慰你，也许更使你［伤感］，由［伤感］而得病' is counted twice by WordSmith, but only once by the CCL tool.

5 In Chinese, 不 (*bù*) has a 4th tone; however, if it is followed by a character with a 4th tone, it is pronounced as a 2nd tone.

6 This corpus is composed of parallel texts from Chinese to English. It is too small to yield reliable statistical information, so I only use it to retrieve some examples.

7 The number also includes its frequency as a noun, though very small; henceforth.

8 *Chǔchǔdòngrén* is a descriptive adjective with positive semantic prosody.

9 The Bank of English gives top collocates based on both raw frequency and t-score. Collocates with low frequency may lead to negative t-scores and are therefore excluded from the list.

10 In Word Sketch, by clicking on the frequency after a collocate, you will get all the relevant instances.

11 Some of the frequency figures presented here are the sum of two figures from its two patterns: 'v' and 'pre-modifier v'. There is no point in distinguishing between its positions in this book, so I grouped them together manually.

9 Conclusions

1 An English–Chinese/Chinese–English parallel (bi-directional) corpus would be more desired, but I am fully aware that it is less likely to be achieved because the translated texts from Chinese into English are much more limited than those from English into Chinese.

2 Comparability is only a matter of extent. Before we solve the problem of the correspondence between English words and Chinese characters, we cannot be certain of the total comparability in size.

3 The ideal composition of a generous corpus is still controversial.

References

Aarts, J. 1998. 'Introduction'. In S. Johansson and S. Oksefjell (eds), *Corpora and Cross-linguistic Research*. Amsterdam: Rodopi, ix–xiv.

Aijmer, K. 1998. 'Epistemic predicates in contrast'. In S. Johansson and S. Oksefjell (eds), *Corpora and Cross-linguistic Research*. Amsterdam: Rodopi, 277–96.

Aijmer, K. and Altenberg, B. 1996. 'Introduction'. In K. Aijmer, B. Altenberg and M. Johansson (eds), *Languages in Contrast: Papers from a Symposium on Text-based Cross-linguistic Studies*. Lund: Lund University Press, 11–16.

Altenberg, B. 1999. 'Adverbial connectors in English and Swedish: semantic and lexical correspondence'. In H. Hasselgard and S. Oksefjell (eds), *Out of Corpora: Studies in Honour of Stig Johansson*. Amsterdam/Atlanta: Rodopi, 249–68.

Altenberg, B. and Granger, S. 2002. 'Recent trends in cross-linguistic lexical studies'. In B. Altenberg and S. Granger (eds), *Lexis in Contrast: Corpus-based Approaches*. Amsterdam: Benjamins, 3–50.

Ameka, F. K. 2002. 'Cultural scripting of body parts for emotions: on "jealousy" and related emotions in Ewe'. *Pragmatics and Cognition*, 10 (1/2), 27–55.

Aston, G. 1999. 'Corpus use and learning to translate'. *Textus*, 12, 289–314.

Averill, J. R. 1980. 'A constructivist view of emotion'. In R. Plutchik and H. Kellerman (eds), *Emotion: Theory, Research and Experience*. New York: Academic Press, 305–39.

Baker, M. 1993. 'Corpus linguistics and translation studies: implications and applications'. In M. Baker, G. Francis and E. Tognini-Bonelli (eds), *Text and Technology: In Honour of John Sinclair*. Amsterdam: Benjamins, 233–52.

—— 1995. 'Corpora in translation studies: an overview and some suggestions for future research'. *Target*, 7 (2), 223–43.

Bamberg, M. 1997. 'Culture, words and understanding'. *Culture and Psychology*, 3 (2), 183–94.

Banczerowski, J. 1980. 'Some contrastive considerations about semantics in the communication process'. In J. Fisiak (ed.), *Theoretical Issues in Contrastive Linguistics*. Amsterdam: Benjamins.

Barlow, M. 2008. 'Parallel texts and corpus-based contrastive analysis'. In M. Gómez González *et al.* (eds), *Current Trends in Contrastive Linguistics: Functional and Cognitive Perspectives*. Amsterdam: Benjamins, 101–21.

Bednarek, M. 2008. 'Semantic preference and semantic prosody re-examined'. *Corpus Linguistics and Linguistic Theory*, 4 (2), 119–39.

Berger, P. and Luckmann, T. 1966. *The Social Construction of Reality: A Treatise in the Sociology of Knowledge*. Garden City, NY: Doubleday.

Bhat, D. N. S. 1994. *The Adjectival Category: Criterion for Differentiation and Identification*. Philadelphia: Benjamins.

Biber, D., Conrad, S. and Reppen, R. 1998. *Corpus Linguistics*. Cambridge: Cambridge University Press.

Boucher, J. D. and Carlson, G. E. 1980. 'Recognition of facial expression in three cultures'. *Journal of Cross-cultural Psychology*, 11 (3), 263–80.

Bowerman, M.1989. 'Learning a semantic system: what role do cognitive predispositions play?' In M. L. Rice and R. L. Schiefelbusch (eds), *The Teachability of Language*. Baltimore: Brooks, 133–69.

—— 1996. 'The origins of children's spatial semantic categories: cognitive vs. linguistic determinants'. In J. J. Gumperz and S. C. Levinson (eds), *Rethinking Linguistic Relativity*. Cambridge: Cambridge University Press, 145–76.

Brants, T. 2000. 'TnT – a statistical part-of-speech tagger'. Paper presented at the *6th Applied Natural Language Processing Conference*, Seattle, 29 April–4 May 2000. http://www.coli.uni-saarland.de/~thorsten/publications/Brants-ANLP00.pdf (accessed: 10 May 2010).

Briggs, J. L. 1970. *Never in Anger: Portrait of an Eskimo Family*. Cambridge: Cambridge University Press.

Brown, P. and Levinson, S. 1987. *Politeness: Some Universals in Language Usage*. Cambridge: Cambridge University Press.

Burr, V. 1995. *An Introduction to Social Constructionism*. London: Routledge.

Casad, E. and Langacker, R. 1985. '"Inside" and "outside" in Cora grammar'. *International Journal of American Linguistics*, 51 (3), 247–81.

Chang, L., Chen, K. and Huang, C. 2000. 'Alternations across semantic fields: a study on Mandarin verbs of emotion'. *Computational Linguistics and Chinese Language Processing*, 5 (1), 61–80.

Chao, Y. R. 1968. *A Grammar of Spoken Chinese*. Berkeley: University of California Press.

Chesterman, A. 1998. *Contrastive Functional Analysis*. Amsterdam: Benjamins.

Cheung, M. L. L. forthcoming. *Paraphrase, Intertextuality and Knowledge Building: A Corpus-based Study of Meaning in Discourse*. Amsterdam: John Benjamins.

Chief, L., Huang, C., Chen, K., Tsai, M. and Chang, L. 2000. 'What can near synonyms tell us?' *Computational Linguistics and Chinese Language Processing*, 5 (1), 47–60.

Choi, S. and Bowerman, M. 1992. 'Learning to express motion events in English and Korean: the influence of language specific lexicalization patterns'. In B. Levin and S. Pinker (eds), *Lexical and Conceptual Semantics*. Cambridge/Oxford: Blackwell, 83–121.

Chomsky, N. 1986. *Knowledge of Language*. New York: Praeger.

Collins COBUILD Advanced Learner's English Dictionary. 5th edn. London/Glasgow: HarperCollins.

D'Andrade, R. 1995. *The Development of Cognitive Anthropology*. Cambridge: Cambridge University Press.

Darwin, C. 1872. *The Expression of the Emotions in Man and Animals/with a Preface by Konrad Lorenz*. Chicago: University of Chicago Press (reprinted in 1965).

Dixon, R. M. W. and Aikhenvald, A. Y. (eds), 2004. *Adjective Classes: A Cross-linguistic Typology*. Oxford/New York: Oxford University Press.

Durkheim, E. 1911. *The Elementary Forms of the Religious Life*. New York: Collier Books (reprinted in 1961).

Dyvik, H. 1998. 'A translational basis for semantics'. In S. Johansson and S. Oksefjell (eds), *Corpora and Cross-linguistic Research*. Amsterdam: Rodopi, 51–86.

Ekman, P. 1973. *Darwin and Facial Expression: A Century of Research in Review*. New York: Academic.

—— 1993. 'Facial expression and emotion'. *American Psychologist*, 48, 384–92.

—— 1994. 'Strong evidence for universals in facial expressions: a reply to Russell's mistaken critique'. *Psychological Bulletin*, 115 (1), 102–41.

—— 2007. *Emotions Revealed: Recognizing Faces and Feelings to Improve Communication and Emotional Life* (2nd edn). New York: Henry Holt.

Ekman, P. and Friesen, W. V. 1975. *Unmasking the Face: A Guide to Recognizing Emotions from Facial Clues*. New Jersey: Prentice Hall (reprinted, Palo Alto, Calif.: Consulting Psychologists Press, 1984).

Ekman, P. and Davidson, R. J. 1994. *The Nature of Emotion: Fundamental Questions*. Oxford/New York: Oxford University Press.

Ekman, P., Sorensen, E. R. and Friesan, W. V. 1969. 'Pan-cultural elements in facial display of emotions'. *Science*, 164, 86–88.

Elfenbein, H. A. and Ambady, N. 2002. 'On universality and cultural specificity of emotion recognition'. *Psychological Bulletin*, 128 (2), 205–35.

Enfield, N. J. and Wierzbicka, A. 2002. 'Introduction: the body in description of emotion'. *Pragmatics and Cognition*, 10 (1/2), 1–25.

Fairclough, N. 1989. *Language and Power*. London: Longman.

Fillmore, C. J. 2003. *Form and Meaning in Language: Papers on Semantic Roles*. Leland, CA: CSLI Publications.

Fillmore, C. J., Johnson, C. R. and Petruck, M. R. L. 2003. 'Background to FrameNet'. *International Journal of Lexicography*, 16 (3), 235–50.

Firth, J. R. 1957. 'Papers in linguistics'. Oxford: Oxford University Press, 168–205.

Francis, G., Hunston, S. and Manning, E. 1996. *Grammar Patterns 1: Verbs*. London: HarperCollins.

Gao, H. 2009. 'Reexamining multiple class membership in Chinese from a cognitive grammar perspective'. *Chinese Language Learning*, 30 (2), 17–24.

Garfinkle, H. 1967. *Studies in Ethnomethodology*. Englewood Cliffs: Prentice Hall.

Gellerstam, M. 1986. 'Translationese in Swedish novels translated from English'. In L. Wollin and H. Lindquist (eds), *Translation Studies in Scandinavia*. Lund: CWK Gleerup, 88–95.

—— 1996. 'Translations as a source for cross-linguistic studies'. In K. Aijmer, B. Altenberg and M. Johansson (eds), *Languages in Contrast: Papers from a Symposium on Text-based Cross-linguistic Studies*. Lund: Lund University Press, 53–62.

Gergen, J. 1994. *Realities and Relationships*. Cambridge, Mass: Harvard University Press.

—— 1999. *An Invitation to Social Construction*. London: Sage.

Goddard, C. 1990. 'The lexical semantics of good feelings in Yankunytjatjara'. *Australian Journal of Linguistics*, 10 (2), 257–92.

—— 1991. 'Anger in the western desert: a case study in the cross-cultural semantics of emotion'. *Man*, 26 (2), 265–79.

—— 1995. ' "Cognitive mapping" or "verbal explication"?: understanding love on the Malay Archipelago'. *Semiotica*, 106 (3/4), 323–54.

—— 1996. 'The "social emotons" of Malay (Bahasa Melayu)'. *Ethos*, 24 (3), 426–64.

—— 1997. 'Contrastive semantics and cultural psychology: "surprise" in Malay and English'. *Culture and Psychology*, 3 (2), 153–81.

Goh, C.-L., Asahara, M. and Matsumoto, Y. 2005. 'Chinese word segmentation by classification of characters'. *Computational Linguistics and Chinese Language Processing*, 10 (3), 381–96.

Gong, Q. 1997. *Zhongguo Yufaxue Shi (The History of Chinese Syntax)*. Beijing: Yuwen Chubanshe.

González, M. d. l. Á. G., Mackenzie, J. L. and Álvarez, E. M. G. (eds). 2008. *Current Trends in Contrastive Linguistics: Functional and Cognitive Perspectives*. Amsterdam/ Philadelphia: Benjamins.

Gu, Y. 1990. 'Politeness phenomena in modern Chinese'. *Pragmatics*, 14, 237–57.

Hanyu Da Zidian. Wuhan/Chengdu: Hubei Cishu Chubanshe/Sichuan Cishu Chubanshe.

Harkins, J. 1994. *Bridging Two Worlds*. St Lucia: Queensland University Press.

—— 'Linguistic and cultural differences in concepts of shame'. In D. Parker, R. Dalziell and I. Wright (eds), *Shame and the Modern Self*. Melbourne: Australian Scholarly Publishing, 84–96.

Harre, R. 1986. 'An outline of the social constructionist viewpoint'. In R. Harre (ed.), *The Social Construction of Emotions*. Oxford: Blackwell, 2–14.

—— 1993. 'Universals yet again: a test of the "Wierzbicka thesis" '. *Linguistic Sciences*, 15 (3), 231–38.

Harre, R. and Finlay-Jones, R. 1986. 'Emotion talk across times'. In R. Harre (ed.), *The Social Construction of Emotions*. Oxford: Basil Blackwell, 220–33.

Hoey, M. 2003. 'Lexical priming and the properties of text'. http://www.monabaker.com/ tsresources/LexicalPrimingandthePropertiesofText.htm (accessed: 10 May 2010).

—— 2004. 'Lexical priming and the properties of text'. In A. Partington, J. Morley and L. Harrman (eds), *Corpora and Discourse*. Bern: Peter Lang, 385–412.

—— 2005. *Lexical Priming: A New Theory of Words and Language*. London: Routledge.

Hu, M. 1996. *Cilei Wenti Kaocha (An Investigation of Chinese Word Classes)*. Beijing: Beijing Yuyan Xueyuan Chubanshe.

Hu, Y. 1995. *Modern Chinese* (revised edn). Shanghai: Shanghai Jiaoyu Chubanshe.

Huang, Z., Harper, M. P. and Wang, W. 2007. 'Mandarin part-of-speech tagging and discriminative reranking'. Paper presented at the *2007 Joint Conference on Empirical*

Methods in Natural Language Processing and Computational Natural Language Learning, Prague, Czech Republic, 28–30 June 2007. http://www.aclweb.org/anthology/D/D07/D07-1117.pdf (accessed: 10 May 2010).

Hunston, S. 2002. *Corpora in Applied Linguistics*. Cambridge: Cambridge University Press.

—— 2007. 'Semantic prosody revisited'. *International Journal of Corpus Linguistics*, 12 (2), 249–68.

Hunston, S. and Francis, G. 1998. 'Verbs observed: a corpus-driven pedagogic grammar'. *Applied Linguistics*, 19 (1), 45–72.

—— 1999. *Pattern Grammar: A Corpus-driven Approach to the Lexical Grammar of English*. Amsterdam: Benjamins.

Ivir, V. 1987. 'Functionalism in contrastive analysis and translation studies'. In R. Dirven and V. Fried (eds), *Functionalism in Linguistics*. Amsterdam/Philadelphia: Benjamins, 471–81.

Izard, C. E. 1971. *The Face of Emotion*. New York: Appleton-Century-Crofts.

—— 1977. *Human Emotions*. New York: Plenum Press.

—— 1991. *The Psychology of Emotions*. New York: Plenum Press.

James, C. 1980. *Contrastive Analysis*. London: Longman.

James, W. 1890. *The Principles of Psychology*. London: Macmillan.

Jiang, S. 2004. 'A semantic study of the classifier *dao*'. In M. Achard and S. Kemmer (eds), *Language, Culture and Mind*. Stanford: CSLI Publications, 429–43.

Johansson, S. and Hofland, K. 1994. 'Towards an English-Norwegian parallel corpus'. In U. Fries, G. Tottie and P. Schneider (eds), *Creating and Using English Language Corpora*. Amsterdam: Rodopi, 25–37.

Johansson, S. and Oksefjell, S. 1998. *Corpora and Cross-linguistic Research*. Amsterdam: Rodopi.

Josephs, I. E. 1995. 'The problem of emotions from the perspective of psychological semantics'. *Culture and Psychology*, 1 (2), 279–88.

Kennedy, G. 1998. *An Introduction to Corpus Linguistics*. London: Longman.

Kilgarriff, A. 2009. 'Putting the corpus into the dictionary'. In V. B. Y. Ooi, A. Pakir, I. S. Talib and P. K. W. Tan (eds), *Perspectives in Lexicography: Asia and Beyond*. Israel: K Dictionaries Ltd, 239–47.

Kilgarriff, A. and Tugwell, D. 2001. 'WORD SKETCH: extraction and display of significant collocations for lexicography'. Paper presented at the *ACL Workshop on COLLOCATION: Computational Extraction, Analysis and Exploitation*, Toulouse, France, 7 July 2001.

Kilgarriff, A. and Rundell, M. 2002. 'Lexical profiling software and its lexicographic applications – a case study'. Paper presented at *EURALEX 2002*, Copenhagen, 13–17 August 2002.

Kilgarriff, A., Rychly, P., Smrz, P. and Tugwell, D. 2004. 'The Sketch Engine'. In *Proceedings of EURALEX 2004*, Lorient, France, 6–10 July 2004, pp. 105–16. http://www.kilgarriff.co.uk/publications.htm (accessed: 10 May 2010).

Kleinman, A. 1980. *Patients and Healers in the Context of Culture: An Exploration of the Borderland Between Anthropology, Medicine and Psychiatry*. Berkeley: University of California Press.

Kondo, F., 2004. 'Words denoting emotions: the case of unhappiness in a Japanese-English parallel corpus'. Unpublished manuscript.

Kövecses, Z. 2000. *Metaphor and Emotion: Language, Culture, and Body in Human Feeling*. Cambridge: Cambridge University Press.

Krek, S. and Kilgarriff, A. 2006. 'Slovene word sketches'. In *Proceedings of 5th Slovenian and First International Language Technology Conference*, Ljubljana, Slovenia, 9–10 October 2006. http://www.kilgarriff.co.uk/Publications/2006-KrekKilg-Ljub-SloveneWS.pdf (accessed: 10 May 2010).

Krzeszowski, T. P. 1990. *Contrasting Languages: The Scope of Contrastive Linguistics*. Berlin/New York: Mouton de Gruyter.

Lakoff, G. 1987. *Women, Fire, and Dangerous Things: What Categories Reveal about the Mind*. Chicago: University of Chicago Press.

Lakoff, G. and Johnson, M. 1980. *Metaphors We Live By*. Chicago: University of Chicago Press.

—— 1999. *Philosophy in the Flesh*. New York: Basic Books.

Lan, C. 1999. 'A study of spatial orientiational metaphors in Chinese: a cognitive linguistic perspective'. *Foreign Languages Teaching and Research*, 31 (4), 7–15.

—— 2002. ' A cognitive approach to Up/Down metaphors in English and *Shang/Xia* metaphors in Chinese'. In B. Altenberg and S. Granger (eds), *Lexis in Contrast: Corpus-based Approaches*. Philadelphia/Amsterdam: Benjamins, 161–84.

Langacker, R. W. 1987. *Foundations of Cognitive Grammar*. Stanford: Stanford University Press.

—— 1999. 'Assessing the cognitive linguistic enterprise'. In T. Janssen and G. Redeker (eds), *Cognitive Linguistics, Foundations, Scope and Methodology*. Berlin/New York: Mouton de Gruyter, 13–59.

Lave, J. and Wenger, E. 1991. *Situated Learning: Legitimate Peripheral Participation*. Cambridge: Cambridge University Press.

Leech, G. 1997. 'Introducing corpus annotation'. In R. Garside, G. Leech and A. McEnery (eds), *Corpus Annotation: Linguistic Information from Computer Text Corpora*. London: Longman, 1–18.

Levin, B. 1993. *English Verb Classes and Alternations: A Preliminary Investigation*. Chicago: University of Chicago Press.

Levy, R. I. 1973. *Tahitians: Mind and Experience in the Society Islands*. Chicago: University of Chicago Press.

Li, C. and Thompson, S. 1981. *Mandarin Chinese: A Functional Reference Grammar*. Berkeley: University of California Press.

Li, J. 1924. *Xin Zhu Guoyu Wenfa (A New Grammar of Chinese)*. Beijing: Shangwu Yinshu Guan.

Liu, M. 2002. *Mandarin Verbal Semantics: A Corpus-based Approach* (2nd edn). Taipei: Crane Publishing Co.

Liu, M., Huang, C., Lee, C. and Lee, C.-Y. 2000. 'When endpoint meets endpoint: a corpus-based lexical semantic study of Mandarin verbs of *throwing*'. *Computational Linguistics and Chinese Language Processing*, 5 (1), 81–96.

Longman Dictionary of Contemporary English, 4th edn. Harlow, Essex: Pearson/ Longman.

Louw, B. 1993. 'Irony in the text or insincerity in the writer? the diagnostic potential of semantic prosodies'. In M. Baker, G. Francis and E. Tognini-Bonelli (eds), *Text and Technology*. Amsterdam: Benjamins, 157–76.

—— 2000. 'Contextual prosodic theory: bring semantic prosodies to life'. In C. Heffer, H. Sauntson and G. Fox (eds), *Words in Context: A Tribute to John Sinclair on his Retirement*. Birmingham: ELR Discourse Analysis Monograph No.18 [CD-ROM publication], 48–94.

Lü, S. (ed). 1954. *Hanyu Yufa Lunwen Ji (A Collection of Papers on Chinese Grammar)*. Beijing: Shangwu Yinshu Guan.

—— 'Guanyu hanyu cilie de yixie yuanzexing wenti (Some key issues on Chinese word classes)'. In S. Lü (ed.), *A Collection of Papers on Chinese Grammar*. Beijing: Shangwu Yinshu Guan, 256–70 (Originally: *Journal of Chinese Language*, 1954, 9 (10)).

Lutz, C. 1987. 'Goals, events and understandings in Ifaluk emotion theory'. In D. Holland and N. Quinn (eds), *Cultural Models in Language and Thought*. Cambridge: Cambridge University Press, 290–312.

—— 1988. *Unnatural Emotions: Everyday Sentiments on a Micronesian Atoll and their Challenge to Western Theory*. Chicago: Chicago University Press.

Ma, B. 1994. 'A statistical method to classify word classes'. *Journal of Chinese Language*, 8 (5), 347–60.

Machakanja, I. 2008. 'Conceptual domains and metaphorical mapping in English'. *NAWA Journal of Language and Communication*, 2 (1), 12–32.

Mahlberg, M. 2005. *English General Nouns: A Corpus Theoretical Approach*. Amsterdam: Benjamins.

Matsumoto, D. 1989. 'Cultural influences on the perception of emotion'. *Journal of Cross-cultural Psychology*, 20 (1), 92–105.

Mauranen, A. 2002. 'Will "translationese" ruin a contrastive study?' *Languages in Contrast*, 2 (2), 161–86.

McAndrew, F. T. 1986. 'A cross-cultural study of recognition thresholds for facial expressions of emotion'. *Journal of Cross-cultural Psychology*, 17 (2), 211–24.

McCawley, J. 1992. 'Justifying part-of-speech assignment in Mandarin Chinese'. *Journal of Chinese Linguistics*, 20 (2), 211–46.

McEnery, T. and Wilson, A. 2001. *Corpus Linguistics* (2nd edn). Edinburgh: Edinburgh University Press.

McEnery, T. and Xiao, R. 2002. 'Domains, text types, aspect marking and English–Chinese translation'. *Languages in Contrast*, 2 (2), 211–29.

Mel'čuk, I. 1988. 'Semantic description of lexical units in an explanatory combinatorial dictionary: basic principles and heuristic criteria'. *International Journal of Lexicography*, 1 (3), 165–88.

Moon, R. 1998. *Fixed Expressions and Idioms in English*. Oxford: Clarendon Press.

—— 2007. 'Sinclair, lexicography, and the Cobuild project'. *International Journal of Corpus Linguistics*, 12 (2), 159–81.

—— 2010. 'What a corpus can tell us about lexis?' In A. O'Keeffe and M. McCarthy (eds), *The Routledge Handbook of Corpus Linguistics*. London/New York: Routledge, 197–211.

Morley, J. and Partington, A. 2009. 'A few frequently asked questions about semantic—or evaluative—prosody'. *International Journal of Corpus Linguistics*, 14 (2), 139–58.

Myers, D. G. 1991. *The Pursuit of Happiness: Who is Happy—and Why*. New York: W. Morrow.

O'Halloran, K. A. 2007. 'Critical discourse analysis and the corpus-informed interpretation of metaphor at the register level'. *Applied Linguistics*, 28 (1), 1–24.

Ooi, V. B. Y. 1998. *Computer Corpus Lexicography*. Edinburgh: Edinburgh University Press.

—— 2000. '"Language games" on the World Wide Web: analysing the language of electronic gaming'. In C. Heffer and H. Sauntson (eds), *Words in Context: A Tribute to John Sinclair on his Retirement*. Birmingham: ELR Discourse Analysis Monograph No.18, [CD-ROM publication], 110–19.

—— 2008. 'The lexis of electronic gaming on the web: a Sinclairian approach'. *International Journal of Lexicography*, 21 (3), 311–23.

Oxford Advanced Learner's English–Chinese Dictionary. 4th edn. Beijing: Shangwu Yinshu Guan.

Oxford English Dictionary Online. Oxford: Oxford University Press. http://www.oed.com.libproxy1.nus.edu.sg/ (accessed: 4 May 2011).

Palmer, G. B. 1996. *Toward a Theory of Cultural Linguistics*. Austin: University of Texas Press.

Partington, A. 1998. *Patterns and Meanings*. Amsterdam: John Benjamins.

—— 2004. '"Utterly content in each other's company": semantic prosody and semantic preference'. *International Journal of Corpus Linguistics*, 9 (1), 131–56.

Ratnaparkhi, A. 1996. 'A maximum entropy model for part-of-speech tagging'. Paper presented at the *First Conference on Empirical Methods in Natural Language Processing (EMNLP)*, Philadelphia, Pennsylvania, 17–18 May 1996. http://acl.ldc.upenn.edu/W/W96/W96-0213.pdf (accessed: 10 May 2010).

Renouf, A. and Sinclair, J. 1991. 'Collocational frameworks in English'. In K. Aijmer and B. Altenberg (eds), *English Corpus Linguistics: Studies in Honour of Jan Svartvik*. London: Longman, 128–44.

Rosch, E. H. 1973. 'On the internal structure of perceptual and semantic categories'. In T. E. Moore (ed.), *Cognitive Developement and the Acquisition of Language*. New York: Academic Press, 111–44.

—— 1977. 'Classification of real world objects and representations in cognition'. In P. N. Johnson-Laird and P. C. Wason (eds), *Thinking: Readings in Cognitive Science*. Cambridge: Cambridge University Press, 212–22.

Russell, J. A. 1991. 'Culture and the categorization of emotions'. *Psychological Bulletin*, 110 (3), 426–50.

Rychly, P. 2008. 'A lexicographer-friendly association score'. In P. Sojka and A. Horák (eds), *Proceedings of Recent Advances in Slavonic Natural Language Processing, RASLAN 2008*, Brno, 5–7 December 2008, pp. 6–9.

Santangelo, P. 2003. *Sentimental Education in Chinese History: An Interdisciplinary Textual Research on Ming and Qing Sources*. Leiden: Brill.

Santos, D. 1998. 'Perception verbs in English and Portuguese'. In S. Johansson and S. Oksefjell (eds), *Corpora and Cross-linguistic Research*. Amsterdam: Rodopi, 319–42.

Sapir, E. 1933. 'Language'. *Encyclopaedia of the Social Sciences (New York)*, 9, 155–69.

Schachter, P. 1985. 'Part of speech systems'. In T. Shopen (ed.), *Language Typology and Syntactic Description, Vol. I: Clause Structure*. Cambridge: Cambridge University Press, 3–61.

Scherer, K. R. 1994. 'Towards a concept of "modal emotions"'. In P. Ekman and R. J. Davidson (eds), *The Nature of Emotion: Fundamental Questions*. Oxford/New York: Oxford University Press, 25–31.

Schmied, J. 1998. 'Differences and similarities of close cognates: English *with* and German *mit*'. In S. Johansson and S. Oksefjell (eds), *Corpora and Cross-linguistic Research*. Amsterdam: Rodopi, 255–76.

Scott, M. 2008. *WordSmith Tools Manual*. Liverpool: Lexical Analysis Software.

Scott, M. and Tribble, C. 2006. *Textual Patterns: Keyword and Corpus Analysis in Language Education*. Amsterdam: Benjamins.

Sealey, A. 2010. *Researching English Language: A Resource Book for Students*. Milton Park, Abingdon, Oxon/New York: Routledge.

Sharifian, F. 2003. 'On cultural conceptualisations'. *Journal of Cognition and Culture* 3 (3), 187–207.

—— 2008. 'Distributed, emergent cognition, conceptualisation, and language'. In R. M. Frank, R. Dirven, T. Ziemke and E. Bernárdez (eds), *Body, Language, and Mind. Vol. 2: Sociocultural Situatedness*. Berlin/New York: Mouton de Gruyter, 109–36.

Shen, J. 1999. *Bu Duicheng he Biaoji Lun (On Asymmetry and Markedness)*. Nanchang: Jiangxi Jiaoyu Chubanshe.

Shi, X. and Feng, B. 2013. 'Contemporary Chinese communication made understandable: a cultural psychological perspective'. *Culture and Psychology*, 19 (1), 3–19.

Shweder, R. 1991. *Thinking Through Cultures: Expeditions in Cultural Psychology*. Cambridge: Cambridge University Press.

—— 1993. 'The cultural psychology of the emotions'. In M. Lewis and J. M. Haviland (eds), *Handbook of Emotions*, 417–31.

—— 1994. 'You're not sick, you're just in love: emotion as an interpretive system'. In P. Ekman and R. J. Davidson (eds), *The Nature of Emotion: Fundamental Questions*. Oxford/New York: Oxford University Press, 32–44.

Sinclair, J. 1985. 'On the integration of linguistic description'. In T. A. van Dijk (ed.), *Handbook of Discourse Analysis*. London: Academic Press, 13–28.

—— 1987. *Looking up: An Account of the COBUILD Project in Lexical Computing*. London: Collins.

—— 1991. *Corpus, Concordance, Collocation*. Oxford: Oxford University Press.

—— 1996. 'The search for units of meaning'. *Textus*, IX, 75–106 (reprinted in Sinclair, 2004).

—— 1998. 'The lexical item'. In E. Weigand (ed.), *Contrastive Lexical Semantics*. Amsterdam/Philadelphia: Benjamins, 1–24.

—— 2000. 'Lexical grammar'. *NaujojiMetodologija*, 24: 191–203. http://donelaitis.vdu.lt/ publikacijos/sinclair.pdf (accessed: 9 November 2009).

—— 2003. *Reading Concordances*. Harlow: Longman.

—— 2004. *Trust the Text: Language, Corpus and Discourse*. New York: Taylor & Francis.

Sinclair, J. and Teubert, W. 2004. 'Interview with John Sinclair, conducted by Wolfgang Teubert'. In R. Krishnamurthy, J. Sinclair, S. Jones and R. Daley (eds), *English Collocation Studies: The OSTI Report*. London: Continuum, xvii–xxix.

Stearns, C. Z. 1993. 'Sadness'. In M. Lewis and J. M. Haviland (eds). *Handbook of Emotions*. New York: Guilford, 547–61.

Stefanowitsch, A. 2004. 'Happiness in English and German: a metaphorical-pattern analysis'. In M. Achard and S. Kemmer (eds), *Language, Culture and Mind*. Stanford, Calif.: CSLI Publications, 137–49.

Stewart, D. 2010. *Semantic Prosody: A Critical Evaluation*. New York/London: Routledge.

Strauss, C. and Quinn, N. 1996. *A Cognitive Theory of Cultural Meaning*. New York: Cambridge University Press.

Stubbs, M. 1996. *Text and Corpus Analysis: Computer Assisted Studies of Language and Culture*. Oxford: Blackwell.

—— 1997. 'Whorf's children: critical comments on critical discourse analysis'. In A. Ryan and A. Wray (eds), *Evolving Models of Language*. Clevedon: Multilingual Matters, 100–16.

—— 2009. 'The search for units of meaning: Sinclair on empirical semantics'. *Applied Linguistics*, 30, 115–37.

Summers, D. 1991. *Longman/Lancaster English Language Corpus: Criteria and Design*. Harlow: Longman.

Sweetser, E. 1990. *From Etymology to Pragmatics*. Cambridge: Cambridge University Press.

Tai, J. 1994. 'Chinese classifier systems and human categorization'. In M. Chen and O. Tzeng (eds), *Essays in Honour of Professor William S-Y Wang*. Taipei: Pyramid Publishing Company, 479–94.

Tai, J. and Chao, F. 1990. 'A semantic study of the classifier "zhang"'. *Journal of the Chinese Language Teachers Association*, 29 (3), 66–78.

Talmy, L. 1985. 'Lexicalization patterns: semantic structure in lexical forms'. In T. Shopen (ed.), *Language Typology and Syntactic Description, Vol. III: Grammatical Categories and the Lexicon*. Cambridge: Cambridge University Press, 57–149.

Teubert, W. 1996. 'Comparable or parallel corpora?' *International Journal of Lexicography*, 9 (3), 238–64.

—— 1999. 'Corpus linguistics—a partisan view'. http://telri.nytud.hu/telri2/newsletter/newsl8.html (accessed: 10 May 2010).

—— 2000. 'Starting with trauer: Approaches to multilingual lexical semantics'. In F. Kiefer, G. Kiss & J. Pajcs (eds), *Papers in Computational Lexicography: Complex '99*. Budapest: Linguistics Institute, Hungarian Academy of Sciences, 153–69.

—— 2004a. 'Language and corpus linguistics'. In M. A. K. Halliday, W. Teubert, C. Yallop and A. Cermakova (eds), *Lexicology and Corpus Linguistics: An Introduction*. London: Continuum, 73–112.

—— 2004b. 'When did we start feeling guilty?' In E. Weigand (ed.), *Emotion in Dialogic Interaction*. Amsterdam: Benjamins, 121–62.

—— 2005. 'My version of corpus linguistics'. *International Journal of Corpus Linguistics*, 10 (1), 1–13.

—— 2010. *Meaning, Discourse and Society*. New York: Cambridge University Press.

Teubert, W. and Cermakova, A. 2004. 'Directions in corpus linguistics'. In M. A. K. Halliday, W. Teubert, C. Yallop and A. Cermakova (eds), *Lexicography and Corpus Linguistics: An Introduction*. London: Continuum, 113–65.

Thede, S. M. and Harper, M. P. 1999. 'A second order hidden Markov model for part-of-speech tagging'. Paper presented at the *37th Annual Meeting of the Association for Computational Linguistics on Computational Linguistics*, College Park, Maryland, 20–26 June 1999. http://acl.ldc.upenn.edu/P/P99/P99-1023.pdf (accessed: 10 May 2010).

Thompson, S. 1988. 'A discourse approach to the cross-linguistic category "adjective"'. In J. Hawkins (ed.), *Explaining Language Universals*. Oxford: Blackwell, 167–210.

Tognini-Bonelli, E. 2001. *Corpus Linguistics at Work*. Amsterdam: Benjamins.

Tsai, M., Huang, C., Chen, K. and Ahrens, K. 1998. 'Towards a representation of verbal semantics: an approach based on near-synonyms'. *Computational Linguistics and Chinese Language Processing*, 3 (1), 62–74.

Tseng, H., Jurafsky, D. and Manning, C. 2005. 'Morphological features help pos tagging of unknown words across language varieties'. Paper presented at the *Fourth SIGHAN Workshop on Chinese Language Processing*, Jeju Island, Korea, 14–15 October 2005. http://www.stanford.edu/~jurafsky/sighan_pos.pdf (accessed: 10 May 2010).

Turpin, M. 2002. 'Body part terms in Kaytetye feeling expressions'. *Pragmatics and Cognition*, 10 (1/2), 271–305.

Viberg, A. 1998. 'Contrasts in polysemy and differentiation: running and putting in English and Swedish'. In S. Johansson and S. Oksefjell (eds), *Corpora and Cross-linguistic Research*. Amsterdam: Rodopi, 343–76.

Vygotsky, L. S. 1978. *Mind in Society: The Development of Higher Psychological Processes*. Cambridge, Mass.: Harvard University Press.

Wang, J. 2009. 'A corpus-based study on the Chinese near-synonymous verbs of running'. In Y. Xiao (eds), *Proceedings of 21st North American Conference on Chinese*

Linguistics (NACCL-21), Smithfield, Rhode Island: Bryant University, 6–8 June 2009, pp. 399–416.

Wang, L. 1955. *Zhongguo Yufa Lilun (A Theory of Chinese Grammar)*. Beijing: Zhonghua Shuju.

Wellenkamp, J. C. 1988. 'Notions of Grief and Catharsis among the Toraja'. *American Ethnologist*, 15 (3), 486–500.

White, G. M. and Kirkpatrick, J. 1985. *Person, Self and Experience*. Berkeley: University of California Press.

Whitsitt, S. 2005. 'A critique of the concept of semantic prosody'. *International Journal of Corpus Linguistics*, 10 (3), 283–305.

Whorf, B. 1956. *Language, Thought, and Reality: Selected Writings of Benjamin Lee Whorf*, ed. J. B. Carroll. Cambridge: MIT Press.

Wierzbicka, A. 1972. *Semantic Primitives*. Frankurt: Athenaum.

—— 1986. 'Human emotions: universal or culture-specific?' *American Anthropologist*, 88 (3), 584–94.

—— 1992a. *Semantics, Culture, and Cognition: Universal Human Concepts in Culture-specific Configurations*. New York: Oxford University Press.

—— 1992b. 'Defining emotion concepts'. *Cognitive Science*, 16 (4), 539–81.

—— 1995. 'Emotion and facial expression: a semantic perspective'. *Culture and Psychology*, 1, 227–58.

—— 1996. *Semantics: Primes and Universals*. Oxford/New York: Oxford University Press.

—— 1999. *Emotions Across Languages and Cultures: Diversity and Universals*. Cambridge, England/New York/Paris: Cambridge University Press.

Williams, G. C. 1998. 'Collocational networks: interlocking patterns of lexis in a corpus of plant biology research articles'. *International Journal of Corpus Linguistics*, 3 (1), 151–71.

—— 2006. 'Book review: Michael Hoey. *Lexical priming: a new theory of words and language*. London: Routledge. 2005'. *International Journal of Lexicography*, 19 (3), 327–35.

Xia, F. 2000. 'The part-of-speech tagging guidelines for the Penn Chinese Treebank (3.0)'. http://www.cis.upenn.edu/~chinese/posguide.3rd.ch.pdf (accessed: 6 August 2010).

Xiandai Hanyu Cidian (A Dictionary of Modern Chinese). Beijing: Shangwu Yinshu Guan.

Xiandai Hanyu Cidian: Bilingual Edition (A Dictionary of Modern Chinese). Beijing: Waiyu Jiaoxue Yu Yanjiu Chubanshe.

Xiao, R. and McEnery, T. 2006. 'Collocation, semantic prosody, and near synonymy: a cross-linguistic perspective'. *Applied Linguistics*, 27 (1), 103–29.

Xiao, R., McEnery, T. and Qian, Y. 2006. 'Passive constructions in English and Chinese: a corpus-based contrastive study'. *Languages in Contrast*, 6 (1), 109–49.

Xu, Y. 2002. *Contrastive Linguistics*. Shanghai: Shanghai waiyu jiaoyu chubanshe.

Ye, Z. 2001. 'An inquiry into "sadness" in Chinese'. In J. Harkins and A. Wierzbicka (eds), *Emotions in Crosslinguistic Perspective*. Berlin/New York: Mouton de Gruyter, 359–404.

—— 2002. 'Different modes of describing emotions in Chinese: bodily changes, sensations, and bodily images'. *Pragmatics and Cognition*, 10 (1/2), 307–39.

Yip, P. 2000. *The Chinese Lexicon: A Comprehensive Survey*. London/New York: Routledge.

Yu, N. 2002. 'Body and emotion: body parts in Chinese expression of emotion'. *Pragmatics and Cognition*, 10 (1/2), 341–67.

—— 2003. 'Metaphor, body, and culture: the Chinese understanding of gallbladder and courage'. *Metaphor and Symbol*, 18, 13–31.

—— 2009. *The Chinese Heart in a Cognitive Perspective: Culture, Body, and Language*. Berlin/New York: Mouton de Gruyter.

Zhang, B. and Fang, M. 1996. *Hanyu Gongneng Yufa Yanjiu (A Study on Chinese Functional Grammar)*. Nanchang: Jiangxi Jiaoyu Chubanshe.

Zhang, R. 2009. 'An interview with Professor Wolfgang Teubert'. *Journal of Foreign Languages*, 32 (2), 84–93.

—— 2011. *A Corpus-based Contrastive Analysis of Sadness Expressions in English and Chinese*. PhD. National University of Singapore.

Zhang, R. and Ooi, V. B. Y. 2008. 'A corpus-based analysis of qing (情): A contrastive-semantic perspective'. In R. Xiao, L. He and M. Yue (eds), *The International Symposium on Using Corpora in Contrastive and Translation Studies*, Hangzhou, China, 25–27 September 2008. http://www.lancs.ac.uk/fass /projects/corpus/ UCCTS2008Proceedings/papers/Zhang_and_Ooi.pdf (accessed: 10 May 2010).

Zhang, Z. (ed.) 1979. *Hanyu Zhishi (On Chinese Language)*. Beijing: Renmin Jiaoyu Chubanshe.

Zhu, D. 1982. *Yufa Jiangyi (Lecture Notes on Grammar)*. Beijing: Shangwu Yinshu Guan.

—— 1985. *Yufa Dawen (Some Questions on Grammar)*. Beijing: Shangwu Yinshu Guan.

Index

Aijmer, K. 29
Altenberg, B. 3, 29–30, 208
Ameka, F. 195

Baker, M. 30, 80
Bamberg, M. 15–16
Barlow, M. 54, 56–8
Bednarek, M. 34
Biber, D. 27, 35
Bowerman, M. 22
Briggs, J. 10

Chao, Y. 63
Chesterman, M. 3, 30
circularity 3, 23–4
clean-text policy 58, 65
cognitive linguistics 2, 33, 45, 208
    see also Lakoff, Langacker
componential analysis 3, 23–4
    see also decomposition
conceptualization 4, 13, 190, 193–5, 204,
    211
    cultural conceptualization 4, 13, 211–12
    metaphorical conceptualization 190, 193,
    195
    specific conceptualization 194–5, 204
contrastive lexical semantics 7–8, 21–2
corpus-based/corpus-driven approach
    33–4, 46
corpus-linguistic framework 6, 34, 208, 211
corpus-linguistic theory 4, 7, 47, 208, 211,
    213
cross-linguistic research 7, 27–31
critical discourse analysis 35
cultural specificity 1, 10, 12, 15, 17, 103
    see also universality

Darwin, C. 9
decomposition 2, 7, 22–3
    see also componential analysis
delexicalization 41, 142

discourse 4, 17, 27–9, 35–43, 45, 47, 51,
    74–5, 92, 96, 101, 105, 113, 127–8, 141,
    194, 197, 204
Dixon, R. 61
Dyvik, H. 31

Ekman, P. 9–11, 69, 116
Elfenbein, H. 10
emotions 1–2, 4–7, 42, 52, 69, 72–73, 97,
    99, 115–16, 153, 155, 156, 169,
    173, 178, 193–6, 204–5, 207, 211,
    212–13
    basic emotions 1, 4, 9, 12, 69
equivalence network 5, 198–9

Fairclough, N. 35
Fillmore, C. 2, 15, 21, 46
Firth, J. 3
form and meaning 34, 37

Goddard, C. 11–12, 14–17

Harkins, J. 14
Harre, R. 11–12, 16, 69
Hoey, M. 4, 34, 37, 40, 44–7, 208
Hunston, S. 33–4, 42, 50–1

introspection 3, 5–6, 19, 24, 31, 43, 206–7
    see also intuition
introversion/extroversion 67, 74, 79, 82, 84,
    87–8, 90–1, 93, 95, 98, 101, 106, 111,
    113–15, 117, 119, 127, 135, 147–8,
    150–2, 154, 156, 162–3, 165, 167, 170,
    172, 186–7, 190, 200–1
intuition 17, 27, 33–4, 46–7, 58, 71, 149,
    198, 206, 208, 210
    see also introspection
Ivir, V. 30
Izard, C. 9–10, 73–4

James, C. 3, 24

James, W. 13
Johansson, S. 29–30
Josephs, I. 12, 15–17

Kennedy, G. 51
Kilgarriff, A. 59
Kleinman, A. 11
Kövecses, Z. 169
Krzeszowski, T. 2, 22–4, 30

Lakoff, G. 2, 15, 22, 190–1, 193–4
  see also cognitive linguistics
Langacker, R. 2, 22
  see also cognitive linguistics
Leech, G. 59
Levin, B. 3
Levy, R. 116
lexical equivalence 2, 22, 24
  see also translation equivalence
lexical item 34, 36, 38–43, 45, 67, 76,
    198–9, 211, 214
  see also (extended) unit of
    meaning
lexical model 4, 40–1, 43–7, 211, 214
lexical priming 40, 44–5
lexicalization 2, 7, 21, 203
Li, C. 63
linguistic manifestation 153, 194–5, 204,
    211
Liu, M. 46
Low, B. 34, 42–3, 46
Lü, S. 62
Lutz, C. 10–12, 14, 69

Machakanja, I. 194
Mahlberg, M. 34
Matsumoto, D. 10
Mauranen, A. 30
McAndrew, F. 11
McCawley, J. 63
McEnery, T. 30, 34
meaning 3–4, 6–7, 12–24, 27–8, 31, 34–47,
    64–70, 208–14
  (extended) unit of meaning 34, 38, 40–4,
    47, 214 *see also* lexical item
  paraphrase 4, 6–7, 31, 34, 37–40, 46–7,
    67, 69, 74–6, 89, 140–1, 151, 184,
    208, 211
    explicit/implicit paraphrase 6, 47,
      67

social construct 4, 7, 35–7, 40, 45, 47, 208,
    211
usage 4, 7, 16, 37, 40, 47, 50, 56, 64, 66,
    173, 195, 207–8, 210–11
Mel'čuk, I. 46
metaphor 7, 16, 18, 83, 97, 110, 113, 115,
    117, 123–4, 137, 139–40, 153, 166, 169,
    173, 177, 179–80, 185, 188–98, 204,
    211–14
metaphorical mapping 18, 153, 191, 198,
    213–14
Moon, R. 50, 208–9
Morley, J. and Partington, A. 43

Natural Semantic Metalanguage 13–15

O'Halloran, K. 34, 37, 46
Ooi, V. 27, 33–4, 45, 52, 169, 204

Palmer, G. 4
parallel corpora 7, 17, 27–31, 55–6, 131,
    208, 211
Partington, A. 34, 42–3, 46
pattern grammar 33–4
POS classification 49, 65–6, 213
primitive concept 3, 24
  semantic primitive 13–14, 16–17, 25
  universal concept 13

Renouf, A. 50
Rosch, E. 17, 43
Russell, J. 9–10

Santangelo, P. 4, 78
Santos, D. 29
Sapir, E. 12
Scherer, K. 11
Schmied, J. 29
Scott, M. 33, 53
semantic profile 40, 51, 66–7, 72
Sharifian, F. 4
Shi, X. and Feng, B. 96
Shweder, R. 11
Sinclair, J. 27, 33–4, 37, 39–45, 47, 50, 53,
    58–9, 65, 142, 208, 212, 214
Sketch Engine 59–60, 213
source domain 153, 191–2, 195
  see also target domain
Stearns, C. 116
Stefanowitsch, A. 18

Stewart, D. 34
Strauss, C. and Quinn, N. 4
structural category 40–1, 43, 69, 208,
    213
    colligation 3–6, 17, 40–2, 44–7, 66–7, 69,
        72, 92–3, 100–1, 105, 107, 111, 119,
        128, 133–4, 138–9, 143–4, 157, 160,
        179, 199, 203, 206–8, 211, 214
    collocation 3–4, 17–18, 27, 31, 34, 40–7,
        51, 53, 66–7, 69, 88, 107, 111, 127, 159,
        168, 191, 203, 206–8, 211, 214
    semantic association 40, 44–7, 51, 66, 69,
        72, 144, 148, 206–7, 209 *see also*
        semantic preference
    semantic preference 3–6, 17, 41–2, 44–7,
        67, 99, 101, 105–7, 119, 134–5, 139,
        143–4, 177, 186, 189, 208, 211, 214 *see*
        also semantic association
    semantic prosody 34, 41–5, 47, 116, 120,
        128, 145, 158, 205, 214
Stubbs, M. 6, 34–5, 37, 41, 44

Talmy, L. 22
target domain 153, 191–2, 195
Teubert, W. 4, 17–18, 27–8, 30–1, 34–41, 44,
    51–2, 70, 79, 208, 212
    see also corpus-linguistic theory
Thompson, S. 63
Tognini-Bonelli, E. 33–4, 37, 41, 46
translation equivalence 10, 28
    see also lexical equivalence

translation equivalent 30, 58, 102,
    123–4, 136, 146, 149, 155, 179,
    195, 204
    see also translation equivalence
translationese 29–31
Turpin, M. 195

universality 1, 9–10, 16
    see also cultural specificity

Viberg, A. 29
Vygotsky, L. 35

Wellenkamp, J. 74
Whitsitt, S. 34, 42–3
Whorf, B. 1
Wierzbicka, A. 1, 13–17, 69, 77–8, 93, 97,
    106, 116, 195
    see also Natural Semantic
        Metalanguage
Williams, G. 34, 37, 44–6

Xiao, R. 29–30, 34
Xu, Y. 203

Ye, Z. 14, 87–8, 195
Yip, P. 81
Yu, N. 195–6

Zhang, R. 37, 169, 204, 212
Zhu, D. 51, 63